QUITTING THE MOB

ALSO BY DARY MATERA

Get Me Ellis Rubin!
Are You Lonesome Tonight?

QUITTING THE MOB

HOW THE "YUPPIE DON"
LEFT THE MAFIA AND
LIVED TO TELL HIS STORY

MICHAEL FRANZESE

&

DARY MATERA

HarperCollins*Publishers*

Illustrations follow page 114

HarperCollins books may be purchased for educational, business, or sales promotional use. For information, please call or write: Special Markets Department, HarperCollins Publishers, Inc., 10 East 53rd Street, New York, NY 10022. Telephone: (212) 207-7528; Fax: (212) 207-7222.

FIRST EDITION

Designed by Fritz Metsch

LIBRARY OF CONGRESS CATALOGING-IN-PUBLICATION DATA

Franzese, Michael.
    Quitting the Mob: how the "Yuppie Don" left the Mafia and lived to tell his story / Michael Franzese & Dary Matera.—1st ed.
        p. cm.
    Includes index.
    ISBN 0-06-016493-X
    1. Franzese, Michael. 2. Criminals—United States—Biography. 3. Mafia—United States—Case studies. 4. Criminals—Rehabilitation—United States—Case studies. I. Matera, Dary, 1955-. II. Title.
HF6248.F674A3 1992
364. 1´092—dc20
[B]   91—50477

92   93   94   95   96   MAC/RRD   10   9   8   7   6   5   4   3   2   1

To Gia, who suffered the most.
Forgive me.

ACKNOWLEDGMENTS

Special thanks to Fran Matera, Ph.D., the Walter Cronkite School of Journalism and Telecommunication, Arizona State University, for the extensive editorial assistance she provided.

Thanks to Bob Greene, Manny Topol, Kenneth Crowe, and Peggy Lundquist of *Newsday;* Peter Blauner of *New York* magazine; James Mills, Edward Barnes, and William Shebar of *Life* magazine; and Craig Neff of *Sports Illustrated.* Thanks in memoriam to Tom Renner of *Newsday,* the nation's foremost organized-crime reporter. Renner died of a heart attack in January 1990; his last story, which he never completed, was an exposé on Michael Franzese.

Thanks are due: Edward McDonald, former attorney-in-charge, and Jerry Bernstein, former special agent, of the Organized Crime Strike Force of New York, Eastern District. Ray Jermyn, attorney-in-charge, Organized Crime Bureau, Suffolk County, New York. Detective Jim McDermott of the Dade County Police Department and Dr. Jay Barnhart of the Dade County Medical Examiner's Office.

Thanks to Beau Matera, Mary Magdelena, Les Share, Phil Steinberg, Leo Suarez, Bernie Welsh, Hank Kaplan, Deborah Corley, Brian Ross, Ira Silverman, Steven Boyle, Ed Kelly, Ellen Burkoff, John Jacobs, Bruce Kelton, Mark Sennet, Joe Valiquette, Robert Davenport, Martin Radner, Tom Bruny, Fred Dannen, George Randolph.

Special thanks to Tina Franzese, Tina Franzese II, Gia Franzese, and to Micki, Mandi, and Macho, for being such joys; and to the Garcia family: Seferino, Irma, Temo ("Rock the Truck"), Rudy, Dino, Sabrina.

Thanks to my agent, Connie Clausen, for her wise advice and counsel, and to my editors, Eamon Dolan and Larry Ashmead, for their talent and sensitivity.

In memoriam to John "Johnny Cakes" Matera, 1926–1954.

—Dary Matera

To my mother and father for making it all possible. To Nana and Tata for all their love and support. To my sister Sabrina for being there with me. To my best friend in the world, Rosita Soto, and to Carol Conners from the L.A. Dance Force.

—Camille Franzese

To my attorney, Bruce Kelton, thanks for your support and friendship. Special thanks to my friend and agent, Jack Gilardi, for making it all happen.

To my wonderful children, Tina, John, Maria, Miquelle, Amanda, and Michael Jr., all of whom have been my motivation and my joy.

To my wonderful wife, Camille, without whom there would be no story. "I love you, forever and always."

—Michael Franzese

There's an old saying that the only way to leave the Mafia is in a coffin. Members are pledged to a lifetime of secrecy, and to quit would be to arouse suspicion that you are cooperating with the police or federal agents. Such breaches of faith the Mob punishes with death.

Michael Franzese says he's willing to take that risk. He will not betray his former crime associates and then disappear into the federal witness protection program....If he holds to what he has promised...it will mark the first time that a high-ranking member of the Mafia will publicly walk away from his past.

> —Edward Barnes and
> William Shebar,
> Life *magazine*,
> *December 1987*

Investigative correspondent Brian Ross and producer Ira Silverman have been tracking the Mob ever since they first hooked up as a team here at NBC fifteen years ago. They've met a variety of characters in their travels, but none as slick as the one they introduce us to tonight...a handsome and high-living young man as rich as royalty, and royalty he is—a Prince—of the Mafia.

> —Tom Brokaw,
> "Exposé,"
> *January 1991*

Michael Franzese has a lot to pray for. Before he was born again, he was a family man. The family was the Colombo crime family. And Michael Franzese was a captain, one of the richest and most powerful men in the Mob.

> —Bernard Goldberg,
> "48 Hours,"
> *May 1991*

Within a decade, Franzese had become…one of the biggest earners the Mob had seen since Capone, and the youngest individual in Fortune *magazine's survey of "The 50 Biggest Mafia Bosses."*

> —Fredric Dannen,
> Vanity Fair,
> February 1991

I wouldn't want to be in Michael Franzese's shoes. I don't think his life expectancy is very substantial.

> —Edward McDonald,
> former attorney-in-charge,
> Organized Crime Strike Force,
> Eastern District of New York

He's a fascinating person. What he did was intriguing. It took a lot of time and energy to dissect what he did.

> —Jerry Bernstein,
> former special attorney,
> U.S. Department of Justice; special agent,
> Organized Crime Strike Force,
> Eastern District of New York

He will get whacked.

> —Bernie Welsh,
> retired FBI organized-crime expert
> and legendary Mob hunter

I pray for Michael every night.

> —Tina Franzese,
> Michael's mother

My love is stronger than my fear of death.

> —Marty Robbins,
> "El Paso"

QUITTING THE MOB

In this book, Michael Franzese tells his own story in the first person, written with the assistance of Dary Matera. Statements and opinions in the first person are those of Michael Franzese. Those portions of the book written in the third person were independently written and researched by Dary Matera and are not to be attributed to Michael Franzese.

INTRODUCTION

They were standing high above the congregation, waist-deep in the warm blue water. Bronze organ pipes lined the walls on both sides, occasionally crying out piercing notes. Above them, the ornate Gothic ceiling was too high to make out the carved rafter patterns and checkerboard bursts of color. Down below, in the water, the two men wore white robes tinged pale crimson by the light bouncing off the blood-red carpet that bathed the entire building.

All eyes were riveted on the chiseled features of the younger man, the slight, dark-haired parishioner to the right of Pastor Myron Taylor in the small, watery chamber. Many in the congregation knew who he was . and what he was. Openly, they had accepted him into their flock. It was the Christian way. There was even an historical precedent that demanded their acceptance: Jesus himself had reached out to the man who had hung beside him on the cross. They all knew the story. It was one of the Bible's most memorable tales, symbolizing forever how easily one can slip into heaven, right up to the last breath of life, simply by believing. One can lead a lifetime of greed, evil, lust, and murder and still escape the postdeath sentence of spending an eternity in a fiery lake merely by whispering a deathbed request to be forgiven.

The example was unmistakably clear. They could argue among themselves about other passages, other verses and other parables, but not about this one. There was no gray area regarding the thief on the cross. They were thus charged with accepting the stranger into their flock, welcoming him with a joyful heart, smiling when they shook his hand, trying not to let their tension reveal itself through muscles jerked tight down the sides of the neck and around the edges of the mouth.

It was God's way.

But privately, they doubted.

Privately, many were afraid.

The good people of Westwood Hills Christian Church in the trendy Westwood section of Los Angeles weren't used to a young man like this one among the congregation of their stately, nondenominational church. The old-fashioned cathedral, which sits precariously between the glitz of the Westwood Marquis Hotel and the youthful glamour of the UCLA campus, was modeled after the ones constructed in Scotland centuries before. Stone arches, varnished pews, and silk-screened shields fill the interior. A large steeple topped by a cluster of sharp-pointed spires dominates the exterior. The church survived as the neighborhood around it grew wild. Traveling businessmen and their high-priced call girls regularly break the Sixth Commandment in the three-hundred-dollar-a-night hotels visible from the church's lawn. College students drink, get high, fornicate, and break most of the other nine Commandments in the apartments and sorority houses that look down upon the spires. Surrounded by sin, the nineteenth-century-styled church, perched on a multimillion-dollar parcel of prime L.A. real estate at the corner of LeConte Avenue and Hilgard, quietly lives on, all but unnoticed.

Only now, this morning, something dark and frightening, something far worse than the congregation ever imagined, had ventured inside.

It wasn't so much that this man was in a church that was so disturbing. The congregation had seen the movies. They knew such men weren't strangers to churches. On the contrary, many had been portrayed as devout. But it was the Roman Catholic Church that had to deal with them, accept their tainted money, hear their bloody confessions, and minister to their meek, prayerful wives and well-behaved children.

They were the Catholic Church's problem.

No longer. Now, one had come their way. A powerful one. A famous one. One who had been in all the newspapers, made all the network news shows. A thirty-eight-year-old Long Island native who had been part of one of the most infamous Mafia families and had sprung directly from one of the most feared crime bosses: an enforcer so cold-blooded and deadly that he had evoked as much fear among his minions as the devil did among his.

That man's son was now standing before them, participating in their most sacred ceremony. And no matter what they thought, how much they feared, Jesus had ordered them to accept. Not to judge, not to cast stones; not even to question the man's sincerity. They were to accept.

It was supposed to be a quietly joyful moment, a humble rebirth for the man who brought himself into the water. The rite is performed many different ways by many different denominations, but this congregation's method, shared with the Southern Baptists and other Protestant sects, was the most dramatic. This wasn't going to be a simple sprinkling of a wailing baby to cleanse it from the Original Sin of Adam and Eve; a baby's sins are incorporeal, an "all have sinned and come short of the glory of God" kind of pseudo-sin. The congregation knew that their pool had been designed to scrub away actual sins.

From this perspective, the scene before them had to be disquieting. Their way was total immersion. In the case of the gangster in the baptistry, the water would surely bubble and turn black as the night.

They also knew about the woman, the one who usually sat among them and was now in the chamber alongside the two men. The story was titillating and romantic. She had brought him here. She had succeeded where all the prosecutors and government task forces and police detectives had failed—she sent him to prison. He went, the story was, out of his all-consuming passion for her. He gave up the money, the power, the family tradition and spent three years locked up because of his love for her.

He put his very life at risk, in the past, in the future, and at that very moment. All for her.

The women in the congregation, those who pondered such things, were skeptical. They couldn't see it. What was so special about this woman? She was pretty, they admitted, maybe even beautiful if one is partial to the dark and exotic. She seemed nice enough and appeared to be a good mother and a faithful wife. She was even a true believer. But to abdicate from an empire, even a criminal empire, for her? To go to jail? Give up millions? For this Mexican woman who sat among them each Sunday with her two little girls and baby son?

The men, those who pondered such things, were less skeptical. In fact, it was the woman who heralded the first ring of truth to the whole bizarre story. She was more than just pretty. They could sense it, almost feel it. Something about her made the heart pound and the knees weak. Maybe she truly had gotten inside him, first making him crazy with lust, then insane with love. The combination could have consumed his every thought and led him down whatever path she desired, including the renouncement of his secret life.

Love can do that. Lust certainly can do that. Combined, they can be an addiction more consuming than money, power, or the strongest drug. Fused together, they can be more enticing than crime practiced at the highest, most profitable levels.

Fanciful thinking. A good story, certainly—the kind of which movies are made. And not surprisingly, Hollywood had called. A television miniseries was in the works. It would be America's version of Samson and Delilah, played out, fittingly, by a mobster and a Latin dancer.

The cynical among the congregation scoffed. Nice story; heck of a movie...now wake up. Lovesickness overtaking a man who reigned over a violent world where the slightest show of weakness could be fatal? Giving up everything and going to jail when he could have kept it all, stayed free, and probably gotten the girl anyway?

Sure.

But the woman had made him weak. Even the cynics could see that. And she made him strong.

Every now and then, the free-floating speculation was interrupted by a scent of death hovering in the distance. Sometimes it floated closer, so close you could feel it pressing against the skin. Would the young man rise out of the water? Would he walk out of the church and make it safely to his car? The underground buzzed with news about the contract. You can't walk away, they say. He had. He had created an unprecedented situation that needed to be corrected. He had violated the Mafia's most sacred oath, the one he had sworn to on Halloween night fourteen years before.

The whispers claimed that his public repudiation had caused such fury that his own father had ordered his death.

Wash away his sins, blow away his life, all in one mad fusion of water and blood and exploding gunpowder mixed with pipe-organ music. Keep an eye on the door. Get ready to duck. The assassins feared the other church, the one with the statue of the Virgin. But did that fear hold true for this one? Or would they just come slithering in and take him out right there where he stood, so vulnerable in Pastor Taylor's arms, waist-deep in a pool of warm water in a blood-red Protestant church?

"Michael Franzese, will you repeat after me: 'I believe that Jesus is the Christ, the son of the living God, Jesus is Lord.'"

The voice that followed was deep and resonant, exactly the voice the congregation expected to hear—a voice more suited to ordering death than to praising a resurrected Savior.

"I believe that Jesus is the Christ, the son of the living God, Jesus is Lord."

"Michael Franzese, upon the profession of your faith in Jesus Christ, you are baptized in the name of the Father, and of the Son, and of the Holy Spirit. Amen."

Pastor Taylor put a handkerchief over the young man's mouth, braced his right hand against his back, and leaned him backward into the water. Michael Franzese arose a few seconds later, dripping wet, his thick black hair pushed back as if it were heavily gelled for a night on the town. He looked down at the congregation, then over to his wife. She had been immersed moments before. Her wet robe now clung to her body, outlining every curve. Her hair danced in wet ringlets across her shoulders. Their eyes locked. She looked more beautiful at that moment than he'd ever seen her before.

The mobster Christian. The born-again don. The yuppie capo, now going onward as a Christian soldier. The senses spin. The brain rejects it. The billion-dollar Mafia swindler. The brilliant schemer who took the blood, guts, and hot lead out of the Mob and streamlined it into a smooth, white-collar operation that made money faster than any old-style gangster ever had. Armed with only his wits, he shook down the labor unions, banks, and financial institutions, then took down the oil-men. He wrapped himself in crisp button-down shirts, Italian silk ties, and Pierre Cardin suits, smiled, winked, and played a blinding billion-dollar shell game on Uncle Sam.

The son proved to be as lethal in the skyscrapers of the business world as the father had been on the streets.

And even after he turned himself in, after he unbuckled his six-guns, raised his hands in surrender, and looked longingly at the Mexican cantina girl, little changed. He merely put on his open-collar shirts, his California-casual Gucci loafers, his Giorgio Armani suits, smiled, winked, and brought the feds back to the table. Follow the pea. Watch closely. Which shell is it under this time? Switch, shift, roll. The hand is quicker than the eye. I'll cop a plea in return for three years in prison, some of it to be served in a halfway house with weekends off. Switch, shift, roll. I'll pay back whatever I owe. Fifteen, twenty million? Okay. I don't have the money now, of course. The billions? The newspapermen exaggerate. It's all gone! Expenses. The family. Those wild and crazy Russians. Everyone taking their cut. Hardly any left for me. But no sweat. Switch, shift, roll. Just let me out so I can work my magic and turn the money faucets back on. And don't worry. I'll do it clean this time! In Tinseltown! The land of stars and dreams and overnight fortunes! We'll be partners: Michael Franzese and Uncle Sam. Got a nice ring to it. And I'll do all the work. What a deal!

What a deal indeed. Uncle Sam squinted down through his bifocals, turned over the shell, and, for once, thought he'd found the pea.

There remain cynics. Not only among the Westwood Hills Christian Church flock but among the FBI, the Organized Crime Strike Force, and the state attorneys in California, Illinois, Florida, and New York. And especially among the Mafia itself. Could this guy possibly be for real? And what's this born-again thing? Is it another great con? Part of the big picture, the Franzese all-the-world's-a-sucker megascam?

If so, what's the angle? He's out of prison. The extraordinary deal he wrangled out of the feds had been cut. He hadn't used his born-again conversion to impress the parole board. And he was baptized after he was out, his time served, with seemingly no one left to scam or impress.

There was no accompanying media extravaganza like at boxer Mike Tyson's baptism. No CNN cameras to record the moment. Just a private ceremony in a mid-sized Los Angeles church. A public proclamation of faith before a congregation of strangers. A dunking that most people, particularly a man of his stature, would find a bit embarrassing. An event that had indeed made the iron-willed Mafia prince so nervous he found it difficult to stand.

Where did this religious transformation fit into the master plan? What *was* the master plan?

Was he doing it for himself? Or was he truly paralyzed by his love for the dark-eyed Latin woman in the wet, clinging white robe? Was this, again, her doing?

Maybe.

Maybe not.

I

SONNY

CHAPTER 1

Phil Steinberg was sitting in his luxurious Manhattan office at 1650 Broadway feeling on top of the world. The rock-and-roll record company he started with two Brooklyn buddies had taken off. The Shangri-Las, a sexy teenage girl-group, hit Number 5 with a song called "Remember (Walkin' in the Sand)." A second group, the Lovin' Spoonful, was a year away from becoming a monster rock band that would release seven Top Ten songs in a row. The record company itself, Kama Sutra/Buddah Records, was destined to become a giant in the industry.

Steinberg was only twenty-three years old. His partners, Artie Ripp and Hy Mizrahi, were just a few years older. Nothing, it appeared, could stop them.

Steinberg's buxom secretary, an Ann-Margret look-alike named Sandy, knocked on his office door.

"Phil, you have a visitor—Morris Levy."

"Send him in."

He smiled as he greeted Levy, a tough-guy record producer who had founded Roulette Records and would one day own Strawberries, an eighty-store record chain. Levy didn't return the smile.

"We have a problem, Phil."

"What's up?"

"The Shangri-Las—nice kids. Great group. Great song."

"Yeah, we got lucky. So what's the problem?"

"They're mine."

"Bullshit."

"They're mine. And I want my cut."

Steinberg felt the muscles in his neck tighten. A burly ex–football player, he suppressed an urge to toss Levy out of his office. That wasn't an option. Steinberg knew the streets: Levy was an associate of Gaetano

"Tommy the Big Guy" Vastola, a vicious soldier in the DeCavalcante Mafia family. He was also the childhood friend of Vincent "the Chin" Gigante, a menacing hood on his way to becoming the boss of the Genovese family.

Levy was big trouble.

"I'll discuss this with my partners and we'll get back to you," Steinberg said, forcing a smile. "I'm sure we can work this out to your satisfaction."

"Make some calls. Check around," Levy advised. "I'm confident you'll do the right thing."

After Levy left, Steinberg called a meeting with his partners. He explained what had happened. They collectively sank into despair. Aside from his connections, Levy had legendary moxie. He had copyrighted the term "rock and roll" and forced record companies to pay him a royalty to use the magic words. The government had to step in and end the hustle by declaring the term generic. With that kind of audacity, and that measure of Mafia weight behind him, Levy wasn't about to back off from the Shangri-Las and Kama Sutra/Buddah.

The upstart record producers were so depressed they hardly noticed when a fourth man joined them, a friend of Phil's who frequently dropped by. The visitor was a stocky, powerfully built man about five-nine, with short black hair sprinkled with gray. He was wearing a tailored, pin-striped suit, a red silk tie, black pointy shoes, and had on the most magnificent black topcoat any of them had ever seen. The brim of his fedora was stylishly turned up. A ring encrusted with diamonds flashed from his left pinky.

The man enjoyed popping into the fledgling record company as he made his Manhattan rounds. Sometimes he brought his wife and children and showed them the bustling recording studios. He especially liked checking on the progress of Phil and his friends. They were street punks from Brooklyn, just like him, and he admired their spunk. They had no business trying to crash the record industry, but they'd pushed their way in and hit it big.

"What's the matter with you guys? You look like all your dogs died," the visitor said.

Steinberg tried to brush it off. He didn't want his friend to know. The man might take it as asking for a favor. He knew better than to ask. You ask, and you keep paying it back the rest of your life.

"Everything's okay. We're just a bit tired."

The visitor laughed. "Tired? You guys should be dancing in the streets. What's wrong?"

Steinberg shrugged.

The visitor grew serious. "Hey, Phil—what? Am I your friend?" he said, tapping his chest with both hands. "You can't tell me your problems?"

Steinberg glanced up. A smile cut through the man's rough but handsome features. It wasn't a "favor," it was a friend offering to help out a friend.

"Sonny, Moe Levy came by today. He said he owns a piece of the Shangri-Las. He wants his cut."

The visitor raised his eyebrows in surprise. "Moe Levy said that? You must be kidding."

"No joke, Sonny."

Sonny Franzese's deep brown eyes panned the room. He took in the worried faces of the three young men sitting at the table. "You boys worked too damn hard to have the likes of Moe Levy shake you down. Don't worry about it."

Steinberg didn't see Moe Levy again until a few weeks later, when they bumped into each other at a nearby recording studio. Levy was all handshakes and smiles, complimenting Steinberg on the Shangri-Las' smash follow-up hit, "Leader of the Pack," along with a third hit Kama Sutra had produced, "Come a Little Bit Closer" by Jay and the Americans. Levy made no mention of his cut. Steinberg searched his eyes for the slightest sign of indignation, any hint that a message had been delivered. He couldn't detect a thing.

The Shangri-Las, Jay and the Americans, the Lovin' Spoonful, Sha Na Na, Gladys Knight and the Pips and scores of other rock performers went on to bring tens of millions of dollars into Kama Sutra/Buddah's coffers. By the end of the 1970s, Buddah Records had become one of the largest independent record companies in the world. No one ever came by demanding any kind of cut again.

Not even Sonny Franzese.

John "Sonny" Franzese was, among many other things, a chameleon. He could change his colors so fast, over such a wide a range of personalities, that he could have fooled any dozen psychiatrists into thinking he was certifiable. Actually, he *was* certifiable. His Army career was cut short in 1944 when the military shrinks made him for a "psychoneurotic with pronounced homicidal tendencies." They recommended that he be busted out of the service without delay. He was.

But the Army docs had focused on a sliver of the Franzese psyche and failed to spot the seeds of the other Sonnys waiting to sprout. By limiting him to his baser instincts, they were the first to make the deadly mistake many of his victims would later repeat: they underestimated him. Behind his menacing eyes worked a shrewd mind honed to a razor's edge. His intellect, often purposely hidden, coupled with his cold-blooded fearlessness to give him his advantage.

Sonny's chameleon ways extended beyond his personality. Early mug shots reveal a gruesome, bull-necked man with dark, close-cropped hair, a widow's peak, a boxer's squashed nose, dark stubble, and squinting eyes that burn demonically. He was a burly 200 pounds, and pit-bull ugly. He looked every bit the street thug he was.

Other photos depict a man so different as to strain belief. Longer, styled hair speckled with dignified flecks of gray. Expensive, tailor-made suits draped over a leaner, 170-pound frame. Knock-'em-dead overcoats cut like a suit and fitting as snug as a blazer. Clean-shaven, meticulously groomed. Beaming smile. A crisp fedora with the brim cocked upward. And the Mafia prerequisites—a diamond pinkie ring and black pointed shoes.

At times, he resembled former middleweight champion Rocky Graziano. As he matured, Sonny's features smoothed out even more. His boxer's nose seemed to narrow, and no longer dominated his face. In a *Life* magazine photo reprinted in 1988, he looks like singer Eddie Fisher, Liz Taylor's ex.

Like the chameleon he was, Sonny Franzese's talent lay in adaptation. The higher he rose in the Colombo crime family, the more handsome and dignified his appearance. Even his body movements changed over the years from a plodding chunk-of-iron to an odd sort of grace, like a mountain lion who mesmerizes its victims with its athletic beauty before slashing them apart.

Sonny grew with each transformation. He was like a corporate executive rising from the mailroom to chairman of the board, and looking the part every step of the way. From the streets of the Greenpoint section of Brooklyn, where he grew up riding shotgun on his Italian immigrant father's bakery truck, to the suburbs of Long Island, Sonny soaked up each new surrounding and changed himself to fit in. On the streets, he enveloped himself in the image of the beast within and could paralyze the most fearless hitman with a stare. When he mingled with the mon- eyed of Manhattan, he could suppress the dragon and terrorize no one. Not only did he learn to fit in, but eventually he would dominate and control any circumstance, any setting. Among the Mafia hierarchy, the affluent, or the nothing-to-lose street killers, he adapted, absorbed, and quickly controlled.

Sonny was born in Naples, Italy, on February 6, 1919, the last son and next-to-last of Carmine and Maria Franzese's eighteen children. Contrary to popular myth, his parents had established a foothold in America long before his birth. The baker and his wife traveled frequently between America and Italy to vacation in the homeland. After sixteen children, it was not uncommon for Maria Franzese to make the long voy- age in the late stages of yet another of her perpetual pregnancies. Thus, Sonny's birth has long given Mafia biographers and feature writers the mistaken impression that he came to America as an infant with a newly immigrated family.

Further confusing is the continued procreative power of the Franzese clan, and their confounding tendency to give similar names to second-, third-, and fourth-generation sons, daughters, nieces, nephews, grandchildren, great-grandchildren, and cousins. Any attempt to sort through the Franzese family tree quickly becomes a logistical nightmare. Carmines, Johns, Michaels, and Marias turn up everywhere, often with as many Roman numerals attached to their names as the Super Bowl. Even the in-laws have become favored in this Italian name-game maze.

In the span of a decade, Sonny Franzese I rose from his father's bak- ery truck to become the underboss and heir apparent of the Colombo family, one of the five Cosa Nostra ("Our Thing") crime families, estab- lished in 1931, who still control the New York area—Colombo, Gam- bino, Genovese, Bonanno, and Lucchese. The Colombo sect evolved from the Profaci-Magliocco family, though few today recognize the names of Joseph Profaci or Giuseppe Magliocco, the founding fathers. (The current Colombo boss is the imprisoned Carmine "the Snake" Per- sico, Jr., who succeeded Joe Colombo in 1971. Acting boss is Vic Orena.)

Sonny was brought into the Mafia by old-time Colombo capo Sebastian "Buster" Aloi. Little else is known about his recruitment and induction beyond the fact that tough street kids were frequently taken under the wing of founding Mafiosi as the five families built their armies in the 1930s, '40s, and '50s.

People's views on Sonny Franzese vary as widely as his personalities. Their feelings, then and now, are rooted in the circumstances of their acquaintance. Unfortunately, those who knew him at his most intense aren't around to offer their insights. These would be the thirty-five or so individuals various law-enforcement officials believe he dispatched into another life, in assorted grisly ways, during his bloody rise up the Mafia ladder of success.

There remain enough of those who escaped his vengeance, who were true friends or hung out in the same neighborhoods, to paint a fascinating portrait of one of the Mafia's most powerful, most vicious, and least publicized figures.

In the late 1940s, Sonny Franzese purchased a parcel of land at Thirty-seventh Avenue and Seventy-sixth Street in Jackson Heights and constructed a personal playground he named the Orchid Room. The homey neighborhood tavern was a den of made men and doubled as a thriving bookmaking operation. Sonny's employees sold spirits and hope, and did well with each.

In the decade following World War II, Jackson Heights was in its heyday. The Queens neighborhood was bustling with nightclubs, restaurants, pizza parlors, and ritzy apartments. Aside from the Orchid Room, things cooked all night at such places as the Dinner Bell, Bud's Bar, and the Blue Haven and Flying Tigers nightclubs. When the young and hip got hungry, they could grab a pepperoni pizza at fight announcer Angelo Palange's Savoy pizzeria on Roosevelt Avenue.

Despite the abundance of apartments and co-ops, it never was much of a family neighborhood, even at its best. It was more of, as one longtime resident recalled, "the place everybody stashed their mistresses."

Lots of things were "stashed" in Jackson Heights in the 1940s and 1950s. Then, as now, the neighborhood was known for illegal activities. But the crime of the 1940s sounds almost romantic compared with today's. Bookmaking, shylocking, prostitution, shakedowns, bar and restaurant skimming, and tax cheating were the mainstays. The occasional "drop and drag" murders—kill someone in a bar or restaurant, then drag the body outside to avoid police hassles—did little to keep the crowds away. And despite the unlawful activities, it was a safe area to take an evening stroll.

Not so today. Much of Jackson Heights has become the New York enclave of Colombian cocaine dealers and their desperate, crack-addicted clients. But that is now. This is about then; and then, Jackson Heights was happening.

"Sonny Franzese invaded the neighborhood like a one-man army," recalls Beau Matera, whose family owned the Dinner Bell Restaurant on Thirty-seventh Avenue and Eighty-third Street.* "His base had been Brooklyn, but Jackson Heights was hot after the war and began attracting the attention of everyone from legitimate businessmen, nightclub operators, restaurateurs to, as always, the mobsters. Sonny's invasion was a bloodless coup because nobody was going to try and stop him. His reputation, suffice it to say, preceded him.

"Funny thing," Matera continues, "Sonny's power had nothing to do with the fact that he was a capo in the Colombo family. Most people didn't know, or didn't care, who he was connected with. His power came from within himself. The neighborhood didn't tremble at the thought of hidden Colombo armies keeping watch—they shook at the sight of Sonny Franzese walking down Thirty-seventh Avenue."

Matera's family eventually sold the Dinner Bell to Tommy Grimaldi, one of Jackson Heights' top bookmakers. Among his other interests, Grimaldi managed the Orchid Room for Sonny. Matera befriended the gregarious, well-dressed, well-connected Grimaldi and frequently dropped by the Orchid Room to pass the time. He claims he wasn't there, however, the night it was Franzese's turn to host a "drop and drag" party.

Those who were there recall it well. Franzese was in a back corner talking with a slim young man. The patrons were aware of this because it was everyone's habit to keep one eye on Sonny whenever he was in the room. Tensions were eased this evening because Sonny and the visitor appeared to be friends. They were smiling, laughing, drinking, and talking. It was early in the morning, two or three A.M.

A shot suddenly pierced through the chatter and silenced the bar. The slim man crashed to the floor, his fingers still locked tightly around

---

*John "Beau" Matera is the coauthor's uncle. He is not to be confused with John "Johnny Irish" Matera, Sonny Franzese's former chauffeur, bodyguard, and fellow murder defendant, to whom the coauthor is not related.

his own unused gun. All who turned their heads saw Sonny Franzese holding a smoking pistol—the literal smoking gun. He quickly slid it back into the holster under his five-hundred-dollar suit and signaled for someone to take over. The slim man's body hardly hit the floor before it was dragged out of the place. The fresh corpse was deposited on the sidewalk a block away. Before the drag men could make it back to the bar, the blood had already been mopped off the floor.

Sonny went about his business as if nothing had happened. No one prepped the crowd on how to handle what was to come; no one had to. Sonny had reacted so fast the would-be assassin never got his weapon aimed, but even a story of possible self-defense wasn't to be told. When the police arrived and questioned those remaining about the stiff down the block, no one in the Orchid Room fessed up to hearing the shot. "Must have been dumped outta a car," more than one person helpfully surmised to the detectives.

Not much was ever known about the victim; he was some small-time hood nobody ever missed. Those at the bar that morning have trouble pinning down the exact year—possibly sometime around 1948 or 1949. What is significant, what they all remember, was Franzese's reaction after the shooting. He sat in his usual corner, sipping a drink, talking with friends, laughing, enjoying himself without a care in the world. He appeared oblivious to the fact that he had come within seconds of being killed, oblivious to the possibility that his life might lie in the hands of one person in the bar, one stranger, one out-of-towner who'd stopped by for a beer and didn't know the rules. If even one person talked, Sonny Franzese was history. The police and the state attorney wanted Sonny bad. This shooting, regardless of who drew first, could have greased his skids into the electric chair.

But nobody talked.

Soon after, it came time for young Beau Matera to decide if he was going to stop riding the edge and join one of the crime families. Was he in or out?

He moved to Las Vegas.

"I figured if you were gonna be a mobster, I mean really be a big-time mobster, you had to have steel balls like Sonny Franzese. You had to be able to take out your assassin, then sit there calmly sipping a drink while the police wandered about, asking everyone questions. I didn't have balls like that. Hell, nobody had balls like that except Sonny."

Steel balls. Those who know Sonny well nod at the description, but quickly add that even that doesn't quite capture the strange measure of the man—or the power he commanded.

Bob Greene, now a *Newsday* investigations editor, chronicled Franzese's life in a riveting feature, "The Hood in Our Neighborhood," published on Christmas Eve, 1965.

He is a prototype of the rising young executive, aggressive, dynamic, moderate in his habits, a good family man, careful with money and so absorbed in his work that lunch, when he manages to find time for it, is usually a quick date-nut bread sandwich at Chock Full O' Nuts. He could be working for IBM, GM or Chase Manhattan. But he isn't.

He is John (Sonny) Franzese, 45...tabbed as the fastest-rising young executive in the Cosa Nostra empire of crime. His business: supervision of underworld rackets in parts of Brooklyn, Manhattan and Queens and in almost all of Nassau and Suffolk counties. The tools of his trade: greed, fear and, when necessary, the gun.

Sergeant Ralph Salerno, then the Mafia specialist for the New York City Police Department, added his expert opinion: "Sonny Franzese is the big comer in the Cosa Nostra. He has an extraordinary talent for organized crime. He knows when to compromise and when to get tough; he knows how to run a business and crime is a big business, and, most important, he is an expert at not getting caught."

Greene continued: "Family boss is Joe Colombo of Brooklyn, an aging executive who is gradually paving the way for Franzese to take over completely. Operating under Franzese are six or more crime lieutenants, each of whom directs from 10 to 30 crime soldati [soldiers], who in turn have their own individual criminal organizations."

As diverse as his personalities were, Sonny toed the line when it came to the Cosa Nostra's strict laws, even when it affected his private life. In the early 1940s, he met and married a voluptuous German blonde named Ann Schiller. After a rocky start, they settled down, had three children, and were relatively content. Then Sonny's other family became involved. Sonny received word that his higher-ups felt the independent-minded Mrs. Franzese, who longed to be an actress, couldn't be controlled. Sonny was given the message that his career prospects would greatly improve if he found a more subservient Italian wife. He promptly left Schiller, a process made easy by a bizarre circumstance.

After they married and Sonny was inducted into the Army, Schiller decided she'd made a mistake. She traveled to Miami and arranged a divorce. Sonny abided by her wishes and signed the necessary papers. When he was bounced out of the Army and returned home, Schiller had another change of heart. She wanted him back. She accomplished her goal by telling Sonny that the divorce wasn't legal. The pair resumed their marriage and continued it for nearly a decade, starting their family. When it came time for Sonny to break it off, he discovered the trickery. The Florida divorce was legal, only the joke was now on Ann: Sonny could simply walk away.

Shortly afterward, Sonny met Christina Capobianco, a slim, seventeen-year-old telephone operator who doubled as coat-check girl and roving photographer at the renowned Stork Club. The exclusive Manhattan restaurant and nightspot had a four-star celebrity clientele that included Marilyn Monroe, Grace Kelly, Ernest Hemingway, Damon Runyon, and radio broadcaster and journalist Walter Winchell. Genovese family boss Frank Costello was also a regular, as were a healthy influx of other top-echelon mobsters. The beautiful, dark-haired Tina was a pet of Stork Club owner Sherman Billingsley and a special favorite of frequent club guest Montgomery Clift, the brooding movie actor linked in the newspapers with Elizabeth Taylor. Sonny figuratively snuffed out Clift, who was struggling with his sexual identity and didn't need to compound his personal angst by scrapping with an infamous killer over a skinny coat-check girl.

Sonny and Tina hit it off. According to one version of their romance, the lovers capped a whirlwind courtship by getting married on July 24, 1951, one day after Tina's eighteenth birthday. Sonny was thirty-two. They were the Mobster and the Coat-Check Girl. Had there been television movies back then, their life certainly would have made for a good one.

Tina had been married before. At sixteen, she had hooked up with a handsome, dark-haired soldier named Louis Grillo. The teenage marriage produced a child, Michael, but barely survived a year. Sonny accepted Tina's infant son as his own. Tina had to return the favor three times over when Sonny's three children showed up on her doorstep after Ann Schiller left them to pursue a career—either of Schiller's own volition or at Sonny's request. Tina filled the house further by having three children of their own. The family swelled with Johns, Carmines, Marias, and Michaels, along with a brand-new line, Christina.

By all accounts, Sonny was a doting father who played in the yard with his kids, took them to the local amusement park, and didn't favor any one child over the other, despite the "yours, mine, and ours" nature of the brood. Sometimes he'd give his wife the night off, proclaim himself to be the world's greatest cook, and make an elaborate calzone dinner for the family. The Italian delicacy consists of stuffing dough with cheese, sausage, pepperoni, peppers, and tomato sauce, or any variation of the above, and baking it in the oven. The excitement of "Daddy's making dinner!" always made for a joyful evening.

When he wanted to discourage his children from various harmful activities, he'd resort to making up wildly explicit stories. The Franzese sons were discouraged from owning or riding motorcycles by Sonny's vivid tale of a grisly accident that transformed a handsome athlete into a drooling, brain-dead paraplegic. Sonny's antidrug speech was dressed up by the tragic story of another "friend" who descended from being a successful businessman with a beautiful wife and family to being a crazed freak who crawled the gutters, coughing, vomiting, and debasing himself a dozen different ways to feed his habit.

The Colombo underboss's insight and ability to adapt, learn, and control can be seen in how he operated in his other family, especially in how he handled their interests in the entertainment industry. Sonny had a piece of the infamous Linda Lovelace film *Deep Throat,* which revolutionized the motion-picture industry by bringing oral sex and hard-core pornography out of the shadows and into neighborhood theaters. He additionally had a cut of the classic blood-and-gore horror film *The Texas Chainsaw Massacre.*

He was also a pioneer of sorts in the record business. In January 1964, the recorded music industry changed dramatically when the Beatles hit Number One on *Billboard's* music chart with "I Want to Hold Your Hand." The song stayed there for seven weeks and was finally toppled by another Beatles song, "She Loves You." By the time the mop-haired Englishmen crossed the Atlantic to appear on "The Ed Sullivan Show," they were already a sensation. The Beatles' American television appearance was the long-awaited explosion of rock and roll, which had burned like a lit fuse during the previous, Elvis decade.

Most of the entertainment-minded mobsters rejected the new long-haired music. They deemed it a passing fad, preferring to place their bets on the continuing success of the kind of music being recorded by Frank Sinatra, Dean Martin, Tony Bennett, Sammy Davis, Jr., Steve Lawrence, Perry Como, Nelson Riddle, Andy Williams, Connie Francis, Brenda Lee, and the McGuire Sisters. Sonny Franzese saw the future, and the future rocked. He made New York's famous Tin Pan Alley part of his rounds, kept a close watch on what was happening in the infant rock business, made friends and took notes.

In the mid-1960s, he formed a lucrative booking agency with Norby Walters, which began with popular New York area performers and rock groups, then later branched out to include a glittering array of black superstars. However, it was Sonny's relationship with Phil Steinberg and Steinberg's upstart record company that provides the most insight into this multidimensional man.

During his Tin Pan Alley rounds, Sonny befriended Steinberg and allowed the young record producer to become one of the few people outside the Mafia who were close to him.

"Sonny was what we called an 'ice man,'" Steinberg said. "When he walked into a room, everyone's blood ran cold."

Steinberg's own story is not without drama, so much so it was optioned as a television miniseries. Much of the drama involves how his life intertwined with Franzese's. Steinberg was a dead-end Brooklyn street kid who teamed up with two partners to form a record company in the early 1960s. They were in the right place at the right time, and the company took off. Along with the previously mentioned superstar acts, the Kama Sutra/Buddah roster included the Isley Brothers, Lena Horne, Rod McKuen, Paul Anka, Charlie Daniels, Curtis Mayfield, Bill Withers, Captain Beefheart, Melanie, and dozens of others. By 1975, the company had crashed and burned, a victim of kinky sex, drugs, bad business, vicious infighting, relentless investigations, and its ominous reputation as a Mob company.

The improbable rise and fall of Buddah Records was aided by Sonny

Franzese—but not in the way it was commonly believed. And not in the way the IRS, the FBI, and the New York State attorney general's office, which hounded Buddah for years, suspected.

Sonny admired Steinberg and became, for lack of a better description, his guardian angel. According to Steinberg, it was all on an unspoken level. To this day, he doesn't even know for certain that Sonny intervened in the Moe Levy incident.

"Who knows?" Steinberg says. "You never knew. He was my friend, a damn close friend, but I never knew. That's Sonny's way. He had a thousand people who owed him favors. But he had ten thousand who thought they owed him a favor but weren't sure. You had to go through that dance in your own mind. That was one of Sonny's strengths, the illusion that a debt was owed."

As he continues to talk, Steinberg's description of Sonny turns increasingly toward one of a benevolent father figure. Sonny was a "great guy" who was always immaculately dressed and who had an unmistakable air of power about him. And he was, without question, a man in control of the killer that raged inside him.

"We were going to a boxing match at Sunnyside Gardens," Steinberg said. "I'm walking with Sonny and he bumps into some big guy in the crowd, nothing hard, nothing intentional, just a typical bump. The guy freaks out and starts screaming and yelling and calling Sonny vile names. I couldn't believe it. I'm figuring Sonny's going to blow him away any second, or rip out his throat with his bare hands. Instead, Sonny just calmly walked away.

"So the idiot follows, still cursing and threatening Sonny. Now I'm getting mad. I'm about to deck the guy when Sonny holds me back. He shakes his head, shrugs, and talks in a soft, calm voice: 'Phil, let it go—let it go. Who cares? He's nothing. We don't have to do anything. Guys like that, somebody will do it for you.' That was Sonny's way of saying the guy had bad karma—that the guy would push the wrong person one day and get his. Sonny didn't feel the guy was worth killing. He wasn't worth the effort. I was amazed at how calm Sonny was, and how, with all his power, he didn't let the guy call his hand.

"Of course," Steinberg adds, "for all I know, Sonny had the guy followed and had his balls sliced off before he got home."

A third incident burned into Steinberg's mental file could have imperiled their relationship.

"It wasn't long after I first met him. How we met, I can't really remember, but at the time, we weren't that close. We were at a party, and I brought my wife. She didn't drink much, so when she had a drink at the party, it loosened her up. Sonny came over and I introduced them. My wife stared at him for a couple of beats, then brightened up and became animated.

'I know you!' she exclaimed. 'I've seen you in the newspapers!' She then brought her arms down like she was holding an imaginary machine gun. 'You're the guy who goes *rat-tat-tat-tat-tat-tat!*'

"I cringed. The room suddenly went silent. It was like one of those E. F. Hutton commercials where everybody shuts up and leans in. Only everybody was holding their breath. The silence lasted for what seemed like an eternity. Then Sonny started laughing. And everybody else started laughing. He put his arms around my wife and said, 'Phil, you got yourself some lady here.'"

Franzese's power extended beyond Brooklyn, Jackson Heights, Manhattan, and Tin Pan Alley. It coursed through the Colombo family, penetrated all the other families, and reached across the country.

"We were out at Al and Nick's in Manhattan one night, having dinner and watching one of the shows," Steinberg recalls. "Sonny was in good spirits, enjoying himself to the hilt. Joe Colombo comes in, and he and Sonny started getting playful. Before you know it, Sonny had Joe's head in a headlock. One flexed muscle and Sonny could have snapped the boss's neck like a stalk of spaghetti. Sonny could have climbed the final rung to the top. But Sonny wouldn't do that. They were just playing. And Sonny ran the family anyway.

"A little later, Frank Sinatra comes over to our table. Sinatra leaned down, took Sonny's hand, and kissed his ring. Kissed his ring! Right in front of Colombo. Unreal!"

There was at least one specific reason why Sinatra may have been so respectful that evening. Sonny usually had a ringside table whenever Sinatra, or Sammy Davis, Jr., or any number of entertainers opened anywhere in New York. He was a regular in their dressing rooms backstage, and far from being an unwanted presence: the superstars were keenly aware of an entirely different power Sonny wielded.

In 1963, some years before Steinberg witnessed Sinatra paying his respects, Frank Sinatra, Jr., was playing at the San Su San nightclub off the Jericho Turnpike in Mineola, Long Island. The crowds were thin and the young singer, struggling to step out of his father's immense shadow, was bombing. A call came to Franzese from Chicago. The next night, and for many nights afterward, it was standing room only at the San Su San. The crowd, mostly hit men, Mob soldiers, bookmakers, and extortionists accompanied by their floozies and favorite prostitutes, cheered wildly and treated every Frank Jr. number as if it were the greatest thing they'd ever heard. Standing ovations followed virtually every song. Buoyed by the boisterous response, young Sinatra cranked it up a few notches and gave a rousing performance equal to the unexpected adulation. The entertainment press was alerted to the San Su San happening, captured the unrestrained enthusiasm in the room, and dubbed Frank Jr. a hit. That brought in the legitimate crowds—and no doubt the elder Sinatra's ring-kissing gratitude.

It wasn't the first or the last time Sonny packed a house for a struggling entertainer. And if Sonny had a good time, there was no favor to repay.

"Hey," Steinberg continues, grabbing onto his interviewer's arm late at night at his Florida home. "I know everything about Sonny. Things I can't even tell you. I knew what he was and who he was and even who he killed. He was a hitter—*the* hitter. He swam in the biggest ocean and was the biggest, meanest, most terrifying shark in that ocean. Still is. I don't care how long he's been in jail or how old he is, he still is. He was an enforcer and he did what he did better than anyone. And he was a great friend. My friendship with him caused me enormous problems with the police, state attorney, IRS, FBI, SEC, you name it. But it was worth it. He was always there for me. Always. Artie, Hy, and I were just kids from the Jewish ghetto running a record company that exploded into a hundred-million-dollar operation before we learned what the hell we were doing. Sonny kept the wolves away. He never asked for anything in return. I love the guy."

It sounds so Hollywood—Sonny Franzese as the Mob enforcer with a heart of gold, the benevolent godfather hovering protectively over some fellow Brooklynites trying to stake a claim in the record business, and protecting them for no other reason than to be a pal. Yet from all accounts, Steinberg's improbable story checks out. The government agencies that tried so hard to figure Sonny's angle in Buddah came up empty.

There are those who laugh derisively at the image of Sonny Franzese as a benevolent godfather—or a benevolent anything. To them, he was a madman and a killer. And although his victims can't offer their opinions, there remain those who insist they were on Franzese's hit list and survived, or survived long enough to record their stories.

The best of these can be found in James Mills's twenty-nine-page *Life* magazine article, published in August 1968. The epic story chronicled Franzese's murder trial. Mills shadowed the Queens County, New York prosecutors for nine months and, as Bob Greene did later with "The Hood in Our Neighborhood," produced a lasting work of journalism. Particularly engrossing were the sections detailing the terror of the witnesses testifying against Franzese. As the trial date neared, the witnesses, including four convicted bank robbers, demanded to be taken to the courthouse in helicopters or armored cars. Their drivers reported that they cringed on the floor of the backseats as they rode to the trial.

The stress of testifying against Franzese and his fellow defendants was even more pronounced in one particular witness, John Rapacki, a convicted robber. " 'If Sonny hits the street he'll kill my wife,' Rapacki, nearing hysteria, told the prosecutors prior to testifying," according to Mills. " 'I know they'll kill her…they know they can hurt me by killing her.

'They're going to kill me. They're going to poison me. They're going to poison me in prison. You don't know how powerful they are. They're more powerful than you…If Sonny beats this, he's gonna figure no one can touch him.' "

Not long after Rapacki expressed these views, the jury returned with its verdict: not guilty. Sonny Franzese walked.

All this talk of murder, blood, guts, and savagery strikes at least one Franzese intimate as a complete fairy tale: the still-slender Tina, his long-suffering wife. Her views of the man she fell in love with, married, and has waited for with a devotion that would make Odysseus' wife, Penelope, blush, are startling in their contrast to the harsher images promoted by law-enforcement officials.

"Boss of this, boss of that…the 'family.' What family?!" Tina exclaims. "I was Sonny's family. My children were his family. Sometimes, when I read the papers, I thought he had another wife and kids somewhere, because they were always talking about his 'family,' and it wasn't us.

"And this stuff about his being a killer. He couldn't stand the sight of blood! If one of the kids scraped their knee, Sonny turned his face away.

He couldn't deal with it. I had to take care of it. Then the next day I'd read in the newspapers about what a bloodthirsty killer he was.

"I didn't know that man in the newspapers. He wasn't my husband. He was the work of somebody's imagination."

Killer. Madman. Army psycho. Capo. Enforcer. King-in-waiting. Unselfish guardian angel. Gentle lover. Squeamish father. In marrying Sonny Franzese, Tina had set an interesting and undeniably confusing course for her son Michael's life.

II

MICHAEL

CHAPTER 2

I remember the policeman.

I was ten. It was a warm afternoon in the late summer of 1961. I was playing catch with a neighborhood friend in the front yard of our Long Island home.

"Throw it high—I want to jump for it!" I shouted to my friend.

He obeyed, hurling the baseball just above my head. I leaped and snagged it in the webbing of my leather glove.

"Throw it higher," I said, tossing the ball back. "I want to catch it like Mickey Mantle did against the Red Sox!"

This time the pitch was too high. The ball skittered off the top of my glove and rolled down the street. I chased after it and found it under the brown wing-tipped shoe of a big man with a craggy face wearing a tan overcoat. The man opened his coat, flashed a badge, and pulled a huge black pistol from a shoulder holster.

"See this gun," the police detective growled, shoving the barrel in my face. "This is for your father. Bang, bang—he's dead."

The detective's words and the sight of the massive weapon froze me in place. The thought of my father being killed paralyzed me with fear. I hated that evil detective, just as I'd grow to hate all the policemen and FBI agents and United States attorneys who wanted to hurt my father.

"Go on, you little punk, get outta here," the cop said, waving the gun to shoo me away. I ran off as fast as I could. But I remember that cop and that gun as if it happened yesterday.

The encounter with the surveillance cop was the beginning of some tough times in the Long Island suburbs. After dinner one evening, about three months later, I hid in the den and listened as my parents' conversation heated up. I hated spying on my parents' arguments, but my fear made me hang on every word. The topic was my stepbrother and -sisters. Mom wanted them returned to their mother. Dad explained for the umpteenth time that his ex-wife wasn't cooperating.

"What am I supposed to do—throw them out in the streets?" my father shouted. "My hands are tied."

My eyes widened as I saw my stepbrother, Carmine, wander by on his way to the refrigerator. Carmine had heard the argument so many times before he had become immune to it. Suddenly, Mom grabbed the barefoot Carmine and pushed him out the door into a blanket of fresh snow that had gathered on the porch. I ran from my hiding place and peered out the window. I saw Carmine hopping on the ice and snow. A wave of terror shot through me. I figured I was next. My mind began working. I wasn't about to be heaved into the snow by my father without a fight. I rushed over to Mom and grabbed her around the waist.

"Stop! Stop!" I cried. "Don't do that to Carmine. Let him in! Let him in!"

My strategy was to show my father that I didn't agree with what my mother had done. Technically, he was my stepfather, but since he was the only father I'd ever known, I never thought of him or referred to him that way. At the time, however, I was just beginning to understand the difference. That's why I hid and listened to their arguments, and why I felt moved to act. I wanted my father to know that I was on Carmine's side, and thus didn't deserve to be by Carmine's side out in the cold. Whatever the childish logic, the tactic worked. Mom cooled off. A shivering and perplexed Carmine was allowed to come back inside the warm house.

I had used my wits to diffuse an ugly scene, but it hardly eased my mind regarding my status in the family. Later that evening, I cornered Mom in the kitchen. I pleaded with her to accept my stepbrother and two stepsisters for my sake. I felt that I was in a particularly precarious situation, one that made me uneasy for much of my early life. Of the seven children in the house, I was the only one who didn't have Sonny Franzese's blood running through my veins. I reasoned that if my mother wanted my father's previous children out, where did that leave me? The most obvious solution to the arguments appeared to be a compromise that banished both the "yours" and the "mine" from the family, leaving only the "ours," the three younger children Mom and Dad had together.

My mother gently assured me that my status was secure, that the union between a mother and her child was unbreakable. She explained that it was that precise union she felt my stepbrother and -sisters needed in their lives. Her explanation did little to ease my anxiety. My insecurities were focused upon the paternal bond I craved.

As my parents continued to debate the issue over the ensuing months, I grew so nervous I tried to run away and live with my grandmother. On the surface, that move appears to be the enactment of a self-fulfilling prophecy—I was so afraid of being kicked out of the house, I left voluntarily. But the action reveals what I feared the most: I didn't want to be there the day my father—whom I absolutely idolized—finally turned on me.

He never did. No matter how coolly Mom treated my stepbrother and -sisters, and how much she believed that "a child belongs with its mother," he never withdrew an ounce of love from me.

I never forgot.

I was born on May 27, 1951, at St. Peter's Hospital in Brooklyn. My father's fast rise in his profession enabled the family to make a succession of moves during my first nine years. We hopscotched from Brooklyn to New Hyde Park, Long Island, and finally, in 1960, settled in a two-story home in Roslyn, Long Island, a bedroom community twenty minutes from Manhattan. Our spacious home, purchased in 1960 for $39,000, was one of my father's better investments. My mother recently put it on the market for just under $500,000.

As a child, my parents tell me, I was every bit the future doctor they dreamed I would become. I was helpful and obedient to my older brothers and sisters, never a brat, and hovered protectively over the younger siblings. My only flaw, according to my mother, was a fierce determination to have my way. "He could wear me down like you wouldn't believe," she once told a friend. "If he wanted something and I wouldn't let him have it, he would sit there with those puppy-dog eyes and just burn a hole through your heart. I'd almost always cave in." Even so, she concedes that I demanded little, and used my puppy-eyed power sparingly.

My father schooled me in athletics. He taught me how to hit and catch a baseball by playing a game called "pepper" in the backyard during the summer. The game entails hitting ground balls to each other from close range. Dad was a firm but encouraging taskmaster, ordering me to bend my knees and keep my body in front of the ball until I could scoop up the sharply hit grounders in my sleep. When it was my turn at bat, I was told to keep my swing level, keep the Louisville Slugger trademark up, and place the ball where I wanted it.

When the weather cooled and the leaves began to turn, we put away our Roger Maris bats and Mickey Mantle signature gloves and brought out a Joe Namath football. The sport was different, but the lessons continued. Dad taught me to fake one way, cut sharply in the opposite direction, then cradle the spiraling leather-and-lace ball into my arms. He taught me how to lead a receiver so the football could be caught on the run without breaking stride.

Whenever the family went to my Mom's parents' house in nearby New Hyde Park, Dad and I frequently slipped away from the gathering and retreated to the backyard to play a game of our own creation called "Off the Wall." We bounced a pink rubber ball off the chimney and tried to catch the rebound before it hit the ground. A catch was worth a point. Hitting the ledge where the cement base merged with the red brick chimney was worth five points. The first one to earn five hundred points won. We played for hours and hours.

As I entered my teens, the chimney game became fiercely competitive. Most matches went down to the wire. We each hated to lose, and each won our share. If Dad fell behind, I had to stay on top of him to make sure he didn't inflate his score. Dad liked to cheat.

We argued and laughed and tossed the pink ball against the chimney until the sun set over Queens and it was too dark to see the rebounds. Our competitiveness heightened our enjoyment of the game.

The backyard contests and training sessions went on for more than a decade. Dad was never too busy to play with me. In my eyes, he was the world's greatest father. I cherished every minute we spent together.

When Dad wasn't grooming me to be a shortstop, the Catholic schools were molding me into a responsible citizen. I started at St. Ann's grammar school in New Hyde Park, then graduated to Holy Cross High School in Flushing. I spent two years as an altar boy at St. Ann's Catholic Church in Garden City, frequently rising at five A.M. so I could get dressed and ride my bike to the church for six o'clock Mass. Early risers could spot me tooling down the road, clutching the handlebar with one hand and holding my black-and-white vestments outstretched in the other.

At St. Ann's, I found myself in the minority. Four out of five students were Irish, and the Irish and the Italians clashed. Playground fights were frequent, and sports teams were usually divided along ethnic lines. When we played "keep away," it was always the Italians against the Irish. There would be forty Irish guys on one side and about ten of us Italians on the other. We usually got creamed.

Fighting and playing against stacked odds toughened me and further elevated my athletic ability. By the time I reached junior high, I was pretty good. Despite facing yet another hurdle—all the coaches were Irish—I worked my way to starting roles as a shortstop on the school's baseball team and a halfback on the football team. I had the most success carrying the ball on the football field. Overcoming a smallish physique (five foot eight, 130 pounds), I was quick enough to dodge bigger, slower players and tough enough to bust through those my own size. The two attributes enabled me to win a junior-varsity Most Valuable Player trophy, which my father proudly displayed in the kitchen. Whenever a new associate came over for a breakfast or coffee meeting, he'd first have to pay homage to the gleaming trophy and listen while Dad bragged about my accomplishments. "He should have three trophies up there!" I once heard him say to a group of associates. "He should have won it the last three years, but those dirty Irish coaches kept stealing it from us. This year, he was so damn good, they couldn't take it away from us!"

He spoke knowledgeably about my achievements because he rarely missed a game. From the time I donned the ice-blue hat and stretch socks of the 'Nuzzi Brothers' Little League team in New Hyde Park, through my tenure as Big Jock on Campus at St. Ann's and Holy Cross, Dad was a fixture in the stands or on the sidelines. Sometimes he'd come right into the dugout, wearing his standard summer outfit of black nylon socks, sandals, and Bermuda shorts—a dowdy contrast to his dapper Manhattan suits and diamond rings. Often he brought his close friends, "nice" men who in another world were notorious figures. My cheering section included Jo Jo Vitacco, "Johnny Irish" Matera, Red Crabbe, Felice "Philly" Vizzari, Whitey Florio, Salvatore "Sally" D'Ambrosio, Anthony "Tony the Gawk" Augello, and Fred "No Nose" DeLucia.

I was always aware when my father arrived at the stadium or ballpark in his understated red Plymouth Valiant or, later, his green Buick Electra. I took note of where he sat in the stands or stood along the sidelines. It was as if I were performing for one person, my dad. At an eighth-grade all-star football game, I broke through the line and jitterbugged down the field for sixty-five yards before being tackled at the five-yard marker. When I got up, I searched the sidelines for my father. I spotted him running down the edge of the field, leaping up and down and throwing his fist in the air. His friends trailed behind. When they caught up, they slapped his back and congratulated him on my heroics. Two plays later, I took it in for what would be the game-winning touchdown, causing more sideline celebrations. I was pumped with adrenaline. I followed by kicking off, dashing down the field and leveling the ball carrier near the twenty-yard line. The public-address announcer reported that another player had made the tackle. I glanced over to the sideline and saw my father run to the broadcast booth, wave his fist in anger, and shout at the announcer. The announcer corrected the mistake.

"You see, Rock," he said to my grandfather as they stood behind the bench, "I knew Michael made that tackle. He ran sixty yards, scored the touchdown, kicked off, and made the tackle! He's a one-man team! That's my boy!"

My athletic success and the pleasure it gave my father led to a changed role in the family. Instead of being the outsider, I was emerging as a star at home as well as on the ball fields. My single-minded desire to please my father in every way was paying off. I brought home report cards filled with A's, stayed out of trouble, and scored touchdowns and piled up base hits.

As I succeeded, my insecurity over being a stepchild eased. Nothing was ever said between us, but my father's unqualified acceptance of me as his son had made an indelible impression. His love and attention combined with all the other qualities I saw in the man. I admired the power that surrounded him, his force, and the way he controlled all the bigger men around him. He was fair, kind, and rarely lost his temper no matter how tense the family situation became.

My father was a role model I felt I could emulate. I made it a point to observe and copy the qualities in the man that I so admired.

Surviving my mother was a problem of another stripe. Although my father provided her with a live-in maid, she was a fanatic about cleanliness and preferred doing most of the cooking, dishwashing, laundry, ironing, and vacuuming herself. The cleaning frenzies stirred tension in the household. The children were forbidden to use the showers and tubs for days after she scrubbed the facilities to a shine. I once became so exasperated with this edict I took a bar of soap out to the backyard swimming pool and bathed there. The children weren't allowed to enter their bedrooms after the rugs had been vacuumed and raked, and I had to wear my Catholic school uniform long into the evening so as not to soil a second set of clothing.

As clean as the house was, the battles that went on there were anything but. My spirited mother's hands-on approach to disciplining the noisy brood included threatening us with wooden spoons, table legs, a guitar, the metal chimes from a grandfather clock, or anything else in reach. She kicked, scratched, and, on at least one occasion bit me. She was quick with her hands, I used to warn my friends, describing her as one might a prizefighter.

Mom was similarly spirited in her periodic spats with Dad, but her weapons were psychological. She argued like she cleaned, furiously and repetitively. She could beat a dead horse into ashes, resurrect it the next evening, and beat it to dust again. No issue was ever settled, no argument too redundant. And no matter what subject initially set off a new round, the verbal sparring almost always shifted to the two main issues of conflict—my stepbrother and -sisters, and money.

I guess one can sympathize with my mother's feelings toward the extra children. She was just a teenager herself when she met my father, and her head was swimming with the excitement of the Stork Club. She married a powerful figure with heavy ties to the entertainment business. But along with the thrilling nights on the town and the ringside tables at the big shows, she was swamped by four, five, six, then seven children.

The money conflict resulted from Dad marrying a woman who was as loose with a buck as he was tight. He had grown up in the Depression, and like many who struggled through that dark period, he never could shake the thought that those bleak times might return, no matter how much money he later made. My Mom harbored no such memories. She loved to spend, particularly on clothing and home furnishings, both of which she was forever changing.

I often wondered what kept my mother and father together. Once, when I was older, I went as far as suggesting to him that they divorce for his peace of mind—an unusual stance to take against one's own mother, but that shows where my loyalties were. He wouldn't hear of it. From his perspective, my mother's few eccentricities were a small price to pay. She was gorgeous, a characteristic that can cover a multitude of sins. Each new expensive outfit only made her look more ravishing. It was comforting for him each evening to walk into a beautifully kept home filled with children who toed the line. And to the outside world, Mom defended him and his children—all the children—with a ferocity that rendered the internal conflicts meaningless.

Although I struggled to narrow my concentration on science—biology—and on fielding ground balls and eluding linebackers, my father's notoriety kept intruding. I was twelve when the articles first began appearing on the inside pages of the local newspaper. The stories would announce that Sonny Franzese had been arrested for some minor crime, then went on to refer to him as a "Mafioso" or "organized crime chief." Dad would show up at home a day or so later as if nothing had happened. No explanation was ever offered. Up until then, I thought he was just a successful businessman, which he was. He owned or had interests in many legitimate businesses, including a dry cleaner, numerous bars, nightclubs, restaurants, and diners, a sportswear company, and a pastry shop. He even had a piece of a major record company and was involved with professional boxing.

I didn't understand the stuff in the newspapers about organized crime. It was finally our English maid, Pauline, who sensed my dismay and confusion. She sat me down one afternoon and, without being judgmental, explained what the terms "Mafia," "La Cosa Nostra," and "organized crime" meant. I was grateful but remained perplexed. As the stories increased, I wondered why Mom and Dad didn't call a family meeting and explain what was going on.

They never did. They ignored it, so I ignored it.

I was fourteen, just getting started in high school and serious athletics, when the stories leaped from the back pages to the front. On December 24, 1965, many of my neighbors and classmates discovered for the first time that I was the stepson of "The Hood in Our Neighborhood." My family brushed off the long, damning story and proceeded with a typical Christmas Eve, feasting on seafood and spaghetti at my mother's parents. Not a thing was different that evening. At midnight, we sat in a circle around the tree and one by one opened a mountain of presents. Dad gave me a gold, ten-speed English Racer bicycle. The sleek bike made my blood rush. (Two days later, it was stolen from in front of a Great Eastern Mills department store, where I had parked it to go exploring inside.)

When I returned to school after the holiday break, there were stares and whispers about the newspaper story, but not as much as there could have been. I attended school under my birth name, Michael Grillo. My mother explained that it had been a condition of her divorce that I go by that name until I was eighteen. After that, I could decide for myself which last name I wanted. The Grillo name worked to shield me from those who didn't know my background. The ones who did were mostly friends, and they kept their feelings to themselves. I was a football star and a popular student and had my own identity.

But there's always someone who has to make trouble. In this case, it was a fat Irish kid who took it upon himself to bring the article to school. Flashing it around the hallways and the playground, he informed everyone within earshot that "The Hood in Our Neighborhood" was my father. Encouraged by the attention he was getting, he decided to taunt me directly. "Hey, Michael, I hear your dad's a gangster," he said in the hall.

I stayed cool, pretending to shrug off the embarrassing incident. Inside, I was furious. It wasn't so much the personal insult as the way the fat kid and his snickering friends were portraying my father as some common criminal. I shadowed the guy for the rest of the afternoon, caught him on the playground after school, and beat him bloody.

That quieted things down for a while. Unfortunately, both the press and the prosecutors stayed on my father's tail. The stories continued. At baseball practice that spring, one of my teammates, jealous over being beaten out for the coveted shortstop position, christened my victory with a cutting jab.

"So what? At least my father's not a hood," he said. I tore after him, but the fight was broken up by the other players and coaches before any damage could be done.

Around the same time, I was given a brief glimpse of my Dad's other side. I went with him to Manhattan one afternoon to visit Kama Sutra Records, check in with Phil Steinberg, and see if I could catch a glimpse of the sexy teenage sisters Mary and Betty Weiss, who made up half of the hot rock group the Shangri-Las. We were picked up by Johnny Irish Matera and Red Crabbe, two bruisers. On the way, Dad ordered Matera to pull down a side street where a stocky, balding man about six feet tall was waiting. Dad told Matera, Crabbe, and me to wait by the car as he went for a walk with the stranger. The two were about fifty feet away when I heard my father screaming and cursing. I looked over and saw him grab the bigger man around the collar with both hands and literally lift him from the pavement. Dad held him up for about thirty seconds, then dropped the man to the pavement. I had never seen my father so furious, and marveled at the almost inhuman strength he displayed.

I noticed that Crabbe and Matera were so tense they were about to jump out of their skin. "This ain't right," Matera kept saying. "This don't look right. We better stay close."

The confrontation ended as abruptly as it started. Dad returned, jumped in the car, and ordered Matera to hit the gas. "That dirty bum," he mumbled as they drove away.

Nothing further was ever said.

A second encounter occurred inside our home in Roslyn. A hapless neighborhood carpenter, a distant cousin with a reputation for laziness, picked the wrong house, and the wrong woman, to irritate. Mom was unnerved by his delays in her latest paneling and redecoration project and got on Dad about it. When the mammoth carpenter finally showed up to complete the job, Dad confronted him in the kitchen. The carpenter offered some lame excuses and my father responded by firing a right cross to his eye, tumbling him to the linoleum. The carpenter got up and tried to slink away. "Get back here," Dad shouted. "I haven't finished talking to you!"

Despite the intensity of the incident, I had to stifle a laugh. I looked at Mom and she too was fighting to keep from laughing. Dad had barked the same command he used with the kids.

When the carpenter left, Mom took my father to task. "I can't believe you punched the guy right here in my kitchen!"

"I did it for you," Dad explained. "Now stop nagging me about him!"

"Dad, you treated him like one of the kids," I said.

We all ended up laughing about it—everyone except the carpenter, of course.

By the early 1960s, law-enforcement officials had placed my father under constant surveillance. Detectives sat in unmarked cars at various locations near our home, disturbing neighbors and making a nuisance. It was no picnic for the officers, either. Their job was boring and mentally numbing, and they grew to hate the family who had put them there. During the hot summers, the detectives would bake inside their cars. They struggled to contain the anger their misery caused.

One neighbor, a woman known for her eccentric behavior, became so sick of the grumpy officers parked in front of her house she decided to take action. She walked to their car, brandishing a garden hose. "You guys hot in there?" she said. "Maybe you need to cool off." She sent a blast of water inside the car's open window, soaking the men and all their detailed surveillance records.

No one parked in front of her house again.

Other incidents were more serious. One evening Dad took us to dinner at the nearby Silver Moon Diner on Lakeville Road. A beefy Nassau County cop with a bad attitude decided to push things. He rode our bumper, flashing his headlights, backing off, then speeding up and riding the bumper again. It frightened the younger children, making them cry. Dad kept his cool, but I could tell he was furious that the officer was making a scene in front of his family. At the diner, he calmed the younger children and seated everyone.

The beefy detective walked in with his partner. "There's the tough guy and his worthless family," he said as he passed.

Dad had enough. "You degenerate bum—you bother my family and I'll kill you!"

The diner went dead silent. Everyone froze. The detective turned and went for his gun.

That only enraged my father further. "Go ahead. Go for it, you pawn—go for your gun. I'll kill you before you get it out of the holster!"

My Mom and I jumped up and held Dad back, while the second detective grabbed his partner. My father and the cop continued to trade insults over our shoulders before settling down.

Dinner proceeded without further incident. The next day, the loose-cannon detective was taken off the assignment and was never seen in the neighborhood again.

His replacements were less overt, but the harassment continued. Fighting boredom, the officers began hassling Mom and the rest of us to pass the time. A confrontation on the lawn led to a detective calling Mom an "asshole." I charged the man but was held back by my mother and my brother Carmine. The next day, I snuck into Dad's Buick, sped out of the driveway, and took two teams of Nassau County detectives on a chase around the neighborhood. When I lost them, I returned to the house. The detectives circled back, spotted the car, and went right to the door and ratted to my father. He wasn't amused. He explained that as unnerving as the surveillance was, it was no game. The policemen were dangerous and were not to be trifled with. I got the message.

Still, the game playing continued on the part of the detectives. Arriving at the door of a high-school date's home one evening, I found myself engulfed in a blinding spotlight. When I turned, a voice bellowed from the beam.

"We just wanted to see which scumbag it was, the little one or the big one."

Before I could answer, my date came to the door. "What's going on, Michael?"

"Nothing. Go back inside," I said, pushing her into her house. "I'll handle it." When I turned to confront the detectives, the light was off and they were gone. I told my date that the men had the wrong address.

A short time later, another teenager from the neighborhood, a cute Jewish girl named Leslie Ross, tearfully informed me that her parents had forbidden her to date me. I blamed the police, as always. I grew up with a strong sense that they were the villains, not us. They were the bad guys. They were crude, nasty, and obnoxious and were always hassling and suffocating us. They were the enemy. The whole neighborhood hated them. My father never taught me to hate or disrespect the police. They accomplished that themselves.

When the family left the house, the detectives and FBI agents sometimes broke in and snooped around, planting bugs, adjusting those that were already there, or randomly searching for evidence of my father's alleged criminal empire. They tried to accomplish this without leaving a trace, but my mother's relentless cleaning had one benefit: she could spot the presence of a long-gone intruder the instant she walked in the door. On one occasion, the footprints across the freshly raked carpet were so obvious even the youngest children could spot them. Mom was enraged, but not because her privacy and civil rights had been violated. The law-enforcement officers had committed a far greater crime—they had walked on her carpet!

When I was sixteen, I was blindsided by a confrontation of a different sort while working after school at a drive-in hamburger joint called Big Bow Wow on Rockaway Boulevard near Kennedy Airport. One afternoon, a thin man with salt-and-pepper hair walked in and asked for coffee. I stared at the man; the man stared back. Our eyes locked, but neither of us said a word. The man sat at a small table, sipped his coffee, then quietly left.

After work, I went to my maternal grandmother's house instead of going home. "I think I saw my father today," I told my grandmother. "I'm not sure, but I think it was him."

Knowing how the uncertainty was eating at me, Grandma made a few calls. She confirmed what I already knew: Louis Grillo had come to set eyes upon his son.

For a long time, I wondered why my biological father hadn't said anything, and why I was also unable to speak. I realized that neither of us had anything to say.

When Dad learned of the brief encounter, he became inexplicably angry. I had long noticed that any mention of Louis Grillo upset him, for reasons he never explained.

I chose not to dwell on the strange meeting or Dad's odd reaction. The memory of the paternal ghost from the past was quickly pushed aside by the growing heat coming down upon the only man I knew as my father or wanted to be my father.

As Dad continued to beat arrest raps and maintain his freedom, the police and prosecutors stepped up the harassment. Shortly before I graduated, my parents decided to throw a party in my honor. They set up a tent in the backyard and put out an impressive spread. Scores of class-mates attended. I gave my first public speech that evening, thanking my father for all my success.

Near the end of the celebration, Dad signaled me to come over near the side of the house where we could be alone. When I arrived, he handed me a small package.

"This is for you. I want you to have it. You deserve it."

I opened the neatly wrapped box. Inside was a ten-thousand-dollar, eighteen-carat-gold Lucien Picard watch embedded with diamonds. My jaw dropped when I saw the extravagant gift. Dad smiled and opened his arms. His eyes glistened. We embraced for nearly a minute.

"You've been a good kid, Michael. I'm proud of you. I'm proud that you're my son."

I had to fight to keep from crying.

Within days of the graduation party, a shower of subpoenas rained on my high school and neighborhood. All the cars driven to the celebration, from teenagers' hot rods to their fathers' Oldsmobiles, had been photographed and their license-plate numbers recorded. The subpoenas, summoning the registered owners to a Nassau County grand jury, went out to high-school kids, their parents, and unknowing friends who had loaned out their cars for the afternoon. Our phone kept ringing with scared teenagers and anxious parents wanting to know what was happening and how to respond. It was terribly embarrassing, airing the dirtiest of laundry in public, but my father took it in stride. He advised everyone to appear before the grand jury and tell the truth. The police and prosecutors knew nothing of any substance would result from the tedious and expensive effort. But in the annals of government harassment, it was a move worthy of the *Guinness Book of World Records*.

A few weeks before I turned eighteen, my father called me into his room and handed me some legal papers. "You're changing your name," he said. "It's all been taken care of. I want you to go see the lawyers."

I found it peculiar that he hadn't asked me if I wanted to change my last name to Franzese. I certainly did, and was overjoyed that he had arranged it; still, I was curious about why he hadn't asked me first.

Especially then. The previous year, the Franzese name had been back in the headlines as we suffered through a series of highly publicized trials; the charges ranged from extortion to murder. The law-enforcement blitz led to a further spate of newspaper and magazine articles starring my father as a Mob-king-in-waiting. I again fought to ignore the stories, ignore the stares of my classmates and the insults of the policemen, and lead a normal teenage life. I had, for the most part, succeeded.

I wasn't so successful in ignoring the effects of the trials themselves. The court proceedings and their aftermath would alter the course of my life.

CHAPTER 3

My father's downfall began with the arrests of four lowlife bank robbers in 1965. Two, John Cordero and Charles Zaher, were heroin addicts; the others, Jimmy Smith and Richard Parks, were hapless criminals of minimal style. Their modus operandi was to sweep into a targeted bank, freeze everyone in the sights of their guns, and send Smith, the designated "jump man," bounding over the counter to grab all the loose cash he could. Then they'd split, usually in a waiting car driven by Zaher, or Cordero's wife, Eleanor. The fact that the critical "wheel man" was often one of the heroin addicts didn't speak well of the group's mental abilities. After completing a half-dozen or so of these reckless robberies, the gang had grown important enough to be targeted by an opportunistic snitch. Their arrest was the first step in what would be a classic example of the criminal food chain.

In prison, the four bank robbers banded together and decided to do some snitching of their own. They agreed to offer up a mid-level Mob associate named Tony Polisi as their mastermind. Polisi was promptly arrested, tried, and convicted.

The bank robbers had been cooperative, but apparently not too smart. Time was shaved, but they still faced hefty sentences. It's not hard to surmise what happened next. Their comrades in prison no doubt chided the robbers for having played their trump card for so small a pot. If you're going to sell somebody out, the jailhouse logic goes, you might as well sell out somebody big and go for a reduction of the entire sentence.

It wasn't long before the four robbers called the prosecutors back into their cells and said it was all a mistake. Tony Polisi was only an errand boy. Sonny Franzese was their *real* mastermind.

My father was arrested and charged with conspiracy to commit bank robbery. He was given the police treatment afforded a Mob superstar. Everywhere he went, from booking rooms, court hearings, and jail cells, he was escorted by a dozen or more shotgun-toting, uniformed officers, prison guards, police detectives, and federal agents.

The case brought against him was difficult to believe. It was unthinkable that he would have thrown in with a band of drug addicts and losers. I didn't know it then, but the two heroin addicts were the key.

The traditional Mob swearing-in ceremony, as recorded by Jimmy "the Weasel" Fratianno in the book *The Last Mafioso,* includes this passage: "There are three laws you must obey without question. You must never betray any of the secrets of this Cosa Nostra. You must never violate the wife or children of another member. You must never become involved with narcotics. The violation of any of these laws means death without trial or warning." This oath was burned into my father's soul. To have led a rat pack of bank robbers that included two junkies was an unquestioned violation of the Mob code. It could have resulted in his death "without trial or warning," a death he would have accepted without protest.

My father's own personal adherence to the oath can be illustrated by a story I learned years later. When Buddah Records began coming unglued, my father could have marched in and taken over. Inwardly, he would have liked nothing better. Dad enjoyed the music scene with its stars and excitement, and the entertainment business had long been a source of relatively clean income. Buddah was a money factory, and my father had an in. Yet, when the lucrative record company was at its most vulnerable, he backed off. The reason? His friend, Buddah co-founder Phil Steinberg, had gotten himself addicted to speedballs, a potent combination of pharmaceutical speed and cocaine.

"When I became an addict, any plans Sonny and the Mafia had for Buddah Records disappeared," Steinberg confirms. "They used to be everywhere, all over the building, then *boom,* they vanished. We had our corporate throats exposed, and suddenly they were gone."

Unfortunately for my father, such dramatic testimony could not be offered at his trial. In the cagey world of the law, defense attorneys wouldn't even consider going into court and saying their client swore a blood oath to the Mob that forbade him to have any dealings with drugs or drug addicts. Nor would the attorneys add that if such were the case, the jury need not trouble itself with a verdict: if the accusation were true, then my father's own "family" was sworn to swiftly enact the death penalty upon him. Such a bold courtroom strategy would be too risky, and far too subtle for a jury to comprehend. The legal rule of thumb back then was, if it comes out during the trial that the accused is a mobster, the jury will convict regardless of how the facts of the actual case stack up.

The trial commenced. The four felons repeated their synchronized stories about meeting with my father in a Long Island motel room in July 1965 so he could map out their reckless bank robberies.

Few people believed the testimony, not even the journalists who had hounded my father for years. "That's not the way it's done," flatly states *Newsday's* Bob Greene. "The guys at Sonny's level, they insulate themselves. They have a soldier deal directly with robbers. Even if he were involved, he would have worked through an intermediary."

Greene had said something similar in his story "The Hood in Our Neighborhood":

> Franzese follows a basic Cosa Nostra policy of protection, police say. It is a policy called insulation. The man who makes book or robs a motel is five persons removed from Franzese himself. Franzese gives the orders over a public phone or in a walking conversation and they are then transmitted down the line through three to seven people before they reach the man who commits the actual criminal act.
>
> So even if the criminal is caught, it would require three to seven people to admit that the original orders had come from Franzese. Somewhere along the line, one of these people would keep silent. This, authorities say, accounts for the inability of law enforcement agencies to imprison him for crimes they know he is masterminding.

"It's my own personal feeling that the testimony was entirely out of context," Greene recalled nearly a quarter century later. "Having seen the way Sonny operated in the past, having investigated him, and having talked with law-enforcement officials who had Sonny under surveillance, it just didn't add up. Sonny was extremely careful. He was the rising star in the Colombo family. At the time, the family was in disarray. Sonny was the guy everyone expected to straighten it out and emerge as the boss. He had brains. He conducted himself with dignity. And he was enormously highly regarded among his associates. For him to do something like that, sitting down with a bunch of flaky guys, masterminding minor bank robberies, something so out-of-control like that, it didn't fit.

"Sonny was one of the highest-profile mobsters around at the time," Greene continues. "He was being written about a great deal [especially by Greene!]. He was being looked on as a comer. The feds might have targeted him."

Another *Newsday* reporter, the late Tom Renner, monitored the trial and sat in on some of the testimony. Renner, regarded as one of the foremost organized-crime writers and authors in the nation, supported his colleague's view.

"I was shocked—really shocked," he said. "That was not Sonny's bag. He didn't get involved with clowns like that. He had such a strict sense of carefulness on who he dealt with and how he dealt with them. This was low-level crime. Sonny was a high-level criminal. Gambling. Entertainment. Bookmaking. He wasn't a two-bit bank robber. It didn't make sense. It still doesn't make sense."

The government tried the case. The bank robbers testified. The defense attorneys did their best. And my father was convicted.

Judge Jacob Mishler completed the dispensation of justice by sentencing him to fifty years in prison. How severe is that? In early 1990, a judge in Phoenix, Arizona, sentenced a bank robber to no jail time at all, just 240 hours of community service. "Fifty years is definitely a long sentence for bank robbery," Greene says. "Sonny got the years because of who he was. Back then it was different. That was before the *Godfather* movies came out and humanized the Mafia. Before that, they were just thought of as inhuman thugs that had to be put away. *The Godfather* was the best thing that happened to the Mafia."

Marlon Brando and Al Pacino came along five years too late for Dad. In the end, the general feeling was that justice had been served. The details were said to be unimportant. A "bad man" got what was coming to him. A "bad man" the government feared was getting too big and powerful. He was put away for the rest of his life so he couldn't re-emerge and continue his climb up the ranks of his empire. This was a big win for the guys in the white hats.

There were no innocent victims.

Except no one considered the teenage boy who watched part of the trial from a seat in the front row. No one considered the effect the trial would have upon me, an honor student heading to college and medical school and a career as a doctor. I had struggled all my life with the confusing concepts of good and evil. I idolized my father, but the newspapers said my father was a criminal. I refused to believe it, even after I knew some of it was true. Now, in this trial, in a United States court, I wanted to see the difference. I wanted to see for myself what was wrong with the strong, honorable man I saw every night at the dinner table. A man who treated my often demanding mother so tenderly, and loved my brothers and sisters so intensely. The man who embraced an insecure stepchild and treated him as a blood son.

I sat in the courtroom and waited for evidence of the alleged evil that made my father such a horrible man in the eyes of the world. I also had to see, in comparison, the good in the upstanding citizens who were pitted against my father—the judges, prosecutors, and law-enforcement officers. I had to understand, so I could know which side to choose.

What I observed were federal judges and prosecutors who accepted without question the improbable and self-serving statements of junkies and robbers. I heard stories about police officers and FBI agents swearing to God to tell the truth in a court of law, and then telling lies so transparent that even a teenage boy could see through them. I listened as my father's associates described an entire system working on the theory that the ends justify the means.

I listened, and I remembered.

CHAPTER 4

Within months of the bank robbery conviction, while free on appeal, my father was arrested for murder, held in jail without bond, and brought to trial again. This time he was charged with ordering the 1964 gangland slaying of veteran hit man Ernie "the Hawk" Rupoli. The Hawk had been shot six times, stabbed twenty-five times, bound, fitted with cinder blocks, and buried in the waters off a Long Island beach. Despite the "expert" work, the mangled body surfaced three weeks later.

My father had never even heard of the guy.

The witnesses against him were the same four bank robbers who had testified against him in the previous trial.

After deliberating for only three hours, a short time for a three-week murder trial, the jury found my father and his cohorts innocent. His friends gathered at the house and we threw a big champagne party to welcome him home.

The next morning, and every morning afterward for the following six weeks, he awakened at six, as he had been forced to do in jail. He'd walk down the hall into our bedroom and wake me in the upper bunk. He used the ruse that he needed someone to make coffee—Mom being a late sleeper—and had designated me for the task. I suspected that he was just lonely. I didn't complain. I loved spending the quiet morning hours alone with him, watching the sunrise, talking sports, trading jokes, laughing, and telling stories. By the second week, my eyes would pop open at 5:45 A.M. as I eagerly awaited his summons to the coffee machine.

His court victory didn't stop the prosecutors in an adjacent district, Nassau County, from trying to get some headlines of their own. They regrouped a few of the bank robbers and charged my father with masterminding a particularly heinous home burglary that was highlighted by the robbers tying up the children in the basement. He was infuriated that he would be linked to a crime against children, but understood that the bigger the smear, the better the chance of conviction.

He decided that my mother should remain out of the courtroom for this trial: he didn't want to risk any more stories about her threatening the witnesses with hand gestures. I took her place and watched most of the proceedings, usually sitting up front with a Colombo family capo named Joey Brancato, a World War II hero with a wooden leg.

When the jury announced its decision, Brancato was so nervous his peg leg began knocking loudly against the bench. He grabbed my hand and squeezed it tight.

The jury found my father not guilty. He turned around and winked, embraced his attorney, then walked from the defense table and hugged me. Outside the courtroom, my father, Brancato, and I waited for the jury so we could thank each member. One of the jurors, an older, gray-haired man, walked over to me.

"You take care of that father of yours, and keep him out of trouble," the man said.

Dad's attorneys managed to delay his bank robbery sentence for three years while they appealed the case. During that time, my mother worked feverishly trying to gather evidence that would reverse the verdict. Hard as she tried, she couldn't come up with anything to sway the judge.

On Holy Thursday, 1970, when I was nineteen, the day of reckoning arrived. The lawyers had exhausted all but one appeal.

Before my father left home, he took me aside. "They might remand me today, Michael," he said, using the legal term for being handed over to the prison system. "If they do, I'm depending upon you to take care of your brothers and sisters and mother for me."

His appeal was rejected. He was taken into custody and transported to Leavenworth, Kansas, where he began a fifty-year sentence for a crime he never committed.

Our family was stunned. He had remained free for so long after the initial conviction we had come to believe he would never have to serve. Following the first trial, there were two court victories and big, post-verdict celebratory bashes. It was hard to comprehend that the long-forgotten, bogus bank-robbery conviction, which now seemed like little more than a bad dream, could take him away.

I was in my first year of premed studies at Hofstra University at the time. I drove around the neighborhood after classes that afternoon trying to come to grips with my grief. I ended up at my grandfather's house. I searched the backyard barbecue cabinet until I found a pocked and fading pink rubber ball in the drawer where my grandfather kept paper plates and plastic forks. I began throwing it against the chimney, softly at first, then harder and harder until the ball hit the ledge with such force it sailed over the neighbor's seven-foot hedges. I didn't bother to search for the tunnel I had burrowed through the hedges when I was younger in order to retrieve errant rebounds.

"Five points, Dad," I said to myself in a voice choked with emotion. "We'll get you out. I won't rest until we get you out."

Returning home, I once again found it dismaying that my parents had never sat the family down and prepared them for my father's imprisonment. He just walked out of the house that morning and didn't come back. We would each have to deal with the loss in our own way.

With Dad behind bars, my mother began working even harder to dig up the nugget of evidence that could prove the frame and set him free. But her understanding of the often frustrating intricacies of the law was limited. In her eagerness, she had her attorneys rush in with motions based on bits and pieces of evidence that appeared important to her but held little legal value. We tried to get her to slow down and build a better case, but she wouldn't listen. From her perspective, the frame was so obvious, the evidence so compelling, why make Dad sit in jail another day?

While debating our next move, I received a call from Joey Brancato. He said family boss Joe Colombo was furious over the FBI's arrest of his son, Joe Colombo, Jr., on the flimsy charge of melting coins for their silver content. Colombo was planning to counterattack by picketing the FBI's Manhattan office at Sixty-ninth Street and Third Avenue. Brancato said that Colombo wanted me and my mother to join him.

The pickets began with just a handful of people, including Colombo himself. That was unprecedented: suddenly, one of the most powerful leaders of a legendary secret society had surfaced from the darkest shadows and was out in the open, walking a picket line and chatting with reporters. Colombo's two other sons, Vincent and Anthony, joined Joe Jr., out on bail, in supporting their father.

At the start of the second week of protests, someone handed me a sign that read: "I am the victim of FBI Gestapo tactics. My father was framed and is serving fifty years." The sign, and the clean-cut college freshman who waved it, was a natural for the media. I received Colombo's blessing in giving interviews and talking about my father's case. A number of newspapers, including the *New York Post,* wrote features.

Each day, as word of the street action spread, the number of picketers increased. Colombo reacted by creating an organization called the Italian-American Civil Rights League. The purpose of the group was to combat stereotyping and ethnic slurs against Italians, particularly the belief that all Italians were mobsters. The fact that the group's leader was himself a bona fide Cosa Nostra don, and might do more to foster the stereotypes than fight them, was brushed aside.*

The picketing went on for months. Colombo, a short, polished man with dark, thinning hair, was tenacious. As the Italian-American Civil Rights League grew in numbers and popularity, Colombo's determination grew with it.

I walked the line every chance I could. I'd attend biology, chemistry, Italian, English, and sociology classes at Hofstra in the mornings and picket in the afternoons. We hounded the FBI agents as they moved in and out of their offices, cursed them, painted them as villains, and generally made them uncomfortable. I found it ironic how the tables had turned. My family had been harassed by cops for much of our lives. Now we were harassing them.

My involvement with the league had a second, more subtle effect. I began striking up friendships with Colombo's soldiers and their associates. They educated me on their operations and offered me jobs and slices of the pie. I didn't commit himself, but I took it all in.

A few months into the protests, I was standing in front of a nearby coffee shop with my mom and another woman. Two men in a convertible approached. They slowed down as they drew near.

"Hey, you dago bastard—fuck you!"

"Come over here," I yelled back.

Before anything could happen, a uniformed officer appeared out of nowhere and grabbed me.

"You should get *them,*" I said, pointing out the men in the convertible. "Why are you jumping on me?"

---

*Similarly ignored was the fact, revealed later, that the FBI had gone after Joe Colombo, Jr., solely to bait the senior Colombo into doing something irrational—which is exactly what he did. "We discovered that if we went after these guys' kids, they'd go out of their minds," confided an FBI agent years later. "We hit the jackpot with Colombo."

"Shut up, Franzese," the officer growled. "You're just a troublemaker. Get across the street with the rest of the greaseballs where you belong."

Twenty years of taking abuse from policemen spun like a scratched record through my mind. I felt my blood rush and my anger swell. I clenched my fist and threw a straight right that dropped the cop to the pavement. Within seconds, a half-dozen officers were climbing all over me, throwing me against a storefront wall and pounding me with their nightsticks. I fought back, cursing and lashing out at the officers. The officers finally gained control and snapped a pair of handcuffs around my wrists. They stopped traffic on Third Avenue, ushered me across the street, and shoved me into a paddy wagon. Meanwhile, my mother had run screaming to alert the picketers. Colombo was quick to act. He ordered the picketers to surround the vehicle and prevent it from leaving. For thirty minutes, the cops and the Italians had a tense standoff. The Mob demanded my release. The cops held firm. Finally, Colombo gave the signal and the crowd dispersed. I was taken to the precinct station, photographed, fingerprinted, and thrown in jail.

Infused with anger and pumped with adrenaline, I taunted the processing officers. A detective told me that my father was outside and wanted the keys to the car. Knowing it was my grandfather, I answered that my father wasn't out there and refused to hand over the keys. The detective went into the lobby, returned, and repeated the request. I again refused, saying it wasn't my father. Finally, the detective caught on.

"Okay, smartass—your *grandfather* wants the keys to the car."

I turned them over.

"I told you it wasn't my father," I said.

Within the hour, Barry Slotnick, a famous New York defense attorney, was in the station house arranging my release. Slotnick, Colombo's attorney, retrieved me from the cell and escorted me to a waiting car. Inside the car was Joe Colombo.

"Are you okay?" the boss asked.

"I'm fine," I said defiantly.

Colombo laughed. "You got some balls, kid. But you have to learn— you don't fight with cops. You can never win."

I shrugged.

"You're a good kid," Colombo said, reaching into his pocket and pulling out a button.

"I'm making you a captain in the league."

The experience left me with a far deeper memory than that of Colombo's gesture. I was impressed by the way Colombo had commanded his forces to stall the paddy wagon, and by the way he had dispatched a prominent attorney to handle things at the jail. For the first time, I got a feel for both the power and the "family" aspect of my father's mysterious life. They had taken care of me. What I had done, slugging a police officer, was a serious offense. People have done hard time in prison for less. Yet I had assaulted a half-dozen cops, verbally abused them, and was out within the hour. The charges were later downgraded from felonious assault to harassment. I was fined $250.

My father's reaction to the arrest was odd. The only thing that bothered him was that I was identified in the newspapers as his stepson. "Where do they get this 'stepson' stuff?" he growled over the phone from Leavenworth. "Why do they write that?"

I said I didn't know. I also didn't know why it bothered him so much.

Despite my promotion within Colombo's fringe organization, and my first taste of Colombo's power, I was becoming disillusioned with the Italian-American Civil Rights League. I had joined solely to help my father, and I wasn't seeing any progress on that front. When I visited him at Leavenworth and told him about what the league was doing, he cautioned me not to expect much. As usual, he didn't spell out why. What he knew, and wasn't saying, was that few of his associates were in a big hurry to see him get out. With him in prison, everyone moved up a notch. His cut was now enriching others. In addition, Joe Colombo had to be breathing easier. My father's power had begun to rival that of the boss. The press had touted my father as the future don, going so far as to proclaim him the real force behind the family.

Although the newspaper stories said Sonny's rise had come with Colombo's blessing, and that he was being groomed to take over, those inside the Mob knew differently. He wasn't being groomed for anything, expect maybe a coffin or a prison cell. Which explains why he advised me and my mother to focus on the legal details of his case instead of wasting time and energy with Colombo's league.

Since he wouldn't come out and explain this, I had to figure it out myself. That took time. I was lost when it came to understanding the treacherous inner workings of my father's organization. It was hard to conceive that his loyal confidants would turn their backs.

A month later, at one of the league's Tuesday-night meetings, my eyes were opened. Between scheduled speeches, a squat Jewish man with a gravelly voice stood and made a speech of his own. "What you are doing is great, but what about Sonny Franzese?" the man asked. "What's being done for him?"

I recognized the speaker as Artie Intrada, a friend of my father's outside the Mob who often invited us over to his spacious home for Passover dinner. Intrada, a shop steward for the laborers' union in Manhattan, had slid me into the closed union the previous two summers so I could work in construction for union wages of $400 to $500 a week.

Anthony Colombo was standing at the podium as Intrada spoke. After fumbling for a second, he started saying that my father was important and was to be remembered. Before he could finish, Joe Colombo sprang from his chair, took the microphone, and changed the subject. The boss signaled for Joey Brancato, who was responsible for Artie, to muzzle his charge. I watched in confusion as Brancato, the peg-legged war hero who had been my father's closest blood brother, removed Intrada from the meeting. Intrada later reported that he had been given a verbal thrashing.

Apparently, that wasn't punishment enough. Two months later, I received a call from Artie's hysterical wife. Through her sobs, she told me that her husband had been murdered. I drove to her house in Queens to comfort her.

At the funeral the following day, in a temple on Queens Boulevard in Forest Hills, a friend of the Intrada family took me by the arm and ushered me up front. We stopped in front of a closed casket surrounded by red, yellow, and blue flowers.

"I want you to see what these animals did to Artie," the woman said, lifting the coffin's lid.

I recoiled in shock. Artie's head was bluish purple and swollen to three times its normal size. Even his neck and hands were rubbed raw and bruised. The tough union steward had apparently gone out fighting. His body had been dumped among the flies and rotting fruit in a trash heap on a side street in Manhattan. Besides being beaten half to death, he had been shot once in the back of the head.

As I sat through the ceremony, the horrifying image of Artie's swollen face spun through my mind. I was further unnerved by the piercing wails of Artie's son, who at four was just old enough to sense that something terrible had happened. I stared at Artie's wife and his pretty teenage daughter, two formerly happy, outgoing women who now sat in a trance, the life drained from their faces.

The air was thick with grief and fear that seemed to radiate from the casket. I felt queasy and wanted to run outside into the fresh air. It was all I could do to make it through the sullen ceremony.

Few inside the temple understood what had happened. Artie had not just been murdered; his death was used to send a message. My father's reign was over. He was in prison, where the family apparently wanted him to stay. Anyone who questioned it would end up in the garbage with Artie.

At the time, I refused to accept or believe it. I immediately made reservations to fly to Kansas and consult with my father, pushing up a scheduled visit two weeks.

"I couldn't even recognize him, Dad," I said in the visitors' area at Leavenworth. "Artie spoke out for you at the meeting. They say that's why he was killed. Could it be?"

"I don't know, Michael," he said with only a trace of emotion. "Could be. That hurt him."

"Why? Why did they go that far? What's going on? Why did they do this?"

As always, he measured his words in the careful manner I sometimes found so frustrating. He always spoke as if every conversation, even those with his family, were being recorded by the FBI.

"Don't think these people, this league of Joey Colombo's, don't think they will do anything for me," he said. "You keep working with the lawyers."

On the plane back to New York, I struggled to comprehend what was happening. What mystified me were the actions of Joey Brancato. Joey would have given his life for my father without hesitation. How could he have turned? It would take years for me to understand. Brancato was a good soldier. Regardless of his decades of friendship and loyalty, if the word from the top was that Sonny was to rot in prison, that was the policy he followed.

That was the family's way.

Which didn't mean Brancato still wasn't Sonny's friend. According to the FBI, he displayed his unofficial loyalty to his former capo a few years later when Coney Island boss Carmine "Mimi" Scialo, a heavy drinker known for his murderous savagery and arrogance, paid Sonny the ultimate disrespect by making a series of boozy passes at the still-ravishing Tina. Brancato and his soldiers moved in on Scialo late one night on Coney Island. Brancato ordered his men to hold the screaming, scar-faced Colombo capo down while he and a gargantuan mobster named Charlie "Moose" Panarella cut off Scialo's testicles, waved the bloody orbs in his face, then stuffed them inside the dying man's mouth. Scialo's mutilated body was transported to Otto's Social Club on President Street in Brooklyn, where it was buried under wet concrete in the basement. The FBI dug up the corpse on October 9, 1974, after an informer cashed his chips by directing them to the spot.

After that, no one would so much as enter Sonny's home to visit Tina unless he was with a group.

Still, despite such violent displays of loyalty, it was obvious that Sonny was being abandoned by the Colombo brass. Michael remained too young, immature, and ignorant of Mafia ways to grasp it.

I continued being active in the league, and continued believing the "family" that had so easily rescued me from jail could do the same for my father. I wasn't afraid that my efforts might cause me to suffer the same brutal fate as Intrada. A son was expected to fight for his father—at least until directly told otherwise.

The Italian-American Civil Rights League rapidly expanded. By 1971, membership had soared into the thousands. Frank Sinatra, Sammy Davis, Jr., Vic Damone, and Connie Francis, among others, lent their celebrity to the cause and gave benefit concerts to raise a war chest. The donations coming in totaled millions. Unknowingly, Joe Colombo had stumbled upon a vast new source of clean money. Italian pride equaled big bucks. But not everyone was overjoyed about what was happening. Colombo's bizarre social activism was frowned upon by the ruling commission of the five Cosa Nostra families. The remaining bosses, led by Carlo Gambino, were aghast at what Colombo was doing and how he was operating in the open. They were seeing him giving interviews on the evening news and reading about him in the newspapers. They were also suspicious of how he was using the donations that poured in and why he wasn't sharing them with the other families. The commission met and ordered Colombo to curtail his civil rights activities and get back to the business of organized crime. Colombo refused. Not only did he rebuff the commission, he made plans for the biggest gathering yet, organizing an Italian pride rally for Columbus Day, 1971, at Columbus Circle in Manhattan. He nailed up posters and sent out a kingly proclamation that all the stores in the surrounding area should close for the holidaylike celebration.

Both Gambino and rival Colombo capo Crazy Joe Gallo ordered the stores to remain open. Gallo and his men went around ripping down the posters promoting the rally. The merchants, caught in the middle of a vicious tug of war, didn't know what to do. Most made their decision based upon whose men were in their store last.

On the morning of the rally, I was surprised when my mother decided not to attend. She was a longtime friend of Colombo, was active in the organization, and had been anticipating the big event. That changed when she awakened shaken by a vivid nightmare of Colombo being gunned down. She reasoned that if she went, it would happen as she dreamed.

Others received more direct warnings. "Don't go to the rally," Crazy Joe advised FBI agent Bernie Welsh, one of the few feds the Mob guys respected. "There's gonna be a stampede." Welsh reported the tip to his superiors and discovered that there was a loud buzz on the streets that something bad was going to go down during the event.

When I arrived, nearly twenty thousand people had gathered in the square. Colombo, flushed with victory, was standing at the podium, going over his speech and preparing for the grandest moment of his life. He spotted me and waved me over. He handed me a stack of programs that outlined the afternoon's events, then asked me to distribute them.

"Look at this crowd," Colombo beamed. "Let them try and stop me now."

I nodded, turned, and started walking down the steps. I was rocked by two successive explosions so loud and painful I instinctively covered my ears. My first thought was that someone had tossed a pair of bombs. I swiveled my head around in time to see Colombo drop.

"Joey's been hit! Joey's been hit!" someone yelled.

I then saw some men pounce on a black man clutching a pistol. The explosions had been gunshots, but I was so close to the discharging weapon that the sound had been deafening. I heard two more bangs, almost as loud but from another direction.

FBI agents on the scene later explained the second set of shots. In a scene reminiscent of Jack Ruby and Lee Harvey Oswald, one of Colombo's soldiers had stuck a pistol through the legs of a policeman and blasted the black man while he lay handcuffed on the pavement. The concussion and the powder burns nearly blew the cop's balls off. The soldier dropped his gun and vanished into the crowd. Within seconds, a half-dozen more revolvers bounced like live hand grenades on the pavement as Colombo's associates rid themselves of their guns before the police backups swooped in.

Meanwhile, the crowd screamed and ran in every direction, crashing into each other and nearly creating the deadly stampede Crazy Joe had predicted.

My first thought was to find my sister and my girlfriend, a blond Hofstra student named Maria. I spotted them standing dazed in the surging, panicked crowd near the stage and directed them into a nearby coffee shop. I ordered them to stay inside. I exited the shop and went to find out what had happened. The word among the organization was for everyone to go home. Joe Colombo had been shot and was on his way to the hospital. He was alive, but barely. The man who had tried to assassinate him, Jerome Johnson, was dead. There was nothing anybody could do.

I returned to the coffee shop, rounded up my charges, and drove them home. I found my mother distressed by both Colombo's assassination and her eerie dream that had foreseen it.

Although I wasn't an initiated member of the family, I was close enough to learn the two prevailing theories of what had happened and why. The first was the most obvious. Colombo's unprecedented activity with the Italian-American Civil Rights League had heightened his profile and that of La Cosa Nostra. It was bringing heat down upon the five families. The Mob's high commission had ordered him to cease and desist, and he had refused. That was a capital offense.

Enter the ever-opportunistic Crazy Joe. Still smarting from losing to Colombo in a power play for the family's leadership a decade earlier, Gallo sensed an opening. He was quick to pick up that Colombo's grip was eroding, and that Colombo's support among the families was nonexistent. Crazy Joe figured the chance would never be better to take his revenge.

This time, however, few figured Crazy Joe had aspirations to take over. A prison term had weakened his power, and his soldiers had never been loyal—a factor attributed to Crazy Joe's tightrope walk with sanity. The feeling was that Crazy Joe, who had met Jerome Johnson in prison, had taken out Colombo for the sheer hell of it.

Then again, at the time, the Colombo family was in its most vulnerable position in its forty-year history. Colombo was off in left field, fancying himself the Martin Luther King of Italians. His two most powerful underbosses, Carmine "the Snake" Persico, Jr., and Sonny Franzese, were both in prison. With Colombo dead and my father and the Snake locked away, maybe Crazy Joe thought he could make one last mad dash for family leadership.

The second theory, the one supported by Persico, the man who eventually took over the Colombo family, was that the government had set up Johnson to kill Colombo because they were afraid of the power he was gaining through the Italian-American Civil Rights League. The plan was, as Persico related, that after the shooting, Johnson was supposed to be arrested, not killed. He was then all set to roll over on some specified Cosa Nostra target, possibly the man who took over after Colombo's death. Johnson would get immunity to testify, go into the Witness Protection Program, and would never have to do a day for the murder. The feds would have Colombo dead and his replacement indicted for murder, a one-two blow that might have destroyed the family.

Whatever the truth, one thing is certain: Jerome Johnson's bullet, which turned Colombo into a vegetable, burst the bubble of the Italian-American Civil Rights League. The organization crumbled into dust.

CHAPTER 5

As Joe Colombo lay in his bed, stripped of his mental capacity, his crime family spun into disarray. Because Colombo had focused on keeping my father in jail and disbanding Dad's loyalists, Carmine Persico's soldiers were allowed to stay together. That placed Persico in a position to mount a successful coup from behind bars. Persico installed Thomas DiBella, an aging, low-keyed capo, as the acting don until his parole.

Following the assassination attempt, my personal life became as unfocused as the Colombo family. I found it difficult to concentrate on my studies. Figuring in medical school and internships, I faced a decade of intense study before I could become a doctor.

There was a quicker route to success. As frightening as the Intrada hit and the Colombo shooting were, there were aspects of the Mob I found intriguing. The stories I heard on the picket line about the money that could be made through various legal and illegal business ventures excited me. I needed money, because I came to believe that money was the key to winning my father's release. I decided to reduce my class load and take a stab at a few business opportunities.

Among my father's many scattered businesses was an automotive body shop in Mineola, Long Island. I used to work there after school and learned how to paint and restore car exteriors. I figured it might be a good place to start. I paid a visit to the new owner, an upbeat man named Frank Cestaro, and explained that I had worked for the previous owner and was interested in the job. It was mostly a ruse to see who had taken over the place. Cestaro, no doubt making the name connection, called me the next day. I said I wasn't really interested in working as an employee but would be willing to lease half the shop and operate my own business. Cestaro agreed.

I began digging wrecked Ford Pintos and Chevy Vegas out of junkyards, restoring them, and selling them for a healthy profit. The two makes, America's first attempt to counter the Japanese small-car market, were so flimsy and cheaply built it took little more than a fender bender for an insurance company to total them out. Many junked Vegas and Pintos were actually in relatively good shape and could be fixed in a day or so and sold for $1,500 to $2,000. Although the effort was profitable, I quickly realized that half-interest in a body shop wasn't going to lead to a mansion on a hill.

I received a call from Tony Morano, a stout man in his late thirties with a head of curly sandy-blond hair. Morano had experience in the auto-leasing business, along with a criminal record, but he wasn't connected to La Cosa Nostra. We hit it off, formed a partnership, and rented a corner lot on Cherry Valley Road in West Hempstead. We approached Mel Cooper, a man I knew in the finance business, and asked him to direct us to a company that would assist with our start-up financing. Cooper sent us to a man named Vince in the garbage business. Vince heard us out and recommended Equilease, a company run by two brothers. We talked the brothers into giving us a $500,000 line of credit to begin our West Hempstead automobile leasing operation. Within a few months, M.B.E. Leasing was turning over ten to twenty automobiles a month. I was pulling down five hundred dollars a week.

Meanwhile, Frankie Cestaro was struggling to turn a profit with the body shop. I took over the operation and moved the equipment to the West Hempstead lot. The business, now in a better location, started turning around. It was soon putting another five hundred dollars in my pocket each month.

Six months later, during my sophomore year of college, Tony and I sectioned off a corner of our Cherry Valley property and opened a used-car lot. This segment of our rapidly expanding operation started kicking a thousand dollars a month into my swelling kitty.

My success in West Hempstead had not gone unnoticed. My father's friends started coming around, looking over the operation and trying to figure their angle. I played them nice and easy, giving up nothing but leaving doors open and making sure no one left insulted. Pretty soon, instead of trying to squeeze their way in, they came to me with partnership offers on other ventures. One was a pizza restaurant in Lindenhurst, Long Island. A friend of my father, Vinnie Perozzi, told me about a location he had scouted in a strip shopping center near the commuter railroad tracks. I checked it out and saw what Vinnie saw—lots of hungry people waiting for trains. I kicked in one month's take from the leasing business, $2,500, and opened a small pizza place. I instructed Perozzi to open early and serve breakfast during the morning rush hour. The strategy worked. The restaurant was soon turning a profit of eight hundred dollars a month for each of us.

I named the place Sonny's Pizza.

In twelve months of part-time work, I had started four successful businesses and was pulling down close to five thousand dollars a month in profits.

Around this time, my love life began to stabilize. Early in my freshman year at Hofstra, Leslie Ross, the neighbor who was forbidden by her parents to date me, introduced me to a coed named Maria Corrao. Maria, the daughter of a well-off Italian jeweler and his Polish wife, favored her mother. She had long blond hair, blue eyes, and the sparkling look of the proverbial all-American girl. An education major, Maria was far more intelligent and refined than the party girls I was used to. She was also more mature and serious. I was surprised to discover that she lived within a mile of my home in Roslyn, and although we were the same age, we had never met. I had dated her best friend for a while, but had never even seen her. She explained that she wasn't the type to wander the neighborhood checking out the guys.

When we were introduced, I was dating a shapely archaeology major from Holy Cross named Barbara DeVito. Leslie Ross despised her and thought that even if I went after Maria, at least I wouldn't be with Barbara. I took the bait and asked Maria to a college dance. Although the relationship started slow, and wasn't grounded in romantic fireworks or a burning physical attraction, I was drawn by Maria's character. Everything about her was nice. It was a quality that my parents picked up on immediately. My mother, who could be a pill with girls she didn't like, approved of the squeaky-clean Maria from the start. Shortly before my father went to jail in 1969, we all spent a happy New Year's Eve together at the Copacabana.

Maria had appeared during the most stressful point in my life—and my mother's. She turned out to be the perfect salve for us both. Instead of being frightened away by the family's reputation and deepening troubles, she grew closer. A nurturing type, she comforted me during my worst days of anger and frustration over my father's conviction and was there to help my mother any way she could. Often, while I was working or out doing other things, Maria would be at the house visiting my mother or baby-sitting the younger children to allow my mother to work on my father's case.

The more stressed and turbulent our lives became, the more understanding Maria became. After the Colombo assassination, a firsthand event that would have telegraphed to a thousand girls that this wasn't the kind of family to get close to, Maria responded by hanging tough. She soared beyond nice into the realm of sainthood.

Everybody loved Saint Maria—my mom, my dad, my brothers and sisters. I cared for her a whole lot, and with my time divided between school and the expanding business interests, a thoroughly undemanding girlfriend like Maria was ideal.

Although Maria and my mother were thick as thieves, what impressed me the most about her was how unlike my mother she was. Maria was low-keyed, easy to please, and, most of all, quiet. She had minimal concern for fancy clothes and material things, knew little and cared less about furniture, and had a healthy notion about the acceptable standards of household cleanliness. She never complained, asked nothing of anyone, and was always there when anyone needed her.

She was, in essence, the kind of woman who would never give her boyfriend any reason to break up. There was no doubt that she would make a perfect wife and mother, a quality Mom pointed out a few hundred times a day.

We were engaged in 1973. We set the wedding for the following year. When the date neared, I stressed out and canceled. I liked Maria and cared for her, but I still wasn't sure if I loved her. And I wasn't ready to give up the less saintly girls, the kind who overflowed with passion and little else.

Maria was crushed, but of course she didn't show it. She just waited for me to come around and set another date.

My near-marriage experience led to a rushed romance with a sizzler named Michelle Celli, a nightclub singer who was two years older than me. We met at the Baldwin Manor nightspot in Baldwin, Long Island, where she fronted a band called Stars and Stripes. Celli, a dark-haired beauty, made my blood boil.

And my mother's.

Unknown to me, Michelle's best friend and Maria's sister, Valerie, both worked for Estée Lauder cosmetics in the same Manhattan office. After Valerie was married, she brought her wedding album to the office to show her co-workers.

Michelle's friend spotted me in one of the photographs. "I know that guy!" she squealed. "He's dating my best friend!"

"That can't be," Valerie responded firmly. "He's engaged to my sister."

Michelle's friend pushed her nose closer into the album. "I'm positive," she said, pointing at the picture. "He's dating my friend Michelle, the singer. His name is Michael—Michael something…Franzese! Michael Franzese!"

Within minutes, the two women had confirmed their stories. Valerie relayed the shocking information to Maria. And Michelle's friend wasted no time telling her that I was engaged.

I had no inkling of the trouble I was in when I drove to Franklin Square that evening and wandered confidently into another popular Long Island nightclub. The moment Michelle saw me, she burst into tears. "You two-timing rat! How could you do this to me?" She ripped my gold ring from her finger and threw it against my chest with such force it stung.

"What the hell's the matter with you?" I asked.

"You're engaged!"

Michelle stayed around long enough to tell me how she had discovered my secret. A wave of panic swept over me. If Michelle knew and her friend knew and Valerie knew, that meant Maria knew. And if Maria knew, that meant my mother knew! Michelle and Maria I could handle. My mother would be impossible.

I lingered at the club, then killed time at another nearby before I ventured home. I hoped my mother would be asleep. No chance. She was waiting up. When I walked in, she gave me a look that could have burned toast.

"You no-good bum," she opened. "How could you do this? Maria knows everything. She's leaving you. You're just no good."

"It's not true, Mom," I lied.

She ignored my explanation and chewed me out good.

The next day, I went to see Maria.

"I trusted you, Michael," she said, the tears streaming down her Madonna-like features. "How could you do this to me?"

"It's not true," I said, sticking to my story.

"It's over, Michael," she said, easing the two-carat diamond engagement ring off her finger and handing it to me. "How could I ever trust you again?"

I felt painfully guilty, but also kind of relieved. I cared for Maria and no doubt would miss her, but the weight of the impending marriage had been lifted from my shoulders.

Not for long. My mother couldn't believe her son could betray an angel from heaven like Maria for a nightclub singer. She treated the breakup like a rug that needed a good vacuuming and raking. She tossed her considerable energy into negotiating a settlement. It took her a month, but she succeeded in forcing me to give up the sexy singer. Maria promised to forgive and forget. My mother invited Maria over so we could officially renew the engagement.

"Let's put this behind us," I said, still traveling the road of complete denial. I handed her the diamond ring.

"Okay. We'll start fresh," Maria agreed, accepting the ring and sliding it back on her finger.

She never mentioned Michelle Celli again.

The damage to the relationship was minimal. The damage to my psyche ran deeper. Because I had been pressured by my mother into renewing the engagement, I was more unsure than ever about getting married. I wanted fireworks. I wanted passion. I wanted it all.

Fate was on Maria's side. My life took a series of turns for the worse. I would soon need a solid, steady companion to comfort me through the rough days ahead.

With all the business deals and domestic dramas whirling around me, I never lost sight of my prime goal—freeing my father from prison. Everything I did was geared toward that. Every dollar I saved was reserved for it. When a private detective named Matthew Bonora, a former police detective, contacted me about the possibility of getting his hands on my father's missing police surveillance records, I jumped at the opportunity. I paid $5,000 to Bonora as a retainer.

Some time later, Bonora called and told me to come to his office at the Mineola courthouse. The first thing I noticed when the detective greeted me was that he was wearing white gloves. Inside the office, Bonora acted nervous and spoke softly, like he possessed something so secretive we were in danger merely by being in the same room.

Bonora opened a locked drawer and gingerly removed a stack of papers. He told me I could look at the material but couldn't touch it or change the precise order of the pages. He explained that they were the original records and were there only so I could confirm that they existed. They would have to be returned that same day, and we couldn't even risk copying them. Bonora explained that if the records were stolen, they wouldn't be allowed in court. I looked them over. They appeared to be exactly as bargained. There were names, times, and dates of every place my father went, everyone he met. I was certain that somewhere in the stack was a sheet covering the exact time and date the bank robbers said they had met with my father—the critical evidence that had mysteriously vanished during the bank robbery trial. I was equally certain it would place my father at a completely different location.

The detective said we would have to try to find a way to legally obtain the papers. I left the office as confident as I had been since the day my father left home and never returned. I told my mother and she was elated.

Unfortunately, Bonora could never get his hands on the records again. He told me his source had dried up, and the papers had been moved. The prosecutors and police continued to deny their existence. I kicked myself for not having grabbed the records when I had the chance. Bonora later told a newspaper reporter the entire incident never happened.

Just as that door slammed shut, another opened by freak accident. Next to Sonny's Pizza in Lindenhurst was a bar called the Village Pub. Although I didn't drink, I occasionally dropped by to sip a club soda and talk with the owners. I became friendly with a waitress named Dee. One afternoon, Dee's latest boyfriend, a seedy-looking dude with dark hair and a bushy mustache, was in the pub talking about the wild and crazy time he had had with his previous girlfriend. She was a woman named Rusty who wore red wigs and had a habit of marrying serious criminals. He said she had told him her husband and his friend had framed some big Mob guy and were in serious trouble.

I had been listening to him halfheartedly. When he mentioned the frame, I perked up. I let the guy go on some more, then asked if the Mob guy they framed was Sonny Franzese.

"Yeah, that's him," the man said. "Franzese."

"That's my father," I said.

The poor guy nearly had a seizure. I told him I wanted to meet Rusty, who I was sure was Eleanor Cordero, widow of the slain hit man Ernie "Hawk" Rupoli and now the wife of John Cordero, one of the bank robbers.

After some arm-twisting, the ex-boyfriend gave me his name, address, and phone number, then promised to arrange a meeting.

The following day, the guy called. He said Eleanor agreed to a meet at midnight in the parking lot of a diner on the Sunrise Highway in Lindenhurst. She would be in a red Mustang parked in the back of the lot.

I told my mother and we contacted our attorney, Herbie Lyons. We discussed the possibility of my wearing a recording device to the meeting. They advised me it would be beneficial, that I might not have the chance to talk with Eleanor again. I considered it, but something inside told me "not this time."

When I pulled into the diner a few minutes after midnight, sure enough, there was a red Mustang in the back of the lot. My headlights flashed through the car. I could see the figure of a woman sitting in the passenger seat. I parked my car, walked over, and entered on the driver's side. Although she was wearing a new wig, I recognized her instantly. "Hello, Eleanor."

She pulled out a .32 and pointed it at my head. "If you're wired, you're dead."

With her free hand, she searched my chest, thighs, crotch, armpits, anywhere the recording device could be. I remembered the debate earlier in the afternoon and breathed a sigh of relief.

"I'm clean," I said.

"You're lucky. What do you want?" she growled.

I stared at her. She was one tough, ugly bitch, about five foot five, chunky, totally unappealing. She had scars on her arms and hands, markings I didn't remember her having before. I marveled at how she never lacked for husbands or lovers, even if they were hit men and junkie bank robbers.

"I want the truth, Eleanor. I need your help."

Eleanor relaxed her grip on the gun but still held it to my head.

"Your father's innocent. They set him up. I know everything. I can get him out. But I want money and I want protection from my husband, and from the government." It was clear Eleanor equated the FBI with her criminal husband. I understood.

Before answering, it occurred to me that maybe *she* was wired. I had to choose my words carefully.

"I'll help you any way I can. But I can't give you money. That would make it appear that I bought your testimony. But if you do this for me, I'll be very grateful."

"What about protection?"

"I can protect you. Don't worry about that. But you'll have to come to the lawyers. You'll have to make a statement."

Eleanor thought for a moment, then pointed the gun barrel between my eyes. She was squeezing the handle so tightly I was afraid it would go off any second.

"If you double-cross me, I'll fuckin' blow your brains out—do you understand?"

"I just want the truth," I said, fighting to stay calm. "That's all I ask."

I gave her my number and told her to call.

She called the next day. We met again. She was less afraid this time, but still armed. To reiterate her demands, Eleanor explained her scars. She said her husband, John Cordero, in a particularly mean mood, had mixed sex, drugs, and an axe one weekend, alternating between the three. He fed her tranquilizers, chopped her up with the axe, then made love to her. He repeated the trio of activities for two days, as the tranquilizers apparently prevented her from bleeding to death. Finally, he told her he was going into the basement to sharpen the axe so he could chop her up into little pieces. When he left the room, she managed to crawl to the phone and dial 911. The police arrived, arrested her husband, and summoned an ambulance to take her, barely alive, to the hospital. She said she ended up with more than two thousand stitches—along with a nasty disposition. Her husband, she said, was kicked loose, a factor she attributed to the fact that he had ratted on my father.

"I need money and protection," Eleanor repeated. "I can't help you unless I have money and protection."

For the next seven months, the most miserable months of my life, I baby-sat Eleanor Cordero. I rented an apartment for her in Hempstead, then later moved her to a house in Huntington. I bought her a car and paid the living expenses for her and her twelve-year-old daughter. I was at her disposal twenty-four hours a day. Soon, she was coming on to me. I fought off her advances.

Before long, I had had it with this woman's constant demands, but I couldn't end it. She was cooperating with the attorneys, giving them everything they needed. They advised me to keep her happy. They needed her to testify at a hearing.

Eleanor's desire for a man just made it worse. I decided to find her someone. I flipped names through my mind. Who did I know who would do the job? Jerry Zimmerman! Six foot five inches, 275 pounds of indiscriminate manliness. I called Jerry, a shaggy dog of a guy, and a happy-go-lucky con man by trade. Not only did Jerry do his job, he liked it.

And more importantly, Eleanor liked Jerry.

She calmed down. The months dragged on. She continued to take advantage of me by making constant demands for money or material things.

If that wasn't bad enough, my mother kept pressing to meet Eleanor and get involved. I figured the two headstrong women would clash like Siamese fighting fish, and saw no reason to dump them into the same bowl. But my mother was persistent, and I relented. As predicted, they instantly despised each other. After my mother's visits, all Eleanor would talk about was how my mother drove a Cadillac, wore expensive clothes and jewelry, and lived in a big house. Eleanor began demanding similar clothing, transportation, and accommodations. I explained that my mother hadn't put Eleanor's husband in jail, and deserved what she had because of her suffering.

Eleanor was unmoved.

Amid all the insanity and the miserable afternoons, Eleanor came through. She swore out affidavits, outlining everything she knew about my father's case and swearing he was framed. She even introduced me to Charles Zaher, another one of the bank robbers. Zaher had gone straight since his bank robbery conviction and was working for the phone company. He was uneasy about meeting me, but eventually backed Eleanor and agreed to cooperate. I was also able to get the letter it had long been rumored that Zaher had written to his wife from prison, a letter that admitted they were planning to frame my father. Things were shaping up. As horrid as baby-sitting Eleanor was, it appeared to be paying off.

The afternoon prior to the hearing, I was at a body shop I owned in Deer Park, Long Island, when I spotted legendary FBI Mob hunter

Bernie Welsh lumbering toward me. Welsh, a giant man whose size and girth contrasted with his baby face and friendly demeanor, was an old-style "Untouchables"-type agent who liked to go toe-to-toe with the toughest Mob enforcers. Far from just shadowing his targets, he sometimes hounded them in an exaggerated fashion. He'd go to a Mob hangout, spot a made man or two, and make a big show of shaking their hands and offering to buy them drinks. Sometimes he'd try to sit down and have dinner with them. The guys hated the act—it killed their conversation and made them look like informers. They'd disappear into dark corners at first sight of the guy.

Welsh loved being an agent and loved the Mob beat. As annoying as he was, he was respected because he was a straight shooter. When he busted a guy, he did it by the book. "I'm gonna get Joey Brancato, and I'm going to get him honest," he'd tell me, alluding to his long battle to turn or convict my father's associate.

"That's a switch," I'd shoot back. "After you guys framed my father, now you're going to start doing it honestly?"

Welsh would just shake his head and laugh, never confirming or denying the setup.

"Michael, come on out. We gotta talk," Welsh shouted from the front of the body shop that afternoon.

"Fuck you, Bernie," I said, in no mood for the agent's games. He persisted, and I reluctantly walked over to meet him. Welsh immediately went into his theatrics. He slowly shook his head and peered at me like a high-school principal looking at a truant student.

"You're getting out of hand, Michael. You've been doing some bad, bad things."

"What now?" I said, figuring it was another famous Welsh stunt.

"We've received information that you were at a meeting and you ordered the kidnapping of Judge's Mishler's daughter."

"What?" I shouted, my blood heating. "I didn't even know he had a daughter. What kind of nonsense is this?"

Then it struck me.

"Did you tell the judge?"

"We had to," Welsh said, shrugging like he hated to do it but was duty-bound.

"A day before the hearing? You son of a bitch! A day before the hearing you tell the judge I'm gonna kidnap his daughter? You fuckers never let up."

I called our attorney, who contacted Judge Mishler. The judge confirmed that the allegation had been brought to his attention. Our attorney quoted the judge as saying that he didn't necessarily believe it, but neither could he discount it.

What effect the FBI's underhanded tactic had upon the subsequent decision is impossible to determine. Under the law, judges are ordered to remove themselves from a trial or hearing if they believe a threat, or even an unconfirmed report of a threat, may cloud their judgment. In practice, however, judges rarely take this step. What is known is that my family received a devastating lesson in the law. We entered the hearing with what we confidently felt was an open-and-shut case. Recanted testimony. Sworn affidavits. A critical piece of written evidence that spoke of the plot to frame my father before the fact. How could we lose?

Easy. Eleanor had demanded and received too much from me. The judge felt she wasn't credible, especially after the state produced a witness who claimed that Eleanor had bragged that she was selling her testimony. Regarding Zaher, a witness reversing prior statements holds little weight in the eyes of the law. Except for rare instances, the only thing that matters is what is said during the trial. Plus, there were three other witnesses who hadn't yet recanted. Since the Zaher letter hadn't been mentioned during the trial, a legal loophole held that it was insignificant. Besides, the judge felt there was some debate over the meaning of the word "frame" in the letter. Guilty men can also be set up like a picture and "framed."

The bottom line was that the government felt the Franzese family was too powerful, and our image too menacing, for anyone to believe that we hadn't frightened, coerced, or bought the testimony of the witnesses. The appeal was rejected.

To say we were shattered doesn't quite capture our feelings that afternoon. The time, the money, and the agonizing effort spent baby-sitting Eleanor had all gone for nothing.

As usual, Maria was right there, comforting me, calming my mother, encouraging us to go on, assuring us in her cheerfully innocent way that the truth would prevail.

CHAPTER 6

The auto-leasing business in West Hempstead was expanding so rapidly I decided to acquire a larger line of credit to float more cars. Our original deal topped off at $500,000. We wanted to fly higher.

A friend introduced me to a banker with a paraplegic son who was being strangled by a mountain of medical bills. It was understood that if I took care of the banker, he would feel obligated to push a credit application through the machinery. All the banker required, initially at least, was for me to purchase a $2,500 mink jacket he claimed to have won in a church raffle. I figured it was a small price to pay for a $2 million line of credit.

The banker's fur coat would haunt me for the next two years. It would lead to my arrest and three trials, destroy my entire business structure, and forever brand me a mobster.

I didn't know anything about furs, but fortunately I shared a roof with an expert—my mother. She could discern a mink from a fox at one hundred paces, and could probably pinpoint the farm where the mink had been raised. She was not only the designated appraiser; if the mink was for real, it would be hers.

I was having a hectic day at work when a friend, Vinnie, arrived with the coat. After waiting around as I took one phone call after another, Vinnie signaled that he would hang the fur on the door. I indicated that I understood. As the day proceeded, I forgot about it. At 5:30 P.M., I locked up and drove home, leaving the mink hanging on the door where Vinnie left it.

The instant I set foot in the house, my mother greeted me by saying, "Where's the coat?" I said I forgot it. She ordered me to go right back and get it. Exhausted and in no mood for another long round trip through traffic, I refused. My mother, in no mood to wait another twenty-four hours for her mink, refused to let up. I finally called an associate and told him to pick up the coat and bring it over. When the man arrived at the office, he couldn't find it. He called me and relayed the information. Figuring someone had put it in a closet or somewhere else, I told him not to worry; we'd find it the next day.

A thorough search of the office the following morning failed to locate the mink. I suspected a young mechanic who we believed had been snatching things from the shop for months. I called the guy in, cornered him, and after some tense moments he confessed. The guy said he had already moved the fur on the black market. I advised him to move it back. The guy promised to try. He then said he needed his Camaro, a beat-up car he had been working on in the shop for more than a week. That made me think he was planning to disappear like the coat. I decided to hold the Camaro and its registration as collateral until the fur was returned.

During the confrontation with the mechanic, an old friend and business associate of my father's, Philly Vizzari, had been in the office. He had just happened by.

The following afternoon, the mechanic called. He said he couldn't locate the coat, but needed his car. I said no way. What the man didn't say was that he was calling from a Nassau County police detective's office. I went out on an errand, then called the office to check for messages.

"The place is swarming with cops!" a near-hysterical employee warned. "They got the Camaro and they're tearing the place apart, looking for the registration!"

I asked to speak to the lead detective. I told the officer that I had the registration and would bring it with me. I arrived a half-hour later, peeled it out of my wallet, and handed it over. The detective grabbed it and ordered the troops to retreat.

The next morning, a Friday, I received a call from a local used-car dealer. "The cops were over here asking if you tried to sell me some beat-up Camaro. What's this all about?"

What it was about was the police were trying to build a case. I called my attorney, John Sutter, and made an appointment to see him. "Don't worry about it. It's bullshit. I'll take care of it," Sutter said.

I drove from Sutter's office back to mine, a ten-minute drive. The phone was ringing when I walked in. It was my mother. She said there were cops all around the house, searching for me. She advised me to make myself scarce. As the words left her mouth, the door of my office was jarred from its hinges and slammed loudly to the floor. A squad of cops, guns drawn, burst inside.

"Get away, quick!" my mother repeated on the phone. "They'll be there any minute."

"Too late, Mom," I said.

I was arrested and charged with conspiracy, grand larceny, and two counts of possession of stolen property (the police viewed the car and the registration as separate entities). Tony Morano was also arrested. The charges, altogether, were punishable by up to ten years in prison.

It was a strange arrest. Because of nothing more than an in-house employee/management hassle, I had been slapped with serious felonies. The newspapers and television stations covered it as big news. I was Sonny's son—a Franzese. I had to be a mobster. Enhancing that image was the fact that Philly Vizzari, the mildly interested observer, was also arrested under the same charges. Philly drove a long Caddy, smoked a fat stogie, and fancied himself Al Capone incarnate. He was not the kind of guy with whom a college premed student wants to get arrested.

What didn't help, and no doubt led to the Gestapo-like police action, was the fact that a parade of Mob guys and organized-crime associates had been observed coming in and out of the leasing office for months. Aside from those hanging around, many of my father's old friends figured they could at least get a good deal on an auto lease. Street guys have a difficult time getting credit. I accommodated them, an action that grew to be a massive headache. More times than not, they lapsed on payments, or made no payments at all. Included among the scofflaws was Philly, whom I had always called Uncle Philly. Not only did Uncle Philly beat me out of a car, he tried to make a deal with Tony Morano behind my back to create a similar leasing company in a neighboring town.

These experiences taught me a lesson I would never forget: friendship and business don't mix, at least not with my father's friends. On top of the aggravation, my association with the Mob soldiers had also brought the police down upon me.

A week after my arrest, another Friday, I entered my office and discovered an ugly incident in the making. Morano was having a heated argument with two bruisers, John "Big Chubby" Verrastro, thirty-four, and his brother Robert "Little Chubby" Verrastro, twenty-nine. Big Chubby was six-three, 300 pounds. Little Chubby was six-four, 350.

Standing behind them was a third monster, Albert Strauss, thirty-one, six foot, 210. A fourth man, Oscar Teitelbaum, twenty-nine, six-two, a tightly muscled 230, waited outside in the car. The "Chubby Brothers" were threatening to tear Morano apart. At issue was an old man's car: Morano had sold it on consignment, then decided to keep the money. The Chubbys and crew had come to collect. I learned what the problem was, did my best to resolve it, then withdrew into my inner office. I put my feet on the desk, settled back, and called Maria.

Boom. The door slammed off its hinges again. The office filled with men carrying shotguns. I didn't know what to think. A hit? A robbery? What now?

"Freeze!" one of the men shouted. "You're under arrest."

The words came as a relief. Of all the possibilities, cops were the best. There were fifteen to twenty police officers this time, twice as many as before. They were inside, outside, in plainclothes and uniforms. The police swept up everyone in sight—me, Morano, the Chubby Brothers, Al Strauss, Oscar Teitelbaum in the car, and two of my employees who chose the wrong time to be hanging around, former love slave Jerry Zimmerman and Peter "Apollo" Frappolo.

I was handcuffed to Big Chubby, who was acting like a caged bull. The big man yelled and cursed the cops and dragged me around like a rag doll. I yelled at him to mellow out, but Big Chubby continued his frantic act all through the ride in the paddy wagon.

At the police station, a familiar officer walked over. "You need anything, Michael?"

"Yeah—get me away from this maniac!"

The officer smiled and uncuffed me.

It took five hours for the police to come up with the charges. I figured I was clear. All I had done was pass through the office. I didn't even know these guys.

When the charges were sorted out, an officer read them: "Conspiracy, grand larceny, extortion, and coercion, against Franzese."

I nearly flipped.

At the arraignment the next day, I stood in the middle, completely dwarfed by the monstrous gang. Aside from the Chubby Brothers and their crew, Zimmerman was six-five, 275 pounds, and Frappolo was five-eleven, 240. In the middle of the prosecutor's impassioned reading of the charges, he stopped, turned with dramatic flourish, pointed at me, and screamed: "And that one in the middle, Michael Franzese—he's the ringleader!"

The theatrics backfired. The judge, and most of the gallery, burst out laughing. Here I was, a twenty-two-year-old college kid, five-ten, 160 pounds, and I'm the boss?

The judge, stifling his laugh, admonished the prosecutor. "Are you sure you got your facts straight?"

When it came my turn to speak, I was equally impassioned.

"Your Honor, I'm going to college and trying to make a living. I don't know what I'm doing here. Every Friday, the cops come in and break down my door and stab guns in my face. Now I'm here with a bunch of guys I've never seen before in my life, and I'm their leader?"

The judge was sympathetic, but not enough. I was arraigned on a $25,000 bond.

The situation at the leasing office remained tense. At midweek, Morano and I had a brief argument. I discovered that he liked to gamble and had been skimming money from the business to support his habit. I overlooked it at first, but finally had enough.

"You go back there in the shop and work it off," I said. "I don't want to see you in here."

I installed Zimmerman and Frappolo as the leasing agents and went about business as usual. The plan was to send Morano a message and get him to stop his pilfering.

Three days later, Friday afternoon, I arrived at the office with two of my father's friends, Jake and Vinnie Perozzi. I walked into the office first. The place was crawling with police officers.

"What the hell's with you guys?" I said. "Every Friday you come to arrest me."

I turned and looked for the Perozzi brothers. They were nowhere in sight. Although they were only a step behind, the veteran players had made the cops and disappeared without a trace.

Zimmerman, Frappolo, and I were arrested and charged with coercion for attempting to squeeze Morano out of his business. The charge began to make everything clear. Morano, in deep with his gambling debts, had borrowed $10,000 from Philly Vizzari. He remained unable to pick a fast horse and had squandered the loan. As a trade-off, he agreed to be wired in an attempt to set up both me and Vizzari.

That explained the commotion the previous Friday. The detectives, listening in, heard the Chubby Brothers going wild and making threats. They figured all hell was breaking loose. They swarmed in, only to discover it was just two giant hotheads trying to collect a small debt. It also explained the police's long delay in trying to come up with charges. The whole elaborate setup was intended to catch me. Instead, they netted a separate gang. Figuring their cover was blown, they jumped upon my disciplining of Morano and tried to cover their losses with the weak coercion charge.

The Chubby Brothers incident turned out to be a lucky break. Had the brothers not bullied and blustered their way in that Friday, and scared the hell out of the listening cops, Morano might have worn a wire around me for months, pressing me and goading me into doing something illegal. (I later became friends with Big Chubby and the rest of the guys.)

At the precinct station, a grim-faced detective sat me down in an interrogation room.

"If anything happens to Tony Morano, we're coming right after you," he threatened.

Growing weary of the harassment, I shot back: "I can't control what happens to a liar."

I paid yet another bail bond, this one for $10,000, and was released again.

At 5 A.M. the following Friday, I was rocked out of the upper berth of the bunk beds I shared with my brother John. A voice out of a bad western movie was blaring from a megaphone.

"Michael Franzese, come out with your hands up."

I looked outside and saw the lawn covered with the flashing lights of police cars. It looked like a discotheque, only the people weren't dancers but yet another army of cops.

A thought pierced my brain: "Tony Morano must have been killed. I'm going down for murder."

The next thing I saw was my mother outside on the porch. "He's not here," she lied.

"We know he's in there. We'll come in and break the door down," the megaphone said.

"He's not here!" my mother defiantly repeated.

Having been forced to clean and repair my office three times already, I was afraid the police were going to burst in and march through the house. I pushed up the bedroom window.

"I'm coming down. Just let me get dressed!" I shouted.

"You have five minutes."

Outside, the officers roughly cuffed my hands behind my back. They were serious and nasty. I was sure Tony Morano was dead and I was going down for murder.

At the precinct house, I spotted Zimmerman and Frappolo sitting in a detective's office, leisurely drinking coffee and eating doughnuts. I couldn't believe it. Here I was, cuffed and shackled, and they were eating doughnuts.

"What are you guys doing here, having breakfast?" I inquired.

"The police called us and told us to come down," Zimmerman said.

What was more incredible was the upshot. I had been dragged out of bed and arrested Dino De Laurentiis-style—with a cast of thousands—merely because a second count had been added to the coercion indictment. It was something that could have been accomplished with the stroke of a pen and then mailed to my attorney. Instead, the blue army invaded under a veil of darkness, ready to break down the door and trample my mother's freshly raked carpet.

It was no coincidence that all the arrests had occurred on Fridays. That's a common police tactic used when they want to get under someone's skin. Since judges work Monday through Friday, nine to five, like most everyone, a Friday arrest, especially a Friday-afternoon arrest, results in a Monday arraignment, which means a weekend in jail for the suspects.

In 1974, I went to trial three times on the fur-coat caper. Prior to the proceedings, my Uncle Philly promptly sold me out, blaming everything on me in an attempt to free himself from the charge.

Visiting my father at Leavenworth, I informed him of his buddy Philly's "loyalty." The news infuriated him, but didn't surprise him. "What did you think he was, a stand-up guy?" he said.

"But he was always around the house. I called him Uncle Philly. I don't understand."

Dad shrugged.

I sensed my father's dismay over my plight. To ease his mind, I tried passing it off as "no big deal." That only made him angrier.

"No big deal! You see my clothes," he said, grasping his prison uniform. "You see these bars. You're telling me it's no big deal? You got more indictments at twenty-two than I've had in my entire life!"

Calming down, he asked me how school was going. That led to more bad news. I explained that I had too many distractions and wasn't into it anymore. It didn't look like I could handle the long haul of becoming a doctor, not with all the legal and financial problems resulting from the arrests.

He looked away. He knew it was the sins of the father coming down upon the son. He was so proud when I had legally taken his name instead of Grillo's. Now, the Franzese name was crippling me.

Despite Philly's undermining, the case was weak. The jury hung each time, 7–5, 10–2, 11–1, all favoring acquittal. The fact that it was tried a third time after a 10–2 acquittal vote was a legal rarity and a waste of taxpayers' money, but spoke of the prosecutors' intense desire to feather their caps with another Franzese.

During the third trial, my mother spotted an attractive young woman from the neighborhood on the jury. She was a substitute teacher who had taught my brother John and sister Gia. Mom alerted me. I started giving the young woman the eye, and we traded glances and smiles the whole trial. I figured I was assured another hung jury.

Unfortunately, Maria was a regular visitor to the courtroom. Near the end of the trial, I made the mistake of giving her a quick hug and kiss in view of the jury box. When the jurors were unofficially polled outside after the 11–1 verdict, it turned out the only one who voted to convict was the substitute teacher.

The "Chubby Brothers" indictment went to trial in the hot summer of 1974. We were dubbed "the West Hempstead Seven" by the press. The prosecutor's case was even weaker than that of the fur coat caper. Even so, the trial became a major ordeal. With seven defendants and six attorneys, such mundane activities as choosing a jury took nearly a month. One problem was my dress and demeanor. I sat among my massive co-defendants in a crisp suit and often entered the courtroom carrying my attorney's briefcase. The prospective jurors kept mistaking me for one of the lawyers.

A few days into the trial, one of the jurors wrote the judge a disturbing note. The judge promptly declared a mistrial. It was never revealed what the note said, but it's not hard to figure. The juror must have suddenly realized he had a relative who knew one of the defendants, or something similar, and could therefore be considered biased.

The attorneys had to start over.

After another tedious jury selection, the trial chugged along in fits and starts. The courtroom was hot, and the stress was intense. My hefty co-defendants started dropping like flies. First the Chubby Brothers went down, fainting and hyperventilating. Then Jerry Zimmerman, Peter Frappolo, and the others fell ill—everyone but me. The paramedics had to keep rushing in with the oxygen, delaying or canceling the proceedings for the day. "This trial must be sponsored by the Red Cross," someone cracked as yet another defendant plopped to the floor.

At one point, the prosecutor made a dramatic announcement that someone had confessed and implicated a co-defendant. A rumble was heard among the defendants. Zimmerman was certain it was Frappolo. He began ranting in my ear. "I knew it. He's no good. I knew he wouldn't last. The man's a pathological liar. I knew he would break. Let me at him!"

The prosecutor made his announcement. "The man who confessed is Jerry Zimmerman!"

I nearly doubled over with laughter. Jerry shot up out of his chair and began screaming that it was a lie, that he was no rat. He had to be restrained.

It turned out that the prosecutors had leaped at some vague statement the verbose Zimmerman had made during his police interrogation. The judge promptly threw it out.

The star witness was Tony Morano. I figured Morano was the state's entire case. Get to him, and the ball game was over. My attorney didn't share that view and advised me against it. I ignored the advice and had a friend set up a meet. Tony was apologetic. He explained that he had gotten in deep with his gambling debts, was being squeezed by Philly, and had no way out.

"Don't worry," he assured me. "I'll bail you out of this. You watch."

Morano came through. He took the stand and double-crossed the prosecutors by testifying in a manner that cleared me and virtually the whole gang.

After that, all the Nassau County prosecutors had left were the tapes from Morano's body mike. The quality of the recordings was terrible. The jurors could clearly hear the words "maim," "kill," "strangle," "murder," and "break you apart" as the Chubby Brothers performed their tough-guy tag-team act, but no one could fill in the gaps. And no one could determine who was threatening to kill or maim whom.

When the tapes fell through, the prosecution's case started unraveling to an embarrassing degree. Before the prosecutors finished presenting their evidence, Zimmerman's and Frappolo's attorneys interrupted and moved that charges against their clients be dropped because of lack of evidence. When the prosecutors couldn't come up with a reason why the judge shouldn't grant the unusual motion, the two men were freed. After the prosecutors finished the state's case, my attorney made a similar motion, which the judge granted.

That left Big Chubby, Al Strauss, and Oscar Teitelbaum. (Little Chubby had been unable to complete the trial for medical reasons and was scheduled to be tried when he recovered.) The defense presented its case and the whole gang was acquitted.

The sad irony is that the person the least involved, Oscar Teitelbaum, ended up doing time. Although he was acquitted, he was just twenty-nine days out of jail when the cops invaded the leasing company. The state slapped Oscar with a parole violation. All he had done was go for a ride with the Chubby Brothers. Long ride—it cost him two years of his life.

The final indictment, the one based on the banishment of Morano to the body shop, eroded. The prosecutors dropped the coercion charge down to a misdemeanor. I refused the misdemeanor. The prosecutors dropped it further, down to a violation. I paid a $250 fine and was done with it.

Although I had dodged a volley of law-enforcement bullets, the damage to my businesses was fatal. The publicity surrounding the arrests and trials, and the six months spent fighting the case, dried up the leasing operation and caused us to lose our critical credit line. The body shop went down with it.

The lawyers consumed my savings. I was down to my last ten dollars. I sat in a Greek restaurant with Maria, scrutinized the menu, and tried to determine how we could both eat, tip the waitress, and stay within my limited budget. It depressed me to have to think that way. I walked out of the restaurant with thirteen cents, and vowed never to have to face such an afternoon again.

Where one door was shut, another was forced open. Vinnie Vingo, a friend from the Italian-American Civil Rights League, operated a bustling weekend flea market on the grounds of the Republic Field Airport in Farmingdale, Long Island. He asked me to help manage it at a salary of $300 a weekend. I accepted, and soon found the flea market to be a hotbed of opportunity. There were six hundred spots available and a list of two thousand vendors trying to get in. Since I was in charge of handing out the locations, I began fielding offers of $20 to $100 to reserve a prime spot. I told Vinnie and we shared the bonus. Only I had a better plan. The vendors needed money to replenish their stock. I figured the cash-laden market was ripe for a good loan-sharking operation. Most of the vendors were regulars whose livelihoods were tied to their slots. They could be depended upon. I began farming out my salary, charging a point a week on any loan more than $1,000 ($10 a week until the principal was paid) and up to ten points on smaller loans in the $100-to-$300 range.

Although I had been repeatedly arrested, indicted, and brought to trial, this was the first time, aside from punching the cop, that I had ever broken the law. Still, lending money to mom-and-pop flea-market vendors didn't make me feel that I was in the same league with Jack the Ripper. Truthfully, it didn't feel like a crime at all. I looked at it as providing investment capital for my clients' small businesses. It was a service they happily lined up to take advantage of.

I guessed right about the vendors' dependability. They were good customers, paid their points on time, restocked their stands, and dutifully paid back their principals. Within six months, I was clearing $1,000 to $2,000 a weekend in shylock interest.

I could look at a restaurant menu again without worry.

The flea-market shylock operation had a limited life. The police continued to track me and started snooping around Vinnie's market. That made Vinnie nervous. He didn't need the attention my presence attracted, especially considering that his employee was operating a lucrative loan-shark operation. He suggested that I go cool off. I didn't argue. Vinnie had done enough. It was time to move on.

The auto business still intrigued me. When I was searching for a bank or credit company to finance the leasing operation, I kept hearing the same thing—banks prefer new-car dealerships. I set about trying to get my hands on one. I put out feelers and got wind of a Mazda dealership on Main Street in Hempstead that was for sale. Mazda had introduced its bold new rotary engines in the early 1970s. By 1974, the cars were dying with startling regularity. The problem was faulty seals between the five pancakelike engine sections. As immobile Mazdas began littering the countryside, the public got wise. Mazda's name was mud.

I wheeled my way into the depressed market and bought the Hempstead dealership from a man named Joe Aveni for the fire-sale price of $75,000. I put down $25,000 in flea-market shylock cash, and financed the rest. I then found a new partner, a wild kid named John Marshall who was making a mint with a fleet of "roach coach" sandwich trucks. I sold Marshall a partnership for $50,000 gleaned from the pockets of hungry workmen on construction sites. That provided some working capital.

The problem we faced was how to make money with cars no one wanted. The answer was factory warranties. While everyone was deserting Mazda, I saw gold hidden in all those broken-down cars. I refurbished the dealership's service area, beefed up the staff, and phoned Mazda and said I wanted my shop to be the main service point in the district.

Mazda, fighting a public-relations disaster, stood behind its warranties and paid dealerships $1,200 per car to repair the hemorrhaging seals. The materials cost next to nothing. The labor took about five hours. After paying the mechanics, that left a $900 profit. Within weeks, the service bay was running full force. Broken cars backed up all over the lot.

It was, however, more difficult getting the sales division rolling. The previous owner had promised that his bank would continue to provide the floor-plan financing. That meant the bank would buy the new cars as they came in and hold the titles until they could be sold off the lot.

As soon as the transfer papers for the dealership were signed, the bank backed out. I learned of the maneuver as a carrier truck with eight new cars pulled into the lot. I called Mazda and convinced the regional sales manager to leave the automobiles without receiving the $80,000 bank draft they were expecting.

"Give me a month to get a new floor plan," I said.

Mazda agreed.

I went shopping banks. I was twenty-four years old, had no credit history, no financial statement, nothing but a trail of negative newspaper articles that I hoped the bankers hadn't read. I was turned away, bank after bank. Time was running out.

I went back to Mel Cooper, the financier who helped start me in the leasing business. "Give me some names—anybody," I pleaded.

Cooper directed me to the Small Business Administration, a government agency, and the Small Business Investment Corporation (SBIC), private lenders who are supported 90 percent by the government. I figured I'd have my best luck with the SBIC. Cooper gave me the name of SBIC Agent Thomas Scharf of Lloyd Capital Corporation in Edgewater, New Jersey. I paid the man a visit.

"Who makes the final decision?" I asked the affable Scharf.

"Me," he said. "I'm the loan committee."

Scharf was intrigued by my description of the Mazda operation. He made arrangements to visit the dealership the next day. Scharf and his accountant arrived as scheduled. Despite Mazda's troubles, the place was impressive. The showroom was large and beautiful. The service bay was hopping. Scharf and his accountant went over the books and the entire operation. "Let me and my accountant meet in private for a moment," he asked afterward.

"Sure," I said, directing them to the manager's office.

They emerged fifteen minutes later. "We got a deal," Scharf said.

It was quite a deal. Scharf offered a $250,000 line of credit at 15 percent, about 3 percent higher than the banks were offering. On top of that, he wanted a $75-to-$150 "consulting fee" per car sold.

"Tom, this is expensive. But you're the only game in town," I said, agreeing to the near-usurious terms.

Despite the financial burden, the dealership prospered. Mazda upgraded its line, began producing conventional piston engines, advertised heavily, and regained a share of the market. Within a few years, the operation began taking in $100,000 a month, $25,000 of which was profit. Everyone was happy.

When the Small Business Administration began a routine investigation of Scharf, I vouched for him. "Without his consulting advice, I'd have never made it," I lied. "He's instrumental to my business."

As word of my financial rebound spread, back came the wiseguys, including prison-fresh entrepreneurs directed to me by my father.

The first was Jimmy. He was said to be a wizard at the fruit-and-vegetable business. My father promoted him highly. I put up $25,000 to open a market in Suffolk County, called Sonny's Farm Circle. The market promptly went under. Jimmy made off with most of the capital.

Next came Joey, a burly truck driver. He told my father about all the money they could make in the long-haul trucking business. All they needed was the tractor. "Michael, I love your father. If anybody hurts you, I'll bring you their head on a platter," Joey promised.

I bought Joey a $12,500 tractor, painted it shiny black, and added new chrome bumpers. Joey nearly cried when he saw the truck. He was so happy he hugged and kissed me and again vowed his undying loyalty. He then got into the truck, threw it in gear, rolled down the road—and was never seen again.

"Dad," I said during my next prison visit, "don't send me any more guys—please."

Undaunted, my father tried again. Another ex-con, Ronny the Shark, came with impeccable credentials as "the best loan shark in town." I fronted $100,000 to put him on the street. Despite getting up to four points a week, at the end of the year, instead of receiving the expected $300,000, I got back $80,000.

The guy was without question a great shylock. He had generated a couple hundred grand in interest. Trouble was, he was a lousy handicapper. He gambled away all of the interest, and part of the principal, on the ponies.

"Dad, *please*—no more guys," I pleaded anew.

In June 1975, I finally quit stalling and married Maria. She had stood by me through all the arrests and trials, never wavering once in her love. I had come to care for her in a way that was deeper and more meaningful than the cheap thrills I thought I wanted. There was no question she would make a perfect wife. She would be devoted and faithful and never give me a moment's worry.

The reception was at Queens Terrace, a catering hall in Queens that was a mainstay for Mob marriages. Six hundred people attended, including a battalion of Cosa Nostra soldiers. Among the people paying their respects was Al Gallo, Crazy Joe's brother. That was ironic: It had long been rumored that my father had ordered the hit on Crazy Joe. Apparently, it was all just business.

But that was just a sidebar to the events of the afternoon and evening. Maria and I were the stars, and it was a union that made both my mother and my father very happy.

CHAPTER 7

Nineteen seventy-five marked another milestone in my life. That's when I decided to go into my father's business.

The offer came by surprise. I was visiting him at Leavenworth, shooting the breeze, when suddenly the conversation turned serious.

"Michael, I believe you've got what it takes. I want to introduce you to my associates downtown. You can take it from there."

I wasn't sure what my father was getting at. He had sheltered me from his business for most of my life. We lived in the suburbs, not in the city or in Brooklyn, where the Mob guys are everywhere and are viewed as celebrities and big shots. I knew the designations "goodfellow" or "made man" meant someone was an inducted Cosa Nostra soldier, and that trusted Mob associates were often called "wiseguys," but I only had a vague sense of what the secret brotherhood was all about.

What I did know was that the organization was my father's heart and soul. If he wanted me in, it was an honor I couldn't take lightly.

"Okay," I responded, emotionlessly.

"What would you do if you had to kill someone?" he asked.

I was taken aback. "If I had to, I could," I heard myself respond.

"Would it bother you?"

"Depends upon the circumstances."

My father smiled. Apparently, that was the correct answer.

I wasn't completely naive. I knew what my father was saying. Before one could be invited to go through La Cosa Nostra's secret, time-honored induction ceremony, a recruit had to "make his bones." Making one's bones meant doing some "work" for the organization. "Work" meant killing someone. As with most Mob terms, the special language was developed to thwart "bugs" and confuse the courts.

Typically, there was never a clear explanation why my father decided at that moment to "straighten me out." The phrase itself is one of the more quizzical of Mob euphemisms and means the opposite of what it might seem. "Straighten out" no doubt developed from the idea of taking a wild, cunning street criminal, embracing him into the Mob, and putting his talents to more productive use.

The term may help explain my induction. Despite my history of legitimate business success, I showed no timidity in venturing over the legal line. My shylock operation at the flea market proved that. I already had a long history of arrests, grand jury indictments, and trials. I had been branded a mobster by the press while I was clean and serious about becoming a doctor. Also, the word among the families was that I was a comer. I was aggressive, motivated, and determined to be successful. I was also proving to be resilient. The Nassau County police and prosecutors tried to destroy me, and I had survived.

My father probably feared one of the other four families might "straighten me out." He figured that if I wasn't going to become a doctor, and I was determined to play both sides of the business world, legal and illegal, I might as well operate under the protective wing of the Colombo family.

A tougher question to answer is why I accepted. I didn't need the Mob. My parents had given me an education. I had the opportunity to become a doctor. I wasn't a street punk from a broken home in search of the "family" I never had. I didn't even believe in that stuff. I was a regular guy with a nice wife and a successful auto dealership.

But I was my father's son. My desire to win favor with my father remained as intense as ever. If he wanted me to become a member of La Cosa Nostra, I wasn't going to question it. And I never did. I never asked him why, or why then. All I knew—and was comforted in knowing that *he* knew—was that it would draw us even closer together. And being close to my father, winning his respect and approval and, more importantly, being accepted as his "son," remained my prime motivation.

There was another unspoken benefit in joining. The way I saw it, my father had been forgotten by the Colombo family because of his long prison sentence. Although he understood the life and never complained, I had a hard time dealing with it. With me in the family, I might be able to use La Cosa Nostra's influence and vast network of contacts and associations to free my father from prison.

My induction was made possible by a Mob high commission decision. From 1955 to 1972, the Mob was a closed shop; virtually no one was inducted during that quarter-century. The ironclad policy was devel-

ht and secret and eliminate the possibility of
nts infiltrating. By 1972, with the ranks thin-
prisonment, the doors were opened. It was

i by Jo Jo Vitacco, a longtime friend of my
man, barely five feet four. He walked with a
ed every bit the street soldier he was. Jo Jo
s than free, and was a barber in prison. He
his size, and up to the time of his death he
ter years, he owned and operated a bar on
klyn called the JV Lounge.
on Carroll Street in Brooklyn. It was a bur-
glar's home that was being used as a meeting place. Jo Jo introduced me
to Colombo family acting boss Thomas DiBella, a big, lumbering man
who had spent fifty years working the unions and the docks. DiBella was
seventy-two years old. He survived in the Mob so long by making sure
he never stepped on anyone's toes. It was that quality, along with his
advanced age, that had prompted Carmine Persico to install DiBella as
boss until Persico could get out of jail.

After acknowledging my father and how warmly everyone regarded
him, DiBella's speech to me that evening was similar to the standard line
given all prospects.

"I want you to understand that La Cosa Nostra comes before anything. You are now on call twenty-four hours a day. There are no excuses.
If your mother is sick on her deathbed, and the family calls, you leave
your mother and come.

"You are no better or worse than anyone else in La Cosa Nostra. You
are your own man. You and your father are now equals. Your father, sons,
and brothers have no priority. We are all as one, united in blood. Once
you become part of this, there is no greater bond.

"Stay close to Jo Jo. Whatever he says, you do. When we are ready
for you, you'll know."

DiBella outlined La Cosa Nostra's capital crimes. Soldiers can never
violate another member's wife or daughter, never raise a hand to another
member, never become involved in illegal narcotics, and never violate
the secrets of the organization.

After the meeting, my name, along with those of the other potential
inductees, was circulated around the five families. This was the Mob's

version of a standard credit check. If anyone had any reason to object to me entering, he would let DiBella know. The name circulation also had a second purpose. If anyone in another family felt he had a claim on a prospect, he was to let it be known.

That's exactly what happened with me. Pasquale "Paddy Mack" Marchiola, a Genovese soldier, raised an objection. He argued that I had done some business with one of his friends, and that made me his recruit. Paddy Mack gambled that this would counter my own father's claim and negate the time I spent walking a picket line with family boss Joe Colombo.

The Mob commission overruled Mack's claim.

A curious factor in the name circulation period was that I was never called in to confirm the heritage of my biological father. La Cosa Nostra only inducts Italians. Stepsons don't count. For all they knew, Louis Grillo could have been Irish, Jewish, or Greek and changed his name. Normally, a recruit would have been scrutinized on that subject. I was never called in to explain. It was thought that someone must have known Grillo was Italian, or that my father had cleared it.

My assigned caporegime was Andrew "Andy Mush" Russo, a cousin of Carmine Persico. One of my first activities during my "pledge" period was to invite Russo in on a nightclub deal I had in the works. The owner of a discotheque on Long Island needed some cash to book star acts into his youth-oriented club. Russo and I kicked in $7,500 each on the promise of getting a percentage of the weekend take until the debt could be repaid. The percentage could go as high as $2,000 if the place was packed—a return that equaled a healthy 13.3 loan-shark points a week.

Norby Walters, a partner of my father's, booked the acts into the club. He provided such national superstars as the Spinners, the Stylistics, the O'Jays, Harold Melvin and the Blue Notes, the Trammps, the Drifters, and the Supremes. The big acts provided a windfall. The lesser-known groups produced less revenue. Regardless, I made sure Russo got his thousand every week, often kicking in my entire share to bring his take up to the maximum. Sometimes, after healthy weekends, I gave my captain my own take, handing over $1,500 to $2,000. I'd explain that it had been an unusually free-spending crowd. My generosity was a calculated move. I wanted Russo to spread the news around that when you made a deal with Michael Franzese, it was going to pay off. That would open the door to bigger stakes in the future.

The "pledge" period lasted nearly a year. The family took this time to train the recruits in discipline and carefully measure their character, all the while waiting for the right low-level "work" to present itself. I spent most of my indoctrination acting as a chauffeur and gofer for DiBella. I was called upon to drive the acting boss around on his daily schedule, usually to meetings and restaurants. Ironically, they almost always used my cars—the chauffeur owned better automobiles than the boss.

Through this minimal activity, I was able to meet various upper-echelon Colombo family members, along with the bosses and captains of the four other New York families. Almost everyone who greeted me paid tribute to my father. The meets were brief encounters in hallways, lobbies, or on sidewalks. I was never invited to attend the actual meetings.

Outwardly, I performed my functions like the eager hopeful I was supposed to be. Inwardly, I was bothered by the servile duties and hated the time they took from my business operations. I also hated Brooklyn, where DiBella's activities were centered. I preferred the wide-open spaces of Long Island, or Florida, or California to the gray, cramped New York cities. I kept these feelings to myself.

As boring as gofering for DiBella was, Jo Jo Vitacco also made frequent use of the yo-yo string I was on. He would summon me to his bar merely to have someone to talk to. I was in the process of building an assortment of businesses and disliked having to spend my afternoons and evenings watching Jo Jo get drunk. I again kept my mouth shut and accepted it as part of the process.

On one occasion, it at least got interesting. Jo Jo was lathered and in mean spirits when I arrived as ordered. He was having trouble with his latest girlfriend, a barmaid half his age. After grousing about her for an hour or so, he leaped off a bar stool and decided to go a few more rounds with her over the telephone. Jo Jo lost again. He slammed the receiver down, retreated into his office, and emerged within seconds waving a .38 Special. He started firing wildly at the telephone and cursing his girlfriend. The phone was set against a concrete wall, and bullets ricocheted off the wall and began whizzing around the bar, shattering mirrors and whiskey bottles. I ducked and lunged for him, afraid that any second a bullet was going to bounce back and catch the little gangster right between the eyes. I grabbed him, wrapped my arms around him, and, after a struggle, calmed him down.

On other occasions, Jo Jo's lounge would be as dull as a graveyard.

These would be the nights FBI agent Bernie Welsh made an appearance. Welsh would waltz in, sit himself in the center of the bar, drink as only an Irishman can, and loudly greet and glad-hand any mobster who entered the place. Soon as they spotted him, they'd get the hell out. "Welsh, you fuckin' bastard—you're killin' my business!" Jo Jo would rant, bobbing up and down like a cork. Welsh would laugh, order another drink, and dig in for the long night.

Whenever he saw me at Jo Jo's, Welsh would really become animated. "Hey, it's my old buddy Michael Franzese! Put it here, man!" he'd shout, extending a meaty paw.

Once, when I refused to shake his hand and ducked into a nearby restaurant, the FBI agent tracked me down. "Michael, I'm insulted," he said, hovering over the table like a storm cloud. "Why didn't you shake my hand?"

"In front of all those people? You jump up like you're my best friend? You must be kidding!"

"You can still shake my hand," Welsh said, standing firm.

"All right," I said, standing. "I'll shake your hand. Now go over to the bar and leave me alone."

"You sure you don't want me to eat with you guys?"

"We're sure, Bernie," I said. "Go to the bar. The first drink's on me."

Careful as I was, I made two mistakes during my training. The first occurred when I dropped off DiBella at Junior's Restaurant on Flatbush Avenue. Instead of waiting in front of the restaurant by the car, I became edgy and started pacing up and down the block. When DiBella came out, I was down near the opposite corner. DiBella chewed me out. "If I tell you to wait out front, you wait out front! You wait there for three days if you have to. You don't walk. You don't go to the bathroom. You stand right there. How did you know I wouldn't come running out and need to leave immediately?"

The second mistake was arriving ten minutes late for an appointment on a cold winter morning. I was left standing on Carroll Street for six hours. I asked the family members who passed by what to do, and they explained that I had to keep waiting. DiBella passed by twice but left me shivering on the corner. After that, I learned that a 3:00 P.M. meeting meant arriving at 2:30, a 4 P.M. meeting meant arriving at 3:30; and if one expected any difficulty arriving at a meeting the next day, you camped out on the spot the previous night. If your car broke down on the way to a meet, you abandoned it and jumped into a taxi or stole another to make it on time.

Aside from the usurious rates on the nightclub loan, I did nothing illegal during my indoctrination. I was invited to go on various stickups and burglaries by soldiers and fellow recruits, but always declined. That was okay. The Mob doesn't choose a job for its members. A numbers runner comes in and stays a numbers runner. An auto thief continues to steal cars. A loan shark lends money. A bookie takes bets. The Mob doesn't try to make the numbers runner into a loan shark, or a bookie into an auto thief. Since I was a businessman, I wasn't expected to rob 7-Elevens. I was free to decline to participate in any activity that wasn't my specialty.

However, when it comes time for a recruit to do some "work," he usually has no such option.

Fortunately, my case was unique. I never received the order. From what I could guess, there were two reasons for the rare break with Cosa Nostra tradition. First, there was such a rush to induct new recruits, especially in the severely weakened Colombo family, that the initiation murder was waived and instead was marked down as a debt to be paid at a later date. Secondly, the number of recruits that the Mob wanted to make far exceeded the number of people the bosses could think of to kill. That made for gangs of eager recruits who were all dressed up with no one to knock off. Whatever the reason, I was spared.*

---

*Others scoff at these explanations and say the Mafia has never suspended the critical initiation requirement. Both law-enforcement and Mob sources—all requesting anonymity—claim that Michael made his bones the old-fashioned way. Michael adamantly denies it.

CHAPTER 8

"Tonight's your night, Michael."

Fitting, I thought, putting down the telephone receiver. Halloween, 1975. I would shed the mantle of the legitimate businessman I had attempted to be and figuratively costume myself in the pinstripe suit and wide-brim fedora of the world's most notorious secret criminal organization.

The caller directed me to a bar on Metropolitan Avenue in Brooklyn where I was to pick up Jo Jo, my sponsor. We drove to a catering house in Bensonhurst. I was escorted to a small office down the hall from the main ballroom where five other recruits were nervously mingling. The only person I recognized was Jimmy Angellino. As I sat and waited, I looked around the room. If the pattern was to mix two guys from each hit squad, and the initiation requirement hadn't been waived for the others, that meant three people had been murdered, maybe more, to uphold the tradition that brought the six of us there.

I was the third recruit called. Jo Jo came out, a big smile cutting through his tight, hard features. He nodded for me to follow.

The lights in the room were dim. The mood was as solemn as the darkness. In the center of the banquet hall, the hierarchy of the Colombo family sat on folding chairs spread out in the shape of a U. As I walked inside the U, I recognized the stern faces of the men sitting around me. The captains were on the edges. The closer to the center, the more powerful the captain. I recognized John "Johnny Irish" Matera, one of my father's soldiers who had risen to be a captain himself. Matera gave me a nod.

In the middle of the U was Tom DiBella, the family boss. To DiBella's left was the family *consigliere*, Alphonse "Allie Boy" Persico, Carmine's brother. Normally, the family underboss would have been to DiBella's right; but at that time there was no underboss.

94

I stood in front of DiBella.

"Are you ready to take the oath of La Cosa Nostra?" the big man asked.

"Yes."

"Cup your hands."

I did as told. A small piece of paper materialized. DiBella lit it and dropped the flaming paper into the pocket formed by my hands.

"If you ever violate the oath of La Cosa Nostra, may you burn in hell like the fire burning in your hand."

I felt only a tinge of heat as the paper was quickly consumed. It was ceremonial, not, as some believe, a show of toughness or the ability to withstand pain.

DiBella grabbed my right hand in his big, rough hand. He held up my thumb and pricked it with a pin. It stung. As the blood formed into a fat drop, DiBella squeezed my thumb. The drop of blood became too heavy and spilled to the floor. Looking down, I could see the splattered drops of blood from the two recruits who had come before me.

"This is a blood tie. Your allegiance to La Cosa Nostra is bound by blood. Should you violate the oath, your blood will be shed."

DiBella squeezed again, hard. Another fat drop of blood fell to the floor. The point was vividly taken. I could feel the breath of death in the room. Violate the oath, and my blood would spill in quarts, not drops. That's what it was all about: life or death. Humanity at its most instinctive level. Follow the rules or die.

"Michael Franzese, do you accept and understand the blood oath and blood tie of La Cosa Nostra?"

"Yes."

"You have now been born again. You are *amico nostro* [our friend]."

I shook DiBella's hand and kissed him once on each cheek. I repeated the procedure with Allie Boy, Johnny Irish, Andy Russo, and the rest of the captains. The congratulations were as serious as the ceremony. The air remained thick and tense. Any one of the men I was shaking hands with and kissing might one day be called upon to kill me. Or I might one day be called upon to kill him. That's what struck me the most about the entire ceremony. Instant capital punishment, often without trial or jury. It was the central theme of the evening—death, murder, and spilled blood.

Yet, leaving the dimly lit room, I was excited. The feeling grew into exhilaration. I was now part of an army of blood brothers. I was locked into a brotherhood few would ever experience or even understand. And more importantly, I had become one with my father. I had bonded. I could never be rejected now, never be banished from the house. That's all that really mattered. My father had accepted me as blood, blood spilled in drops on a wooden floor, but blood nonetheless.

After the last recruit was made, we all, new family members and old, sat down at a large banquet table. We drank wine and ate pasta, veal, and chicken. The solemnity slowly lifted.

Outside in the foyer after it was over, Jo Jo appeared at my side. "Now you can pick up your bag of money."

My fellow inductees raised their eyebrows. Jo Jo and the men around him started to howl. It was Mob humor, an old joke played on the recruits. I got the joke, and would never forget the meaning behind it. There was no bag of money waiting for the newly made men. There never would be. We weren't given a salary or put on somebody's payroll. It was up to each man to make his way. In fact, it was up to each man not only to carry his weight but to kick a healthy share of his earnings into the family kitty. Essentially, from a purely business standpoint, the Mob was an elaborate, criminal pyramid scheme.

As I drove home, the seriousness of what I had done began to overwhelm me. Did I know what I was doing? I had given over my life, not for a few years but forever. What if I didn't like it? What if I *hated* it? There was no way out. No excuse. No "Take this job and shove it." You can't quit. You quit, you die.

I wasn't like the others. It wasn't my lifelong dream to be in La Cosa Nostra. I hated Brooklyn. I didn't enjoy the initiation. I didn't get off on the violence like some of the others. I wondered whether I had made a terrible mistake. Had I just signed my own death warrant?

No. It was the right move, I told myself. I was part of a powerful organization that stretched out across the world. Anywhere I went, I would be welcomed and sheltered by my special brothers. There was a great feeling in knowing that.

Besides, my father was in. It was my father's life. It was what my father wanted for me. It couldn't be wrong.

I kissed Maria upon arriving home, then sat down on the couch. The doorbell rang. I called for my wife, but she was upstairs. I went to the door.

The machine gun was the first thing I saw. Then the fedora and pin-striped suit.

"Gimme all da candy or I'll blow ya away."

It was a just a kid—a straggler making a last few grabs at stuffing his trick-or-treat bag before calling it a night. I looked around the room and spotted the bowl of Kisses, Snickers, and candy corn Maria had provided for the stream of masqueraders.

"Hold on, tough guy," I said.

I grabbed two big handfuls and dropped them into the kid's bulging shopping bag. The boy's eyes became big as silver dollars. "Thanks, mister!"

"Were you really going to shoot me?"

The kid looked up, waved the toy machine gun, and affected his meanest snarl. "Trick or treat. That's the rules, mister."

I went to work the next day as usual. I didn't feel any different. Nothing changed. Some of the other recruits changed drastically. They put on the sleek suits, flashed diamond-and-gold pinky rings, and began walking with a swagger. That wasn't for me. That wasn't even the way of the family. The rule was, you never tell anyone who you are. You don't wear your credentials on your sleeve. You don't hand out business cards saying "Michael Franzese, Cosa Nostra Soldier." The people who need to know will know, or will be told.

The key was in the introductions.

"This is Tony. He's a friend of ours." That meant Tony was in.

"This is Joey. He's a friend of mine." That meant Joey was not in. Joey was merely an associate.

But after a few months, even that wasn't necessary. I found that everybody knew. Somehow, everybody knew. I was treated with awe and respect. The mantle was there. I couldn't see it or feel it, but everyone around me felt its weight.

For the next few years, my activities were limited to attending weddings and funerals, the two big Mob social events. Among the funerals was that of Joe Colombo. The former boss had vegetated for seven years after being gunned down in the middle of his most glorious moment. As they lowered Colombo's casket into the ground, I thought back to the day he was shot. I was only a few feet away. I was a college kid then, a future doctor; yet there I was, in the middle of a major Mob hit.

So much of my life had been like that. Cops hanging around the house and harassing my family. Assassinations right in front of my eyes, the sound of the gunshots ringing in my ears. My father's frame and fifty-year "death sentence" jail term. My own grand jury indictments and trials, all based on false accusations and police harassment. The Mob had shaped every part of my life.

And most of it was bad.

My first payoff came when an associate introduced me to Gerard Nocera, a vice-president at Beneficial Leasing Corporation. I wanted to get the Mazda dealership out from under the strangling floor-plan financing arrangement I had with Lloyd Capital. Nocera was the first example in a long line of what the prosecutors would later claim to be my greatest talent—finding legitimate businessmen who liked to play on the edge. The Beneficial man, who had relatives associated with the Mob, came through with a $600,000 floor plan. And instead of having to pay Tom Scharf $75 to $150 a car, I only had to pay Nocera $25 to $50. With Nocera, however, there wasn't even a thin veil of "consulting" involved. The payments were slid under the table.

My best friend, a high-living embalmer and Mob associate named Larry Carrozza, unearthed another nine-to-fiver looking to increase his profits. Louis Fenza had worked his way to vice-president of Japan Lines, an international marine cargo company. I formed a shipping-container repair firm, and Louie Fenza began writing the work orders. It started at five to one, meaning for every container my firm repaired, Fenza would bill Japan Lines for five. The ratio grew to ten to one, fifteen to one, and finally twenty to one as the scam continued to go unnoticed. We were pocketing $2,000 a week for phantom work.

I rolled the Japan Lines money in with my Mazda profits and put $100,000 on the streets, an investment that produced two to three shylock points ($2,000 to $3,000) every week.

As time passed, I developed a three-point strategy to guide my new life. Two and three were to succeed in business and to be a good Mob soldier. Number one was the same as always: getting my father out of jail. My passion in that area became my weakness. Anyone wanting to get close to me, set me up or shake me down, used my love for my father to his advantage.

In 1978, my father had a critical parole hearing scheduled. He had served nine years, enough time to earn a legitimate parole. Still, he was Sonny Franzese, and the chances appeared slim.

Enter a rival car dealer who claimed to have connections with the parole board. For $150,000, he said, he could ensure that my father would be freed. He wanted the money up front.

He told me they had to work through a specific attorney, Harold Borg. I knew Borg from the "West Hempstead Seven" trial; Borg had represented one of the Chubby Brothers. I hired Borg but balked at pay-ing the bribe money to the dealer. Instead, I offered to pay $75,000 when my father was granted parole, and the second $75,000 when he walked free. The split was made because the actual release of a prisoner can be as long as six months after the parole hearing. The lag time is filled with snags.

To make my point, I filled a suitcase with $150,000 in shylock cash borrowed from the Colombo family, sat it in the corner of my office, and invited the car dealer over to take a look.

In September 1978, my father's parole was granted. I didn't pay. From my own intelligence gathering, I determined that Borg was totally legitimate and knew nothing of the hustle. The parole was gained by the attorney's efforts and my father's good behavior, not through any connec-tions. In fact, when Borg later learned of the bribe agreement, he advised strongly against paying the money.

The car dealer and his secret partner, if there was one, were appar-ently gambling on a good attorney and the timing of the hearing. If my father made it, they could claim credit. If he didn't they'd claim a last-minute foul-up.

"You don't know what they'll do. These people can have you killed," the dealer threatened when I refused to pay.

"I'll take the chance," I shot back.

"They'll have *me* killed."

"Buy a bullet-proof vest," I advised.

Dad came home five months later, in February 1979. We threw another big welcome-home champagne party to celebrate. The next day, my father and I resumed our six A.M. breakfast meetings from a decade earlier. I set my alarm for five A.M. so I could shower, shave, dress and make the ten-minute drive from my home in Jericho to my parents' house in time to operate the drip coffee machine. Only now, intermin-gled with conversations about sports and entertainment, we talked shop.

My father began educating me about the ways of La Cosa Nostra. He told me which family members could be trusted, whom to be wary of, and whom not to trust. He advised me never to say anything of consequence on the telephone or in an enclosed room, and to treat all strangers as if they were undercover FBI agents. "Don't let your tongue be your worst enemy," Dad said.

I gave my father an office and a job as a Mazda salesman, one of the conditions of his parole. I then waited for the earth to shake under Sonny Franzese's feet as it had before.

My father requested that I transfer to his army. Andy Russo, my capo, vehemently protested. The Colombo ruling council decided that I belonged with my father.

Although my immediate family was elated to have my father home, things didn't work out as I had imagined. The strict parole conditions severely hampered his renewed activities. His once loyal and feared army had dissolved during his decade-long incarceration. Among those still alive or free, the only one who asked to transfer back was Jo Jo Vitacco, and he was refused. Officially, the Colombo family still viewed Sonny Franzese as being either too hot or too dangerous, and did nothing to help return him to power.

My father knew the score. He remained low-key, explaining to me that "there's no rush."

Because of this, I never got to see the Sonny of the 1960s, the legendary Sonny Franzese whom Phil Steinberg knew. I knew the reasons, and I knew how the parole handcuffed him, but still it was disappointing. I had always idolized him. For the first time, I realized he was just a man.

I was once again angered by the Colombo family's refusal to give my father his due. It wasn't surprising after the way they'd treated him while he was in prison, but I always believed things would be different once he was back on the streets. Besides, I was now part of the family. Where was the brotherhood? Where was the respect my father earned for keeping his mouth shut, giving up a decade of his life?

Complicating matters was the success of Carmine "the Snake" Persico, Jr. He was paroled around the same time as my father and promptly took over the family. Persico had been all but washed away in my father's furious wake. But his fall, from a lower perch, was softer. He kept his army together during his incarceration, installed the aging DiBella in his place when Colombo was shot, and powered his way to the top. The

Snake was a throwback, a don right out of Central Casting. He was a tough, gritty man who stood five feet seven and ate, drank, and slept the Mob. He was a veteran of the street-war days and was comfortable with the violence so often associated with organized crime. To the Snake, murder was a vital cog in the business machinery of the Mob.

A forceful, aggressive leader, Persico brought an iron-fisted rule back to the Colombo family. My father's fortunes would never return; but with Persico in power, mine would soar.

CHAPTER 9

Carmine "the Snake" Persico wasted little time flexing his muscles. A parole board's worst nightmare, Persico left prison determined to settle a list of old scores. By chance, there had been a breakthrough in one of the oldest and most painful. In the early 1960s, an insanely courageous band of young toughs hit upon a wild scheme of making quick cash by kidnapping Mob soldiers and holding them for ransom. The families paid off, more to silence the insult to their image than to protect the lives of their men. They ground their teeth and handed over the money, vowing never to rest until all the kidnappers were identified, hunted down, and killed.

Nearly two decades later, few remembered and even fewer cared about the kidnappings. Among those who did remember, many held a grudging admiration for the accomplishment of the reckless band. Plus, it was widely believed that some, if not all, of the kidnappers had eventually joined the five families.

Shortly after Persico took over, someone erased a heavy shylock debt by playing an ace carried for twenty years. The guy fingered some of the kidnappers. An investigation was launched and the information was confirmed. Not surprisingly, one of the former kidnappers had become a trusted Colombo family associate. He was a tough, fiercely loyal man who was part of my growing crew. Both my father and I respected him, knew his wife and children, and considered him one of our most valued and dependable associates.

In late 1978, I received a call from Persico that unsettled my world. The family boss explained that he had ordered the death of this man.

It was the first time I had to face anything like this. I didn't know what to do, so I did what came naturally: I protested. My strong feelings for the man prompted me to tread on dangerous ground. I challenged the order and questioned the accuracy of the information. Persico tolerated it and took the trouble of outlining the case against the man. There was no doubt; the associate had unquestionably been part of the gang of renegade kidnappers.

I tried another tack. The offender had been a raw and ignorant kid back then. He had since matured into a faithful associate. I argued that his value to the family was worth more than the value of the revenge.

Persico took it all in, but was unmoved. "We respect your efforts on his behalf," he said. "However, the crime he committed is unforgivable. The guy's got to go. That's the end of it."

Persico's last statement indicated that he wouldn't allow any more second-guessing. Two weeks later, I heard that the hit had been successfully carried out.

On January 15, 1979, Larry Carrozza rushed into my Mazda office with some disturbing news. One of the middlemen in the Japan Lines scam, a short, thin, dark-haired Italian named Joey Laezza, had been nabbed and was going to sing. I called a meeting of my men and had Larry repeat the information. Before I finished, five different associates volunteered to kill Laezza that same day.

"Just give the word, Michael," Larry said.

Now I was on the other end. Instead of just being notified about some "work" that was going to be done, I faced the ultimate responsibility of giving a death order.

"We got to do it, and do it fast," Champagne Larry continued. "Joey's gonna finger you, Michael. We've got to take the bastard out. We can't let him do that to you."

I knew why my best friend was so concerned: Larry had made the introduction. Joey was Larry's responsibility. If Joey rolled over, Larry would have to pay with his life. That was the rule.

I weighed my words carefully. "Let's get some more information. Let's be absolutely certain."

The men appeared upset. They were distressingly eager to kill. I could see that they were also fiercely loyal and totally dependent upon me. They would do anything, kill anyone to protect the income and lifestyle I was providing. A strange and disquieting sense of power swept over me. It was wrong, and it was evil, but it was intoxicating.

At 10:30 A.M. the following day, January 16, the body of Joseph Anthony Laezza, thirty-six, was discovered slumped in the front seat of his car at 18 Gravesend Neck Road in Brooklyn. He had been

*stabbed eleven times, six times in the face and head. The placement
of the wounds made the medical examiner marvel at the murderer's
skill and knowledge of anatomy. The blade of a long, thin knife had
sliced through the right eyebrow three inches below the top of the
head, a location that would take it through the sinus cavity and into
the brain. A second puncture entered the upper right eyelid, finding
the same route to the soft brain tissue. The third and fourth wounds
were spaced a half-inch apart vertically on the right temple, four
inches below the top of the head—another critical passageway to the
brain. The final two facial gashes were a half-inch apart horizontally
on the right cheek, five to five-and-one-half inches below the top of
Laezza's head, just under the cheekbone.*

*If the blade itself didn't kill Joey, the blood flooding his sinuses
would have drowned him.*

*The five stabs to the body were similarly precise. The first pene-
trated the upper left chest fifty inches from the right heel, as patholo-
gists measure, hitting nothing but "intercostal space," meaning the
blade found a clear route through the ribs into the internal organs.
The second was in the upper left chest forty-nine inches above the
left heel, again in intercostal space. The third was placed in the left
chest forty-eight inches from the left heel. This one deftly skirted the
clavicle to slice apart the subclavian vein. The fourth entered Joey
Laezza's body forty-two-and-one-half inches above the right heel,
and cut through the diaphragm and peritoneal cavity to find its
mark—the liver. The fifth stab, probably the first one delivered, hit
Laezza's right forearm.*

*The wounds were so deadly and so exact, it appeared as if the
knife had been wielded by a surgeon.*

*Close. Champagne Larry Carrozza owned a funeral parlor. He
was a mortician and embalmer.*

*"We had to do it," Carrozza reported later that day. "It was too
close to home. We followed him and saw him talking with the cops.
He was gonna take Michael down."*

In the end, I never had to order the killing. It was taken care of for
me. As I drove home that evening, my conscience began jabbing at me. I
had vowed to stay away from the bloody side of the Mob. I had thought I
could do my business bit and leave the messy stuff for the Brooklyn sol-

diers. But no one stays clean. I viewed myself as a white-collar criminal—and still the bodies were starting to pile up around me.

Not long afterward, I was summoned to a dinner in Brooklyn. As I was leaving to make the long, hated drive into the city, an associate entered my office.

"Michael, Tommy was hit last night."

"What? Tommy! What the hell for?"

"I don't know. Something he did long ago. He was probably one of the kidnappers. Someone's ratting them all out."

Tommy Genovese was another one of my men. He had recently gotten out of jail after a long stint, and I felt sorry for him. I knew from my father how hard it was for the long-termers to readjust. Tommy's wife had waited for him faithfully for nearly a decade. My father and I befriended both Tommy and his wife. Now, after she waited so long for her husband to come home, he was shot through the brain and stuffed into the trunk of a car. It didn't seem right.

The wasted lives and constant killing gnawed at me as I drove into Brooklyn. At the gathering, held in an associate's house, I was introduced to four new recruits. They were young, hard-looking toughs from the streets of Brooklyn. They were pumped so high I suspected they were on something. They were—they were flying on adrenaline. This was a party to celebrate the recruits having "made their bones." They had apparently accomplished it by killing my friend Tommy Genovese the night before. I surmised that I had been invited as a way of informing me, without ever saying a word, that the hit was "in family" and there was no need for retaliation.

"To a job well done," said Johnny Irish Matera, the recruits' sponsor, raising a glass in a toast. I was lost in thought. Jimmy Angellino nudged me. I saw the glasses raised. I raised mine.

"To a job well done," I said, clinking my glass with those of the recruits. As I drank the blood toast, the words of a made man friend echoed in my mind.

"You know, Michael, we're all sick. The lives we lead, we're all sick."

CHAPTER 10

Nearly ten years after the photo-album flap at Estée Lauder exposed my affair with rock singer Michelle Celli, the ill-fated relationship was set to pay off in another way. Celli's brother was a six-foot-two-inch, 230-pound bear of a man named Rafael "Big Red" Celli. The nickname derived from Rafael's scarlet hair and beard. Big Red was in the construction business, and had found himself in a quandary over a massive apartment-house renovation project. The three-thousand-unit Glen Oaks Apartments in Glen Oaks, Queens, was going co-op. The owners, Gerald and Reuben Guterman of Guterman Homes, wanted to keep costs down and profits high. The powerful New York labor unions swooped in, pressuring the owners for an expensive union contract. If they succeeded, the influx of three hundred union tradesmen and laborers would triple the costs of the renovation, decrease the quality of the work, and postpone the completion date.

Big Red recalled that his sister once had dated a man with connections. He tracked me down and asked if I could do anything to help, warning that the union representative was a "heavy guy." "I don't know if you can handle it," Big Red said.

I asked who the union rep was.

"Bob Cervone."

I smiled. Basil Robert Cervone was another in a long line of characters who were born to do the job they did. He was a big, fat man in his sixties who sported a cigar, wore a fedora over a shaved head, loved flashy clothes in loud colors, and drove a shiny Eldorado convertible. He always traveled with a wiry little dude who was his man Friday. Cervone had been an AFL/CIO and Laborers' International Union official for nearly forty years. He knew every psychological pressure tactic ever invented. Builders trembled at the sight of him.

I told Big Red I'd give it a shot, but I needed to speak with the Gutermans first. An introduction was arranged. Reuben Guterman confirmed that they wanted my intervention. Ideally, the goal was to keep the union out. Second-best would be a sweetheart contract. I explained that I would negotiate an arrangement, then get back to them with the terms.

Bob Cervone agreed to meet me at the Silver Moon Diner, a popular eatery off Union Turnpike in Long Island. Cervone arrived as described, complete with shiny head, hat, cigar, and man Friday. I got right down to business.

"Glen Oaks. Reuben Guterman. Gerry Guterman. They're with me."

A big smile appeared on Cervone's face. "That's terrific. Whatta you want?"

"No union."

"Okay."

It had to be harder than that, I figured. "Are you going to do this out of friendship?"

Cervone smiled again. "Come on. The Jews are loaded."

Cervone had done his homework. Among other things, Gerald Guterman owned a fine art collection valued at $40 million.

"We've been contacted by the plumbers, carpenters, painters, and you," I explained. "We'll make a deal, but I want you to handle everybody. Can that be done?"

"Certainly."

"Talk to your people and get back to me."

We spent the next week trading offers. Cervone demanded $200,000 paid up-front in cash, just for starters. That would be on top of a fee per apartment. I told Basil Bob he was dreaming. After a week of haggling, we eventually settled upon a price of $50 per room, which came to $150 to $250 per apartment, depending upon the number of rooms. The numbers laid out like this. The renovations using nonunion labor were expected to cost about $2,000 per unit. With union labor, the cost would rise to $6,000. For $250, I saved the Gutermans $4,000 per unit. About two thousand of the three thousand apartments were eventually renovated; the remainder were inside-price pickups by current rental residents wanting to stay on. When the project was completed, I had saved the builders $6 million to $8 million. The union ended up with a long-term payout of about $400,000 for doing nothing.

To slip some frosting on the deal, Cervone reserved the right to provide the bricklayers. He did so from a company he partly owned with a man named Ralph Perry. (Perry later testified against Cervone when Cervone was convicted of receiving union payoffs for an unrelated project.)

In return for my services, I became Glen Oaks' general contractor. I formed four companies to handle the duties: Flexo Contracting, Close-Rite Windows, Bentwood Carpentry, and M.R.C. Business Relations. Among my functions was to facilitate the cash payments to the unions. Union bosses don't like to accept traceable checks for work never performed.

The Glen Oaks renovation went so well, I worked with Guterman Homes on a half-dozen more projects. These included Cryder Point in Queens, Hamilton House in New Jersey, the Parc Vendome and Colonnade co-op conversions in Manhattan, and the Water's Edge in Patchogue, Long Island. I was able to keep all the unions out except for the painters' union on the two high-profile Manhattan projects. And even with them, I arranged a "sweetheart" deal.

In return, I put $2 million in my pocket from my general contracting services.

The relationship profited Gerald Guterman in more ways than in his wallet. The art collector had an interest in backing promising entertainers. I sent him 1980 *Penthouse* Pet of the Year Cheryl Rixon, a blond work of art with an eye on a singing career. The two formed a brief, symbiotic relationship.

Things continued to get bigger and better for me in the business world. The owner of Rumplik Chevrolet in Suffolk County, Thomas O'Donnell, enlisted my financial help in making a run at buying the Twentieth Century Hotel and casino on Tropicana Avenue in Las Vegas, a former Howard Johnson's, now named the San Remo Hotel. I lent O'Donnell $70,000 at two points per week. O'Donnell said he needed the money to clear some debts at his dealership so he could pass the Las Vegas Gaming Commission's licensing investigation.

O'Donnell, who loved to gamble, promptly defaulted on the $1,400 weekly interest payments. He offered his 75 percent share of the dealership to cover his debt and to divest himself of the dealership's problems to stave off the Vegas investigators. Although the price of the fifty-year-old dealership was dirt cheap, included in the deal was the burden of taking on $320,000 in long- and short-term loans. I went to my financing buddy Gerard Nocera and brought in a new, $1 million floor plan.

O'Donnell and I then became partners on the Las Vegas venture. I arranged for a $5 million financing package to help the Irishman swing the deal. Everything was set. It all hinged on O'Donnell's receiving a critical casino license.

It wasn't even close. The commission blew O'Donnell's application away, collapsing the deal.

O'Donnell turned out to be quite a character. He left the Chevy dealership with such a maze of shady paperwork it eventually strangled the operation. Included among O'Donnell's tricks was financing cars twice from different banks, or selling them for cash and sending through paperwork claiming they were purchased on credit. A Mercedes Benz sold to New York Jets quarterback Richard Todd had been financed twice, complete with Todd's forged signature on a second set of papers. The former University of Alabama star was unaware of the chicanery until the second bank came after him for back payments.

O'Donnell was later convicted of grand larceny and fraud, made a deal, and vanished into the Witness Protection Program.

The former owner's problems resulted in some unpleasant déjà vu. Shortly after I took over the dealership, a squad of twenty-five Suffolk County police officers charged into my new office, breaking down the door with an axe. They were attempting to confirm my position as Rumplik's new owner and dig up records of illegal financing activities. I had been tipped about the raid by an informant inside the Suffolk County Police Department. I made sure that neither I nor any worthwhile records were present when the police squad paid its visit.

Another business opportunity found its way to me when I was contacted by Daniel Cunningham, president of the Allied International Union, a lucrative Great Neck, Long Island security-guard union. Cunningham needed help.

He wanted to align himself and his growing union with a connected guardian angel before someone tried to squeeze him.

Although I found the sloppy, freckle-faced Cunningham to be personally repulsive, I did like the man's cash-heavy union operation. I explained that I would be happy to give him protection.

I installed one of my men, Japan Lines executive Louis Fenza, as vice-president of the security-guard union. Together we received an

education in union skimming. Among the scams, Cunningham was paying about $6,000 a month for a health and dental insurance plan for his
members, then turning around and billing the union $20,000. The extra
$14,000 went into his pocket.

Cunningham's big plan was to expand his union into the hotel and
casino hotbed of Atlantic City. He enlisted my help in convincing the
security guards to sign the cards needed to push the union issue to a
vote. First, I arranged a meet with Philadelphia boss Nicky Scarfo.
Atlantic City's bartenders and waitresses were already unionized under
the protection of the Scarfo and Gambino families, and I had to go
through proper channels. Scarfo gave his approval, and Cunningham
opened an office in Atlantic City.

The unionization drive blew up much the same way the Vegas casino
hotel project had crumbled. Cunningham was indicted on fifty-two
counts of union fraud. When the New Jersey press got wind of the
indictment, the stories effectively choked the union drive. Cunningham
was subsequently convicted of forty of the fifty-two counts and was sent
to prison.

Once again I was having a difficult time selecting the reputable front
men I needed to shield my operations from government investigators.
The legitimate business world was overflowing with thieves.

Which is not to imply that the union operation died with Cunningham's conviction. Anthony Tomasso, Cunningham's underling, took over.
Not long afterward, Tomasso had a heart attack. That left one Louie
Fenza as the new union boss. A few dominoes had fallen, and I found
myself in control of a million-dollar security-guard union.

At the same time, I was contacted by a man with Mob connections
who wanted me to arrange the killing of his father-in-law, who he
believed was going to testify against him before a grand jury. I reported
the request to Persico. The boss affirmed what I already knew: La Cosa
Nostra does not kill people for associates. Contrary to popular belief, it
doesn't even kill for hire (although some soldiers will quietly hire themselves out on the side). The Mob kills for Mob business only. In those
instances, the hit men or hit squads are never paid for their services. The
idea of a "contract" being put out on someone's life, while it exists in
other areas of society, is merely figurative when it relates to the Mob. All
Cosa Nostra soldiers are expected to be killers. I explained to the man
that I couldn't help him with his father-in-law, but I did use the opportunity to get involved in the man's business.

During this period, I also found myself back in the flea-market game. The part-owner of a flea market in the Bay Ridge section of Brooklyn was having problems with his partner. The man had become addicted to drugs and was dealing on the grounds to support his habit.

"I'll get him out," I assured the owner. "And then I'm your new partner."

I dispatched two of my men to scare off the unwanted partner. One of the enforcers was a jumpy Vietnam vet named Anthony Sarivola, better known as "Tony Limo" for his job of driving a hearse for Larry Carrozza's funeral parlor. Tony Limo bullied the flea-market junkie and told him to hit the road.

Three days later I received a call from Jimmy Angellino, now a Colombo captain and a fast-rising star in the family. Angellino told me that John Gotti, then a soldier in the Gambino family, wanted a meet.

We met the next day at a restaurant in Queens. Gotti, currently the much-publicized Gambino family boss, arrived with a soldier named Angelo Ruggiero. I brought a Colombo soldier with me.

The meeting turned into a classic example of a high-stakes Cosa Nostra sit-down. Contrary to previously published reports—including the version that was used as the basis of the "He's going around town saying 'Fuck Michael Corleone'" scene in *The Godfather, Part III*—there were no heated arguments, cursing, or trading of insults. We all spoke calmly and treated each other with respect, as decreed by family policy. It was the subtlety of the verbal sparring that provided the fascination.

After we'd politely introduced ourselves, Gotti took the lead. "This kid at the flea market, he's with me."

"How can that be, John?" I countered. "He's a drug addict and a dealer. You know the rules."

"You don't know that," Gotti said, feigning surprise.

"It's been confirmed. He's using and selling. How can a man like that be with you?"

"If he's doing drugs, we'll make him stop," Gotti said, being careful not to admit any prior knowledge of his alleged associate's drug use. "And even so, his interest in the market is still mine."

"If he's into drugs, then you can't be associated with him. If you can't be associated with him, then you have no interest in the market," I said.

"That's not the way it goes," Gotti countered.

"You know the rules, John."

Sensing I had Gotti cornered, I decided to take the offensive.

"Who you kidding, anyway? He's not with you. He ran to you after we threw him out."

"No, no," Gotti insisted, shaking his head. "He's been with me a long time. A long time."

"If he's been with you a long time, then how come you aren't aware that he's using and selling drugs?" I had him pinned.

We repeated our positions. Gotti promised to make the guy kick his addiction and clean up his act. I repeated that the man's long-term drug use severed any tie Gotti had to the rich, unpoliced market, and added that no matter what they decided, the guy was out.

"We can't have a junkie around the market," I insisted. "It's no good. You can't argue that. And since when are we in the drug-rehabilitation business?"

"I'll install somebody in his place," Gotti offered.

"I'm not convinced you have claim to begin with."

Although Gotti's position was weak, his towering ego wouldn't let him lose. We decided to take it up with our captains and meet again. I went to Persico and told him Gotti was full of shit. Persico gave me the okay to press the issue.

The day before the next meet, I received a call informing me that there was a third partner in the flea market, and that partner was aligned with Collie Dipietro, a soldier in the Genovese family. That further muddied the waters. It also confirmed to me that Gotti was lying. If he had been with the flea market for as long as he claimed, he would have known about the Genovese connection.

I knew Collie; he had served time at Leavenworth with my father. He was in his mid-forties, dressed sharply, chewed a fat cigar, and possessed an ego that rivaled Gotti's. If the waitress sneezed during our meeting, both Gotti and Collie would claim that the woman had been overwhelmed by their manliness.

We met at the Bergin Hunt and Fish Club in Ozone Park. I suspected that Collie and Gotti would join forces against me, which is exactly what happened. Right off, Collie showed his cards by acknowledging Gotti's claim on the market. That negated my assault on that front. I also knew I couldn't coexist with these two egomaniacs. The tactic now was to have them buy me out.

Collie had a different plan. "Look, we know that each of our guys is a thief," he said, slandering our associates. "I have the solution. There's this Jew I know, a real business whiz. We'll have him run the market and look out for all of our interests."

I stifled a laugh. Collie's Jew wouldn't look out for anyone's interest but Collie's. I countered that my man had founded the market and was its backbone. There was no way I could justify giving anyone say over him. We ran this around for a while and finally decided to kick out the junkie, replace him with Gotti's representative, and bring in Collie's Jew on a trial basis. If it didn't work, then one party would have to buy out the other.

It didn't work. By the third weekend, the new flea-market partners were at each other's throats. Another meeting was set. I convinced Collie and Gotti to put up $70,000 to buy out Scarola's interest.

I came out of the flea-market meetings $20,000 richer—my share of the $70,000—and, more importantly, with valuable experience. The negotiations were Mob business as usual, infused with deceit, lying, and twisted gamesmanship. Yet I discovered I could not only hold my own under those circumstances, I could win.

I was also left with a grudging admiration for John Gotti. I found the future Gambino boss to be a true mobster who loved the life and everything about it. He was sharp and tenacious, and it was obvious he was going to reach the top—or die trying. I wasn't overwhelmed, however, by Gotti's show of toughness. Gotti was tough, but he was no Sonny Franzese.

"Who's John Gotti?" I remarked to an associate prior to the third meeting. "Remember, I came from the best."

It was a psychological edge I carried throughout my Mob tenure. By comparing every opponent to my father, I could never be intimidated.

Within a year, the flea market wheezed, sickened, and eventually died. The business whiz Collie installed to run the market was convicted of an assortment of felonies relating to his handling of the operation.

A few years later, a high-flying John Gotti entered P. J. Clarke's bar and restaurant on Manhattan's East Side and was smitten by a sexy singer performing in the lounge. He pursued her to no avail, suffering a severe bruise to his immense ego. Finally, the woman confessed why she was brushing him off. "I'm still in love with Michael Franzese."

The singer was Michelle Celli. Gotti was so infuriated he has since taken every opportunity to lash out at his perceived rival.

Gotti fared better when he stayed within his own family. On December 16, 1985, police and prosecutors believe, a squad of his henchmen blasted Gambino boss Paul Castellano in front of Sparks Steak House in Manhattan. As Castellano's life and blood simultaneously spilled onto the New York pavement, police feel Gotti was engineering a successful move to take over the Mafia's largest family.

While John Gotti was on his way to the top in Brooklyn, Michael Franzese kept on quietly doing what he did best—generating huge amounts of money.

It was obvious to even the most fringe Mob associate that my father was lying low and was no longer a factor in the organized-crime hierarchy. Still, the government feared him. In June 1982, his unheralded return to freedom ended much the same way he had originally lost it: the government screwed him.

As part of his parole, he was obligated to prove he could be a decent, civic-minded citizen. To show he was moving in that direction, he joined the Brooklyn Kiwanis Club and dutifully attended the organization's Tuesday-night meetings. A few times a year, the Kiwanis hosted joint meetings with brother chapters around the New York area. The gathering that summer was at the Georgetown Inn in Brooklyn.

In the past, he'd often asked me to join him at the meetings. I begged off, finding them boring. This time, for whatever reason, he didn't mention it. Had he, I never would have allowed him to attend. The Georgetown Inn was a popular Mob hangout, so popular that it was constantly under surveillance. The bartender was an FBI informant who wore a wire.

As soon as my father and a number of other felons were spotted entering the inn, the surveillance team outside perked up. A call went out to James Stein, my father's parole officer. The bartender was alerted to keep watch. In the course of the evening, my father bumped into two old friends, a Gambino capo named Carmine "the Doctor" Lombardozzi and an unidentified man he had met in prison. He spoke briefly to each, and no criminal activity was discussed. Both conversations were reported to last longer than the three-minute limit set by his parole guidelines.

One of the conversations occurred at the bar, right under the nose and hidden microphone of the bartender.

At age twelve.

At age two, posed on a pony.

My father (left) with his friend and look-alike, middleweight champion Rocky Graziano, after Graziano knocked out a challenger in the mid 1940s. (Jay Sharp)

An army of heavily armed police officers and detectives nervously shadowed my father's every move during a string of arrests in 1966. He was charged with everything from bank robbery to murder—whatever would stick. *(Newsday)*

A bizarre police sting goes awry and results in my arrest in January 1974. I was a premed student at Hofstra University at the time. It was part of a rash of harassment arrests that worked to drive me out of college and into the Mob. I'm shown here with the "Chubby Brothers," John and Robert Verrastro. *(Newsday)*

Frankie Cestaro.

Frankie "Frankie Gangster" Castagnaro.

Peter "Peter Nap" Napolitano.

Jerry Zimmerman.

A quarter-ton of fun—Lawrence Iorizzo with his attorney Robert Palstein. *(Newsday)*

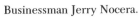

Businessman Jerry Nocera.

THE GANG

Iorizzo's "daisy chain" gas tax scheme brought us unprecedented riches. A federal aerial surveillance photo shows my former estate in Brookville, Long Island.

Champagne Larry Carrozza with his father Tony.

My sister Gia.

Cammy Garcia at age seven. (Mitch Quinones)

This odd shot symbolized the dichotomy of Cammy's turbulent childhood. Her desire to be a cheerleader ostracized her from her gang friends in the Chicano barrio of Norwalk, California. (Mitch Quinones)

Cammy was destined to change the face of organized crime in America.

om the moment I first saw Cammy emerging m a swimming pool in Fort Lauderdale, my e changed. Up until then, I had kept a harness my emotions. Then, without warning, I fell love.

Love blooms in Fort Lauderdale for a hunted New York Mob Prince and a feisty Mexican dancer from Norwalk, California. I was never happier. A movie photographer caught us together during a break in the filming of *Knights of the City*.

With Cammy, singer Smokey Robinson and actor Leon Isaac Kennedy during the final days of *Knights of the City*.

My father, out of prison for a brief time on parole, attended my arraignment in 1985 with my mother, Tina. (*Newsday*)

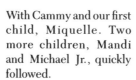

In prison in Terminal Island, California.

With Cammy and our first child, Miquelle. Two more children, Mandi and Michael Jr., quickly followed.

I married Cammy and promised that I'd give up my Cosa Nostra empire, accept a prison sentence, and quit the Mob. She made me an offer I couldn't refuse. (Lawrence Lesser)

Dining with Cammy and her parents, Seferino and Irma.

One of the last photos taken of me as a member in the Colombo crime family. I walked to the altar, said "I do," and vowed to do the impossible, "Quit the Mob." I've never had a moment's regret. (Lawrence Lesser)

The following day, my father received a call to meet with Stein. At the parole office, Stein informed him that he had violated his parole by "consorting with known criminals" and would have to surrender. He was taken back to the Metropolitan Correctional Center in New York.

"Dad, what happened?" I asked him over the phone when I heard the news.

"No good," he said.

My father's crime was a technical violation that should have netted him no more than six to nine months. After the hearing, during which Stein testified about my father's activities at the Georgetown Inn, he was given ten years. Ten years!

I was enraged. I blamed Stein. I felt the duty of a probation officer was to help keep his subjects clean, not sit in on stakeouts to catch them in a violation.

Outside the hearing, I found myself face-to-face with Stein.

"I'm sorry, Michael—that's how it goes."

"You know, Stein, you're a real scumbag."

"What?"

"You heard me," I said, my voice rising. "You were supposed to let him know if there was a problem. They said in there that he was under surveillance the past seven months. You're obligated to warn him. You're a scumbag and you betrayed him!"

A few days later, two FBI agents visited me at my Rumplik Chevrolet office. I ushered them out to the parking lot to talk in private.

"We understand you threatened the life of James Stein," one of the agents sternly said. "We know about it. If anything happens to him, we're coming after you."

"I didn't threaten his life!" I exploded. "I called him a scumbag. He *is* a scumbag, and I'll say it again—the guy's a scumbag! I never threatened the guy in any way."

"That's not the way we heard it."

"Why don't you come inside and explain all this to my attorney. I want it on the record."

The agents refused.

"I don't have time for this nonsense. Get the fuck off my lot!" I ordered.

It wouldn't be the last of the "scumbag" incident. My heat-of-the-moment hallway conversation with Stein was filed away to use against me. The first use was immediate. The FBI set up an undercover "sting" operation to seduce me into offering a bribe to free my father. An informer named Luigi Vizzini teamed with undercover FBI agent Chris Mattiace, and they presented themselves as middlemen who had national parole board head Benjamin Malcolm in their pocket. Numerous meetings were arranged, most held at the Atrium Club in Manhattan. The wired and highly trained undercover agent and his associate tried to cajole me into offering the bribe.

From my perspective, it was an excruciating balancing act. I didn't want to be suckered by an informant, nor did I want to eliminate the chance that the men really had a connection that could free my father. If they were legit, I'd have been more than willing to pay a bribe. My father was my weakness, and everybody, good and bad, knew it. But until I was positive, I took the precautions my father had taught me during all those six A.M. breakfast meetings: "Treat every stranger as if he were an undercover FBI agent." Along with that advice, some internal warning system alerted me to be especially careful with these two. It turned out to be the first of a long line of instances where my eerie sixth sense kicked in and saved my ass.

Relying on verbal adroitness, I kept the doors open while never saying anything on the tapes to clearly implicate myself. Assistant U.S. Attorney Charles Rose deemed all the recordings useless and killed the investigation. (I didn't learn until four years later, at a bond hearing, that Mattiace was an agent and that the conversations had been recorded.)

Despite the elaborate failure, the FBI tried to trap me again. In 1983, the agency launched a heavily financed sting operation aimed at bringing down famed boxing promoter Don King by linking him to the Mob. A former member of Muhammad Ali's entourage, Reggie Barrett, had been turned by the FBI and was being used as its entry into big-time boxing. Barrett was paired with a Latin undercover agent named Victor Guerrero. Guerrero, operating under the pseudonym Victor Quintana, proclaimed himself to be a mega-rich South American trying to buy his way into boxing. The duo were first introduced to my father by fight manager Chet Cummings shortly before my father's parole was revoked. Cummings made the intro at a boxing match in Atlantic City. Guerrero and my father became fast friends, dining together and frequently playing racquetball. My father advised his new buddy that I was the man to see to get to King. Although I didn't know King, my father figured I could do anything.

At that point, Guerrero and Barrett must have thought they had struck gold. The operation had barely started and they already had met Michael and Sonny Franzese. The mob don/boxing Don link was all but established.

I met with Guerrero and Barrett more than fifty times during the next year. The FBI put on a first-rate show. Guerrero opened an office in a high-rent district of Manhattan, drove a Rolls-Royce, wore thousand-dollar suits, and threw taxpayers' money around with abandon. He expressed an eagerness to enter all of my businesses, from cars to movies. We traveled together to Florida and California, spending the hours chatting away. During the flights, Guerrero frequently adjusted his position and complained of a back problem. He was probably covering for the discomfort caused by the wrapping that secured his voice-activated body microphone.

We talked and talked—and I gave up nothing. My sixth sense was on alert again. As usual, it wasn't strong enough to blow the deal away, just strong enough to make me wary. Finally, unable to get a clear fix on the man known as Victor Quintana, I agreed to arrange a meet with King. But first I wanted to see the $15 million Quintana claimed he had. The FBI set up a banker in Illinois to confirm the deposit, complete with official bank statements.

I got to King through the Reverend Al Sharpton, the infamous New York rabble-rouser. Sharpton is a "player" who has friends in the Gambino family; I was introduced to him through his Gambino connections. We used to meet at the offices of Spring Records in Manhattan and discuss our mutual interest in labor unions and entertainment. In public, Sharpton can be grating, especially to the white power structure. In private, he's a gentleman and a good guy. He struck me as someone who believed strongly in his various causes. During our meetings, Sharpton offered to use the considerable black-power forces he commands to assist me in any way. I took him up on it during the drive to unionize the security guards in Atlantic City. Before that effort blew up, Sharpton was planning to organize his people to picket the casino hotels.

I later read an article where Sharpton claimed he was associating with me merely to gather information for the FBI. I doubt that. I think he was just covering his considerable ass when he found himself in a little hot water. Either way, he never did anything to hurt me.

Before bringing Guerrero to Don King, I had a private meeting with the flamboyant, wild-haired boxing promoter. He turned out to be pretty much as advertised—boisterous, verbose, always smiling, always happy. I could believe his off-repeated claim that his hair sticks up that way naturally. The man appears to be electrically charged.

I respected King because he came from the streets and climbed up the hard way. Personally, he struck me as a tough negotiator, but once you had a deal, he'd keep his word. Those who've cried foul in dealing with him weren't cheated. They were simply outnegotiated.

"Don, these guys say they have $15 million to invest," I said. "I confirmed the money, but I haven't been able to qualify them. I want you to play it straight. Play it as if you are talking to FBI agents."

King met Guerrero and Barrett and handled them as advised. A promotion was set for Atlantic City, all aboveboard. When Guerrero failed to come through with the initial seed money, a few hundred thousand, both the deal and the connection collapsed. Apparently, an FBI budget cruncher decided the agency wasn't in the fight business and pulled the plug on the operation. Had the FBI put up the money to promote a few fights, both King and I might have softened.

Guerrero was left with fifty-two taped conversations with me. None amounted to anything. In fact, they backfired. When King was later indicted for tax evasion, I had my attorney send him the tapes that pertained to him. King's lawyers used the recordings to show the lengths the government had gone to sting the colorful promoter. The jury frowned upon the tactic and found King innocent. Following the trial, King sent me a note: "Thanks. I owe you one.—Don King"

CHAPTER 11

In 1981, Sebastian "Buddy" Lombardo went to my father with a problem. Lombardo's boss, Lawrence Iorizzo, was being shaken down by a gang of thugs attempting to move in on Vantage Petroleum, Iorizzo's multimillion-dollar wholesale gasoline business. My father referred Lombardo to me.

I checked out Iorizzo. The information I received on the gas man raised my eyebrows. Larry Iorizzo was the son of a jazz saxophone player who had worked on Broadway and in Brooklyn burlesque houses. The younger Iorizzo grew into a mammoth, six-foot four-inch, 450-pound businessman who ate pizzas the way most people eat Ritz crackers. Since he was the size of two men, he apparently decided he needed two wives—not a then and a now, but two at the same time. He'd spend half the night with one, usually from dinner until three or four A.M., wake up, tell her he needed to check his gas stations along Long Island's highways, then bed down the rest of the night with his other wife. He followed this schedule for more than ten years, routinely having dinner with Wife I and breakfast with Wife II. Between the two women, he had seven children.

In addition to his bizarre domestic life, Iorizzo had gone through a much-publicized spat with Martin Carey, the brother of then New York governor Hugh Carey. The squabble over Carey's cut-rate gasoline business led to a lawsuit. (Iorizzo later testified before a congressional subcommittee that Carey was blending gasoline with cheap, hazardous waste to jump his profits and provide funds for his brother's successful re-election campaign for governor in 1978.)

I could accept the girth, the wives, and the mixed brood of offspring. However, the lawsuit and rumors that Iorizzo had cooperated with the government were something else. Although Iorizzo's gas business was a plum, I passed.

Lombardo wouldn't give up, pushing me "just to meet him." After seven months, I relented. We met at Peter Raneri's restaurant in Smithtown, Long Island. Iorizzo was seated when I arrived. Although I could tell that there was a mountain of flesh bubbling under the table, I was surprised that from the neck up, Iorizzo looked like a normal person. And even below the neck, he wasn't sloppily fat. There were no rolls of lard flopping around his body or hanging down like melting wax from his arms. He was definitely one obese man, but was solidly packed.

As he picked at his food, Iorizzo outlined his impressive operation. He owned or supplied three hundred gas stations in and around Long Island, an operation that grossed millions of dollars a month. His problem was that despite being rich and successful, he lacked power. He was having trouble with a group of men who were trying to extort him and muscle in on his supply stops.

"I'd be very appreciative if you could help me with this problem," Iorizzo said.

I asked who was shaking him down. It turned out to a band of small fry, just associates of another family. Eradicating them wouldn't be a problem. I was more concerned with learning about the Martin Carey incident. The fat man explained that it was a civil suit, meaning it was a personal battle between businessmen that didn't involve anyone ratting out to police or prosecutors. That made a difference. (What Iorizzo didn't say was that he had previously reported Carey to the police and the FBI.)

As I listened and observed, I noticed that Iorizzo ate very little. It was notable because I had been told that the man had once eaten fifty hamburgers at one sitting, then consumed two large pizzas for dessert. During our entire relationship, I would never witness such a display. From the beginning, Iorizzo kept to a policy of hiding his gluttony from me. I took it as a sign of respect, a sign that Iorizzo had something on the ball.

Fixing Iorizzo's problem was easy. I sent out a squad headed by Vincent Aspromonte, a menacing figure who sported an ugly scar across his forehead. A butcher by trade, Aspromonte had acquired his image-enhancing scar in a knife fight or an auto accident, depending upon which story one believed. Whatever, the result was effective. The shakedown artists took one look at the scar and never were seen again.

"Larry, your problem is solved," I announced, visiting him at his Vantage office. The moment the words left my lips, I sensed a change in Iorizzo. He could feel the power I commanded and felt that he had tapped into the flow.

"Here's how I'll repay you," Iorizzo said. For the next hour, Iorizzo proceeded to outline how we could milk hundreds of millions in illegal profits from his gasoline operation. The key was the incompetence of the federal, state, and county governments in collecting gasoline taxes. Together, the three governing bodies demanded a twenty-seven-cent bite out of every gallon of gas sold. Demanding it and getting it were two different things. The lax collection enabled Iorizzo to stall having his owned or leased stations pay the gas taxes for as long as a year. By that time, they could close the station, the owners would vanish, and then, a month or so later, the station would reopen under new management and start again.

Iorizzo further snarled the works by having all his companies registered in Panama. Under Panama's bearer stock law, the owner of a company was the person who had his hands on the stock. That meant the "official" owners of the stations, and of Iorizzo's umbrella operation, could be, and often were, two guys with machetes out in a Panama sugar-cane field. When the government agencies went looking for their tax money, that's who they'd have to find.

We opened a new Panama company, Galion Holdings, to oversee our joint operation. Vantage, which was mired in Iorizzo's past shady tactics, supplied Galion Holdings with the gasoline, and Galion supplied the stations. I installed John Garbarino, a retired union official, as Galion's president. Aspromonte was made V.P. I then bounced most of the current station managers and lessees and began inserting my growing coterie of men in their place. Each of my associates was given three to six stations and paid a salary of $500 per week per station. All the remaining money would come back to Galion.

My deal with Iorizzo was that 20 percent of the profits, off the top, would go to the Colombo family. The remaining money would be split fifty-fifty between us. Iorizzo handled the paperwork, while I protected the stations and dealt with other suppliers.

With the tax money skimmed, the operation began producing millions of dollars, a good percentage of which was delivered in grocery bags full of cash that reeked of gasoline.

In 1981, the state of New York figured out how it was being beaten for tens of millions in gas tax dollars and decided to change the law. Instead of the gas stations being responsible for the taxes, the burden was shifted to the less numerous wholesalers. Since the change couldn't happen overnight, the state alerted the operators and gave them a year to make the switch. The grace period gave Iorizzo ample time to figure out how to play the shell game on the wholesale level. Actually, what he discovered thrilled him: the state had made it easier and far more profitable to steal the tax money. No longer would we have to rely upon collecting bags of money stinking of gas from the service stations. We could rake it off the top of huge wholesale shipments.

The method Iorizzo developed was known as a "daisy chain." Under the new law, the gas could be sold tax-free from one wholesale company to the next. The last company to handle the transaction, the company that sold directly to the retailers, was responsible for the tax. Iorizzo would take a shipment of, say, a million gallons into Company A and sell it to his stations and those on his growing supply route. On paper, however, instead of the gas going to the stations, it would go to Company B, then to Company C, and finally to Company D. On paper, it would denote Company D had sold to the stations. Companies B through D were shell firms that consisted of nothing but a phone number and some stationery. Company D, the one responsible for paying the taxes, would be owned by those same guys down in the Panama sugar-cane fields. After a few hundred million gallons of invisible gasoline passed through Company D, it would declare bankruptcy. When the state and federal governments tried to collect their tens of millions in tax money, they'd have to go on the mind-numbing paper trail from Company A through Company D. At the end of this grim rainbow was no pot of tax gold but the "burnout" firm, owned by some guy named Juan in Panama, current address unknown.

Since Company A was selling tax-free gas to the stations, Galion Holdings could undersell everyone in the area—except those who were also stealing. Station owners, who could in turn sell the gas tax-free to their customers, began begging to get on Galion's supply route—a direct contrast to charges leveled by prosecutors that the station owners were forced into buying Iorizzo's gas by my goons. Galion didn't have to force anybody to purchase gas at ten cents a gallon less than he could anywhere else. Even the stations supplied by Mobil, Shell, Exxon, Texaco, and other major oil companies shuffled their paper so they could illegally purchase from Galion or one of its subsidiaries. They would call and ask Iorizzo to make deliveries at two A.M. to avoid company spotters.

Instead of being ripped off, the New York public actually benefited in one way from the Robin Hood–like operation. Gas prices dropped in New York City and Long Island as station owners had an extra profit margin to work with. Since the wholesalers were responsible for paying the taxes, the gas stations were in the clear. Station owners and managers buying Galion gas could undercut everyone else in the area and still make a larger profit.

As the operation grew, Galion swallowed up large and small independent suppliers all across New York and Long Island and into New Jersey, Connecticut, and Pennsylvania. Galion also purchased the valuable wholesale distributors' licenses from these companies to keep their daisy chains going.

We created so many shell companies that finding names for them got to be a chore. We alleviated the monotony by giving them humorous names, as I had done in the construction business. Among the multitude created were S.O.S. Oil; Southern Belle Petroleum; Dine, Dance and Drink, Inc.; and Down to Earth Management.*

With the money came the toys. Galion Holdings purchased a Lear jet, a Bell jet helicopter, and a twenty-five-foot Chris-Craft speedboat and a forty-foot Trojan yacht, *John-John*, both docked at my half-million-dollar home in Delray Beach, Florida. Galion also custom-ordered the *Trump Princess* of Winnebagos, a $370,000 mansion on wheels furnished better than most doctors' homes. I purchased an assortment of condominiums and settled Maria and our three small children in a multimillion-dollar Brookville, Long Island mansion complete with its own racquetball court and satellite television system.

Whatever guilt I had about thievery on this level was erased because there was no real victim. I wasn't stealing from people but from institu-

---

*There was nothing "down to earth" about the money pouring in. Michael and the fat man split $2 million to $4 million a week. Michael drove into Brooklyn and delivered bags of $250,000 to $500,000 to the Colombo family as their share, downgraded from the 20 percent cut he arbitrarily established before the income soared. He'd hand the cash to Persico or to whatever bug-eyed acting boss, underboss, or captain happened to be around.

tions. And the institution I was stealing from in the gas business was the government—the same government that sent my father to prison for fifty years on the testimony of lowlifes.

To celebrate the gas gang's continuing good fortune, I hosted a dinner-and-dancing party every Monday night at the Casablanca nightclub on the Jericho Turnpike in Huntington, Long Island. I owned a share of the club and closed it for a night of private frivolity. Between fifty and a hundred guys and dolls showed each week. For a few hours during these spirited Monday-night parties, I met with various associates or prospective associates. They entered, paid their respects to me like I was Don Corleone, then stated their business.

Iorizzo was so fond of these weekly galas that he rarely missed one. Quick to become intoxicated despite his great girth, he once became so giddily drunk he picked up a flower pot, put it on his head, and danced around the room. By then he was pushing five hundred pounds. His surrealistic Carmen Miranda imitation made for an unforgettable sight. Later that evening, I drove the big man home in his brand-new Cadillac.

"With the money we're making, we don't need anything," Iorizzo said, inebriated as much by cash and power as by alcohol. "We don't need this car."

With that, he ripped the door off the glove compartment and threw it out the window, howling with laughter.

"We don't need this arm rest!" He ripped that off and tossed it out.

"We don't need this sun visor!" That went next.

Iorizzo proceeded to strip the inside of the car, piece by piece, bouncing parts of the lavish interior down the highway.

"We don't need nothing, Michael! I can just buy another new Cadillac tomorrow!"

They were the best of times.

There were, however, a few problems. Iorizzo went on a power trip that knew no bounds. During the next three years, he asked me to kill at least fifty people who had offended him in various ways. I refused every request, telling him that murder was bad business. On the streets, my men were also becoming drunk with money and power. They made their own requests to hit this person or that, or raze rival stations and trucks. I always turned them down. It was unnecessary.

The men didn't limit their bullying to outsiders. Frankie Gangster walked into Galion's office one afternoon, pulled out a .45, and stuck it in Iorizzo's face.

"If you ever sell Michael out, I'll kill you," he warned.

Things became so unruly that I was forced to call a meeting of the troops. I summoned them to a large basement assembly room in one of Galion's offices in Commack, Long Island. When everyone was seated and accounted for, there were more than fifty in attendance. I stood before them at a podium like Lee Iacocca addressing his top executives. My topic that evening was violence and the new Mob.

"Violence is bad business," I said. "Violence will destroy us. Peace is profitable. This isn't the 1930s. This isn't Al Capone. Those days are gone. We are in a new era. We are not shylocks and pimps and bookmakers. We are businessmen. We have a good thing going here and we can all make a ton of money if we're smart. Murder is not smart. If bodies start showing up everywhere it will bring the police down upon us. We don't want that.

"We want to be friends with our competitors so we can win them over and bring them into our operation. We don't want to extort them or bully them or beat them up. The age of the bent-nose enforcer is over. We can offer our competitors a service they can't get anywhere else. We can offer them profits they can't make anywhere else. We don't need to force them. They'll join willingly.

"From this point on, there will be no violence of any kind unless I personally approve it. There are no exceptions. If you have a problem, bring it to me and I'll solve it. If I can't, we'll use our muscle as a last resort. But only as a last resort."

At the end of my speech, I ordered an associate to pass out more than fifty beepers. I instructed all my men to wear them twenty-four hours a day. Prosecutors would later dub us "the Beeper Gang."

Not long after the meeting, Iorizzo broke the rule and proved me prophetic. The fat man and a Long Island wholesaler named Shelly Levine had a difference of opinion over $270,000 Iorizzo claimed Levine owed. The sum was a pittance considering the sums we were raking in, but Iorizzo was a power junkie and needed to throw around his considerable weight. He called the frizzy-haired Jewish man into his office and slapped him around. When I heard about it, I was livid. Levine had a big operation that I was looking to sweep into Galion. I came down hard upon Iorizzo, a process amplified by the fact that he was terrified of me.

Shelly Levine did exactly what I feared he would do. He ran and got his own muscle. The man Shelly ran to was stubby, cigar-chewing Joe "Joe Glitz" Galizia, a soldier in the Genovese family.*

Iorizzo and I were basking in the Florida sun when the call came. Joe Glitz was so eager to settle things he told me he was flying to Florida for the meet.

"See what you did?" I scolded Iorizzo. "We could have had Shelly with us. Instead, you smacked that guy and now I've got to deal with fucking Joe Glitz."

Joe Glitz arrived the following afternoon with Shelly Levine in tow. I met them on the outdoor patio of the Marina Bay Club in Fort Lauderdale. The first thing I did was order Glitz to bounce Levine from the meet. I didn't want to talk interfamily business with an outsider.

"Shelly's with me," Glitz said, chomping on his cigar, thumping his chest and offering the traditional Cosa Nostra opening. "He's been with me for a long—"

"Don't bullshit me," I growled. "Larry smacked him, so he ran to you. Don't hand me that 'long time' shit. And if Shelly's with you now, then you're responsible for the $270,000 he owes us. That's the first matter of business. Without that, we have nothing to talk about."

Glitz didn't argue. The Genovese soldier agreed to pay the debt and put it on record with his family. It wasn't hard to figure Glitz's angle. "I want to get into the gas business with this guy," he said. "We need your help. Give us a line of credit so we can get rolling."

I had no alternative but to agree. It was a courtesy one made man expected of another. In the end, I got what I wanted: Shelly's extensive operation would be swept under Galion Holdings along with everyone else. Only trouble, there was now another gangster fly in the ointment.

After a satisfied Joe Glitz departed, I confronted Iorizzo.

"Slapping Shelly was the stupidest thing you've ever done. You just introduced another family into the business," I lectured. "Don't ever chase anyone away from us again."

After that bit of unpleasantness, we shifted to one of our reasons for being in Florida. We had expanded our operation to the Sunshine State

---

*Joe Glitz, a stubby man who chewed a cigar, was suspected in Mob and police circles of having made his bones by killing his sponsor, Michael's flea market adversary Collie Dipietro. The event no doubt shocked the hell out of Collie in those few short seconds between comprehension and death.

through a Fort Lauderdale company called Houston Holdings. Within months, we were moving forty million gallons of tax-free gas a month, taking in another half-million per week each.

Iorizzo quickly got back into my good graces by updating me on a side operation he had going. In the Lear jet on the way from New York, while we feasted on shrimp and steak, Iorizzo laid it out. "We're going to make a bundle this weekend," he announced.

Iorizzo had bought off the dispatcher at a New York gasoline loading dock. From Friday night to early Monday morning, he sent a succession of tanker trucks to the station to fill up. As we worked on our tans, Iorizzo kept a running tab of how much gas he was stealing. With each report, he sang, danced a Jackie Gleason jig, and toasted another successful hour of thievery. By Monday morning, he had emptied the tanks of three million gallons of gas, which we immediately sold for a pure profit of $2.5 million.

The fat man already had all the money he could ever spend. Didn't matter. He was stone-cold hooked on the thrill of stealing and the vicarious power he wielded through me.

My success was not going unnoticed in Brooklyn. Although Persico was back in prison, he issued an order that was quickly relayed down the pipe. I received a call requesting my presence at a designated house in Brooklyn. When I arrived, I was greeted by Jimmy Angellino and other family members.

"The boss says he wants to make it official," Angellino said. "You are now a captain in La Cosa Nostra. Congratulations, Michael."

I thanked them and returned to Long Island. Becoming a *caporegime* meant I could officially be the leader of a band of soldiers and associates. I was already doing that, and had been for years, so as far as my day-to-day activity went, it didn't change anything. But the title gave me increased authority, more recognition among the made men and Mob associates on the street, and more power in dealing with members of other families. It also meant that along with recruiting my own crew, made men soldiers would be assigned to my command.

There was a down side. Being a captain gave me more responsibility, and tied me in closer to the central command in Brooklyn.

At the same time Iorizzo and I were running our gas scam on Long Island, a flamboyant mobster named Michael Markowitz was running his own billion-dollar gasoline scheme in and around New York City. For most of the 1980s, Markowitz, a jowly man with thinning, curly brown hair, reigned as the king of the mysterious wave of Russian and Eastern European immigrant gangsters who settled into areas like Brighton Beach in Brooklyn. While me and my army of kinder and gentler mobsters were ushering organized crime into the 1990s, Markowitz and his fellow Russians were dragging it back to the violent 1930s.

A similar invasion of Cuban immigrant thugs, dumped ashore during the 1980 Freedom Flotilla, was ravaging Miami. The connection wasn't missed by the New York media. Markowitz, alternately referred to as a Russian and as a Rumanian, extended his ethnicity into a third area when he was dubbed "the Jewish Scarface."

Actually, it was a fourth description, bringing in still another ethnic group, that was more fitting. Once the money started pouring in, the heavy-set Markowitz began enveloping himself in what he obviously felt was the chic clothing of a successful young American. His version consisted of screaming sport shirts open to the chest, shiny John Travolta disco suits, thick gold chains, and a fistful of gaudy diamond rings, reminding many who met him of the shoulder-shimmying, pseudo-hip Czech brothers created by comedians Steve Martin and Dan Aykroyd on "Saturday Night Live."

As his operation grew and his bankroll increased, Markowitz glittered around town in his tasteful Rolls and tasteless wardrobe. The high profile led to another lesson in Americana. He had made himself a target for both the state regulatory office and for various shakedown artists trying to cut into his operation. His problem was the same one that previously faced Larry Iorizzo: he had immense wealth but no power. He needed a protector.

At the end of 1982, Markowitz's empire was about to come to a crashing halt. The state pulled his wholesale license just as the shakedown vultures were closing in. Desperate to keep his massive business alive, he sought help.

Markowitz came in contact with Vinnie Carrozza, the brother of my close friend Champagne Larry. Vinnie asked me if I could collect a $7,500 debt for Markowitz from a gas station operator. The insignificant amount dramatized the Rumanian's lack of influence. I got the money that same afternoon. Vinnie then scheduled a meet 'at an oversized Mobil station in Brooklyn which Markowitz owned and used as his headquarters. With Markowitz were his Russian-born partners, David Bogatin and Leo Persits.

I stifled a laugh when the gaudy Rumanian walked in looking like a rug salesman who had just hit the lottery. Yet, as we talked, I could see we had a lot in common. We were both more educated than those around us. We both idolized our fathers. We both had a knack for business. We liked high-risk operations that produced big numbers. I also liked Markowitz's partners. They were tough, honest Russians who had clawed their way out of Russia, come to America, and made a fortune. Bogatin had an especially rough background; he had served three years of hard time in a Russian prison.

Putting aside my warm feelings for the men, I cut a deal that was ice cold. I would take over the Russians' billion-dollar operation for 75 percent of the pie. They would get the remaining 25 percent.

They agreed.

The deal increased my authority and expanded my influence. My inner circle of lieutenants, soldiers, and top-level associates grew to about forty men, thirty-five of whom would have killed on my order. Beyond them, there were hundreds of men who were under our command, and hundreds more clamoring to come aboard.

The size of my "army" was somewhat ironic. I had never actively recruited anyone. People were just drawn to the success of the operation and came to me. I could pick and choose whomever I wanted.

Personally, the success, the money, and the level of power I achieved were both exhilarating and tiring. There were people around me catering to my every wish, my every desire. I could issue an order pertaining to anything, from business to matters of life and death, and it would be carried out without question.

I was happy that I had a strong, wealthy crew that everyone wanted to join, but with it came a tremendous amount of work and responsibility. The Mob is not a business, it's a life; and that life consumes all your time and energy.

I also knew that as my profile increased, I was becoming a bigger target. The police and prosecutors—or one of my own men—would one day be coming after me.

At this point, the money pouring into the Franzese/Iorizzo operation started resembling the gross national product of a mid-sized country. Conservative estimates have Michael and the fat man personally making between $5 million and $8 million a week, every week for nearly three years.

Despite the enormity of those numbers, some prosecutors privately admit that the government underestimated the take to stave off embarrassment. A closer inspection bears this out. At the height of its operation, Houston Holdings, which swallowed up Galion Holdings, and its fifty different paper subsidiaries were moving 300–500 million gallons of gasoline a month in five states. Figuring that they offered discounts of five to ten cents a gallon to monopolize the market, a ball-park estimate is that they were stealing twenty cents a gallon.

That's $60–100 million a month in stolen taxes alone, not counting legitimate profits. How much of this money found its way to Michael Franzese, and where he stashed it, is anybody's guess.

In comparison, John Gotti, the head of the largest of the five New York Mafia families, is said today to make "only" between $5 million and $10 million a year.

With Markowitz and his crew aboard, the Monday-night parties at the Casablanca reached new levels of both monetary intoxication and personal surrealism. Iorizzo would lug his 450 pounds to the club, do his Carmen Miranda imitation, and rip apart a luxury automobile. Markowitz would follow, proudly displaying twenty pounds of gold jewelry splashed over his latest hideous suit. Both men would arrive with their swelling entourages, including Markowitz's quizzical band of Russian-speaking criminals.

On occasion, Markowitz returned the favor by hosting a gala event of his own at a favored Russian bar in Brooklyn. The Soviet-styled parties included an endless procession of trays piled a foot high with steamed lobsters. There were oceans of wine and vodka to wash them down, and dancing girls to entertain during dessert.

Regardless of where the parties took place, lording over the proceedings, and taking requests in an inner office, was a slim, handsome, bespectacled Italian named Michael Franzese.

Michael's power inside the New York Mafia families grew with every dollar. His legend outside the Mafia grew even larger. A deputy attorney general in the United States Department of Justice reported to a congressional subcommittee that Michael's operation had grown so large that he had been awarded his own Long Island–based family and had jumped from being a Colombo captain to a full-fledged, Marlon Brando–like Mafia don. That was an exaggeration. The

Colombo family wasn't about to allow their golden goose to escape. Still, it's not hard to see how the feds got that impression. Counting all his subordinates in the wide-reaching gas industry, along with the savage Russians he had organized under his ever-expanding wing, the thirty-two-year-old Mafia prince commanded an army that was as large and as financially powerful as the five New York Mafia families combined.

CHAPTER 12

hampagne Larry Carrozza had been my best friend for ten years. He was a happy, upbeat, sharp-looking college graduate with dark, curly hair, copper eyes, and a quick wit. He loved fast cars, flashy double-breasted suits, and painted women. He especially loved Dom Perignon champagne, a taste that had earned him his nickname. He was also aggressive, arrogant, and had a blazing-hot temper. He was quick with his fists, a knife, or a gun.

I had met him in 1973 through Jo Jo Vitacco. Both Jo Jo and my father knew Larry's father, Tony Carrozza, a Brooklyn dock worker and convicted loan shark.

Champagne Larry's wild and colorful life-style belied his profession. The party-happy champagne connoisseur was an embalmer by trade and a funeral director by profession. When not toasting the world with Dom, he was draining the blood out of bodies and pumping them full of preservatives.

The contrast provided an endless stream of laughs. We frequently went out together to Manhattan and Long Island nightspots. I liked to bust his chops by goading him into telling his prospective lady friends what he did for a living. Larry would beg off, kicking me under the bar, making faces and motions, trying to get me to cool it. My prodding so intrigued the party girls they would pester Larry themselves until he confessed. Invariably, the same women who draped themselves over my handsome friend would recoil in revulsion when he revealed his profession. It never failed, and never failed to break me up.

Larry was forever trying to get me into his Brooklyn funeral home to watch him prepare a body. I always declined, sickened by the creepy thought. But squeamish as I was, I couldn't resist the opportunity to take advantage of Larry's profession in order to play ghastly pranks.

One evening, we were drinking at Jo Jo's bar. Larry said he had to leave because he had made a run and had a body in the back of his sta-

132

tion wagon. I knew that although Jo Jo had turned a few dozen breathing souls into corpses during his long career, the tough guy was nevertheless terrified of them. I instructed Larry to go to the car, unzip the body bag, and lay a towel over the front. In the meantime, I told Jo Jo we wanted him to go somewhere with us.

We positioned Jo Jo in the backseat, inches away from the body. Driving around the block, Larry asked Jo Jo to retrieve something from behind the seat. "It's right under the blue towel," he instructed.

Jo Jo slid the towel off and came face to face with a bulging-eyed, blue-skinned corpse.

"There's a body back there! Get me the fuck out of here," he screamed, clawing at the door. Larry pulled over and Jo Jo shot out. He ran to his place, where he steamed and vowed to get even. Within the hour, he was laughing and colorfully relating the story to patrons at the bar.

Although Champagne Larry was an educated man with a successful business, he was also a Brooklyn street kid who grew up idolizing made men. It was his dream to be straightened out. He made himself available, originally hooking up with Jimmy Angellino. After my operation took off he requested a transfer. Both DiBella and Persico refused. Even so, Carrozza spent more time with my crew than with Angellino's. He was part of the Japan Lines scam and carved up the potential informer when the deal came unglued. He was also partners with me in a loan-shark operation, another flea market, and some stock-and-bond investments.

We had some of our best times, and pulled our most enjoyable scams, in Las Vegas. I hooked up with Dunes Hotel casino manager Robert Amira, a nephew by marriage of former Dunes owner Morris Shenker. Amira, a close friend of infamous mobster Anthony "Tony Pro" Provenzano, was infatuated with the Mob and gave the wiseguys special treatment. Anything I wanted—the best suites, the most beautiful women—Amira provided. He also provided a $50,000 credit line. Instead of gambling the money away, Champagne Larry and I would make a conspicuous show at gambling by whooping it up, flashing expensive jewelry around our necks and knockout women on our arms, betting heavy, and frequently switching tables and games to give the illusion that we were dropping tens of thousands. We would actually dump just four or five thousand this way, then quietly cash in the rest of the chips. We'd return from Vegas $45,000 richer than when we arrived. The casino would bill us for the balance. We would pay a thousand here, a thousand there, and Amira, figuring we had blown the money and the casino had it back anyway, would write off the rest.

We also made a killing with airline tickets. The major Vegas casinos routinely pay the air fare for VIP guests. Every time I went to Vegas, sometimes twice a month, I would print ten to fifteen bogus first-class tickets from a travel agency I had an interest in. I'd present them to the hotel and they'd hand me a check for up to $15,000 to comp my gang of ghost riders.

Between the credit write-offs and the ticket scams, Champagne Larry and I became $500,000 richer thanks to the Dunes Hotel.

Amid all the schemes and partying, we grew so close that Larry was the godfather of one of my three children with Maria, and I was the godfather of Larry's eldest. Larry was a wonderful companion, and I cherished our friendship.

> In May 1983, Michael received an urgent message from Jimmy Angellino to meet him at Lolly's coffee shop on Avenue V in Brooklyn. When he arrived, the look on Angellino's face warned him that the news wasn't good.
>
> It was worse than he had imagined.
>
> Angellino soldiers had been tailing Champagne Larry Carrozza for months. They had conclusive evidence that he was having an affair with Gia, Michael's darkly beautiful, nineteen-year-old sister. They had confirmed sightings in Brooklyn, Long Island, and even Florida. They had the pair nailed dead to rights—"dead" being the operative word, because that is what it meant to Larry.
>
> "This is a grave dishonor to Sonny, and especially to you, Michael. A grave dishonor. It must be taken care of," Angellino said.
>
> Michael sat stunned. He waited for the other shoe to drop. Would he be ordered to kill his best friend?
>
> "It will be handled the way these things are handled. We will take care of this ourselves out of respect to you and Sonny," Angellino said.
>
> It was the Mafia equivalent of a morals charge, and the penalty was death. Champagne Larry's marital status had doomed him. Had he been single or divorced, and had the affair been grounded in love, it would have been okay provided Michael and Sonny gave their blessing. Had either man objected, Larry would have been allowed to back off.

But a married man making a mistress out of a family member's teenage daughter or sister—that was intolerable.

"This can't be right," Michael said. "Let's exhaust every possibility to make sure it's absolutely true."

Angellino shook his head. "Been done. Not only that, but Larry's dealing cocaine."

The second revelation Michael hit like a sledgehammer. He was so shocked he couldn't even mount an effective argument on his best friend's behalf.

Angellino cautioned him to make no mention of this to Carrozza or Gia. He then asked if he was aware of Carrozza's drug dealing. He answered honestly that he hadn't known. If his best friend was into that, he was smart enough to hide it from Michael, who abstained from alcohol and narcotics.

Champagne Larry had broken two of the Mafia's irrefutable death-penalty rules: the "dishonor" of someone's sister or daughter, and dealing in narcotics. Either one, on its own, was enough to get him killed by Angellino's soldiers.

Driving out of the hated city, Michael was torn as he had never been before. How could this have happened? His best friend. His sister. Both knew the rules and the consequences. How could Larry betray him? How could he be so stupid and deal cocaine? How could he throw his life away over a woman? They had all the women either could ever want. They could go to Las Vegas and have five a day, five at a time if they wanted, the most beautiful women in the world. It was stupid. Insane.

His best friend's arrogance had done him in.

Michael was emotionally battered by an onslaught of conflicting thoughts. On one side was Larry's betrayal and ignorance. On the other was the fact that the Colombo family was doing this for him. They were showing respect by taking care of this messy problem. His friend had become a cancer. There was a measure of satisfaction in that. And finally, after years of insult and neglect, the family was paying Sonny respect, even if in a twisted, bloodstained way.

There was a third angle, one not quite so noble. Angellino had never liked Larry and was jealous of his friendship with Michael and their profitable business operations. Angellino was waiting for Larry to slip and had put extra effort into catching him. Tracing the affair down to Florida was extraordinary. The expense involved was unpre-

cedented. The act revealed an ugly personal hatred hiding behind the "pristine" Mafia law. And Michael knew it wasn't as cut-and-dried as presented. These things had happened before. Past offenders had been warned, busted up, and demoted in rank and stature. They didn't always have to die for testing the lucrative drug market or for a sexual indiscretion that is rampant in the rest of society.

What troubled him the most was his own sense of loyalty to his best friend. Despite the betrayal with Gia, should he warn Larry? Should he confront him? Should he give the guy a fighting chance? They had been closer than brothers. But at what cost? He had been ordered not to interfere. To do so would make him as guilty as Larry. And it wasn't just his honor involved; it was Sonny's as well.

He wavered over what to do. If it was just the affair, it might be worth the risk. The drugs made it different.

A week passed. He jumped in a start virtually every time the phone rang.

It was late when I pulled into the funeral home. I had told Larry to meet me there. I wanted to talk on Larry's turf. The door was open when I arrived. I entered slowly, tentatively. The room was dark. A smattering of soft lights peeled away the darkness at various points around the room. It took me a few seconds to realize what the lights were for. I edged closer. The light drew me to the body of an elderly woman in a crisp blue dress reclining in a casket by the wall. I turned. A child lay in a smaller casket. I turned again and saw a plump man with bushy eyebrows sprawled out in an elaborately engraved coffin. There were dead bodies and dying flowers everywhere. The soft lights illuminated a sea of waxy, lifeless faces.

"Larry!" I shouted, unnerved by the surroundings.

"Down here," a distant voice said.

I exited through a side door, climbed down some stairs, and entered a subterranean chamber. This one looked like Dr. Frankenstein's laboratory. There were nude bodies on slabs and tables and a maze of freaky-looking equipment.

"Over here," Larry said.

As I approached, I could see that Larry was in the process of draining the blood from a young woman and replacing it with embalming fluid. She had tubes running in and out of her body. It was a ghastly sight, made even scarier by the late hour and the darkness of the room.

"Auto accident," Larry said. "She was a pretty one. Nice tits."

I felt queasy. Normally, I would have sprinted out of the nightmarish dungeon. The only thing that saved me was my anger—and my desire to help my friend.

"What's up? I've been trying to get you down here for years."

"We've got to talk," I said, diverting my eyes from the dead woman in front of me.

"So talk. I'm backed up."

"I know about you and Gia."

Larry closed his eyes and dropped his head. He took a deep breath. "We were going to tell you about that, I swear, Michael. I'm in love with her. I'm going to get a divorce."

"You're lying, Larry. You'll never leave your wife and kids."

"I swear, Michael. I swear. Ask her."

"It doesn't matter. You know better than that. You can't do this."

"Oh, come on—do you really believe that shit?"

I grabbed Larry by the collar and faced him. "You think this is a game? You think our life is a game?"

"Fuck that bullshit."

As I looked into my friend's eyes, I could see something was wrong. There was an odd glint, a fire I had never seen before. I searched the table. I no longer saw the bodies or the embalming instruments. I did see the vial. I picked it up.

"What's this?"

"Some chemicals for the fluid."

"Bullshit. You think I'm stupid? They know, Larry. You're dealing. You're using too, aren't you?"

"So what?"

"You're going to die, Larry. Don't you understand?"

"For what? I didn't do anything wrong."

"You know better. I talked to Angellino. The deal's done."

"Fuck him."

"Do you hear what I'm saying? You're a dead man. You're no more alive than that girl on the table."

"Leave me alone, okay! I can handle myself."

"Larry, you're high. You're not right. Listen. I'll give you money. However much you need. Take it. Take it and take your wife and kids out of the country. I'll send more. Just get out of here. Tonight."

Larry turned and embraced me.

"You're a good man, Michael. A true friend. I'm sorry about Gia. I really am. I do care for her. But I'm not leaving. This is my home. Don't worry about me. I have my own crew. They're tough kids. They'll take on anybody."

"Are you out of your fucking mind? What's happening to you? You can't beat this."

Larry shot me a scathing look. " 'This'? Don't you mean 'us'?"

I said nothing. I knew what was coming.

"They never straightened me out. Why? Why didn't they? If that fucker Angellino would have straightened me out, all this wouldn't have happened."

"Is that what this is about?"

"You wouldn't understand. It all came easy for you. You could have sponsored me."

"You're under Angellino. You know that. My hands are tied."

"Bullshit."

"You know the truth. We tried. We have rules."

"Fuck the rules."

I could see the conversation was getting nowhere.

"My offer still stands. Consider it. For your wife and kids, consider it."

"I don't need it. I can make a million selling cocaine in one deal. I've got everything under control."

I lifted the vial and held it to Larry's face. "Then why are you using? This stuff will destroy you. It's already destroying you."

Larry let out a chilling laugh. "Look around you, Michael. Take a good look. What do you see? Bodies. Death everywhere. You would never come here and see what I do. And now you're asking me why I get high?"

"Don't give me that. You can leave this."

"Not if I stuck with you guys. I'd be here forever. I'll be able to leave it now. A few big scores and I'm out."

"If that's the way you feel, I can't help you, Larry."

I turned to leave. As I reached the door, Larry called my name.

"Don't worry, Michael. I've got it under control."

A few days later, on May 20, 1983, two weeks after the meeting with Angellino in Lolly's coffee shop, Brooklyn police officer Malcolm

Padaetz pulled off the side of Shore Parkway near Thirteenth Street and found the body of Champagne Larry Carrozza slumped on the ground near the trunk of his green 1979 Chrysler Newport. Carrozza had been shot once behind the right ear. He died in view of the Verrazano Bridge that connects Brooklyn to Staten Island. He was wearing a tan knit jacket over a tan shirt, brown striped pants, brown shoes, and matching brown socks.

Angellino gave me the news.

A few hours later, I received a call from Louie Fenza. "Michael, Larry's been killed!"

"I know."

"We gotta do something."

A group of my men gathered in my office. They were angry and agitated and ready to hunt down Larry's killers and repay them in kind.

I spoke calmly and deliberately. "Although Larry was close to us, he was not with me. He was not part of my crew. Secondly, this has to be left alone. It was business. Larry made a terrible mistake and it cost him his life. He knew better, and he still did it. This is what we live by. We all know that. We've all accepted that. Leave it. Accept it."

The men turned and silently trudged out of the office.

We regathered a few days later at Larry's funeral. As I observed Larry's distraught widow and bewildered children—one my own godchild—the anger welled up inside me. La Cosa Nostra was supposed to be about family, yet when it came to real families, there was little concern shown. The Mob laws never considered the innocent victims. What about Larry's wife and children? The rest of their lives could be an economic and emotional struggle. Larry had sinned and paid the price. His family was left behind to suffer. Wouldn't it have made more sense to punish Larry in another way, and let him continue to take care of his wife and children? Isn't there a better solution than death?

I kissed and comforted Larry's widow, then left with my men. I felt as responsible for Larry's death as the man who pulled the trigger. This was my life-style. I followed the code.

Larry Carrozza was dead and buried. I lived on with yet another bloody scar on my soul.

Following Larry Carrozza's death, it was widely believed among law-enforcement officials and Mafia insiders that Michael killed his friend upon his father's order. It was a logical assumption, since the

Franzeses were the offended parties, and Carrozza died without a struggle, meaning whoever killed him had been a trusted friend.

"No question, Michael did it," insists an informed source. "Carrozza had been warned. He was on the alert. He knew it was coming. Only one person could have gotten that close to him at that time, and that was Michael Franzese. The son of a bitch blew his best friend's brains out without blinking. He's as cold and deadly a bastard as his old man."

However, no legal proof was ever presented to substantiate this. Michael vehemently denies he killed his friend, and that his father ordered it. He says both he and his father anguished greatly over the whole affair.

Gia Franzese was seven when her father went to prison. A lovely woman who already suffered from a lack of self-confidence, she was shattered by the murder and fell into substance abuse and depression. She later moved to London, England. For years Gia denied the affair that cost Larry his life. Recently, during an overseas telephone conversation picked up by an illegal wiretap, she made a startling confession.

"I did it because of you, Michael. I idolized you and everything about you. I wanted to be like you, be close to you. I wanted to be close to that life."

CHAPTER 13

On April 21, 1983, representatives from eleven separate state, county, and federal law-enforcement agencies marched like suited soldiers into the basement of the federal courthouse in Uniondale, Long Island, to hold what would be the first of three-dozen intensive, day-long meetings convened over the next twelve months.

Seated around a large U-shaped table was an impressive array of government muscle. Assigned to the massive interagency crime-fighting squad were Ray Jermyn, special assistant U.S. attorney and the driving force behind the Long Island Organized Crime Oil Industry Task Force; Edward McDonald, attorney-in-charge of the powerful, Brooklyn-based Organized Crime Strike Force of the Eastern District of New York; Jerry Bernstein, McDonald's tenacious assistant and a special attorney with the U.S. Department of Justice; Bill Tamparo and Kevin Craddock, special agents with the IRS; Danny Lyons, head of the Long Island FBI office; Dick Guttler, special agent, FBI; John LaPerla, United States postal inspector; Jack Ryan and Vincent O'Reilly, special assistant U.S. attorneys representing the New York State Attorney General's Office; Jim Wrightson, special investigator, New York State Attorney General's Office; Joel Weiss, Rackets Bureau chief, Nassau County District Attorney's Office; Detectives Frank Morro and Al Watterson, Rackets Bureau, Suffolk County Police Department; and Detective Bob Gately, Rackets Bureau, Nassau County Police Department.

After a few organizational meetings, the scope of the investigation was broadened even further. Joining the joint task force were Sam Badillo, special agent, U.S. Department of Labor, Office of Labor Racketeering; Tom Sullivan, special agent, Florida Department of Law Enforcement; and Fred Damski, assistant state attorney for Broward County (Fort Lauderdale) Florida.

The massive, fourteen-agency government task force had one assignment—to bring down the Mafia's youngest and most financially powerful new superstar, Michael Franzese.

The basement meetings were the antithesis of Michael's Casablanca disco celebrations. Instead of dancing to the pulsating music and feasting on lasagne, veal, pasta, wine, scotch, vodka, and beautiful women, the law-enforcement agents rolled up their sleeves and went to work. They paused only to dash across the street to a Roy Rogers fast-food outlet and bring back sacks of cold hamburgers and greasy french fries, which they ate while they worked through lunch.

Under the direction of McDonald and Bernstein, the group, known unofficially as the Michael Franzese Task Force, pooled their resources, shared information, plotted strategy, and struggled to keep up with their target's rapidly expanding criminal empire. When conflicts arose over jurisdiction and assignments, the FBI's Lyons settled the disputes and acted as sergeant-at-arms. That wasn't a difficult assignment. Egos were suppressed as the prosecutors, government representatives, special agents, and police were united behind the single-minded cause of bagging the "Yuppie Don."

It took months just to untangle the maze of Michael's far-reaching criminal domain. The squadron of government agents shook their heads in amazement when Lyons displayed a large, colored chart that outlined Michael's interests. Jermyn counted twenty different Magic Marker colors on the chart, each representing a rich vein of illegal income.

Although the colorful lines on the FBI's chart led to Michael like streamers to a maypole, the chain of evidence needed to build a court case usually broke down before it reached the young Mafia kingpin. That was by design. Michael had taken mental notes during those six A.M. breakfast meetings when his father sipped freshly brewed coffee and explained the art of insulating oneself from everything except the flow of cash.

I was unaware of the force gathered in Uniondale. Still, my antennae began alerting me like never before. I could almost feel the weight of the mysterious army that was now shadowing my every move. The cars that followed me to restaurants and nightclubs and parked outside my home and offices no longer were easily identified as pesky Nassau and

Suffolk County police units. They didn't even appear to be vehicles operated by FBI agents. These were cars and tags of men that gave off an eerie aura which I had never felt before, not even in my father's heyday.

It was time, my senses warned me, to relocate my base of operations as far from New York as possible. Time to laugh, have fun, and escape to a place where the air was warm, the sun was bright, and people played in the sand. I needed a sensory diversion strong enough to blunt the increasing realization that I was a fox that had stolen one too many chickens, and that the cloud of dust hovering over the horizon was being kicked up by a charging herd of snarling bloodhounds and furious farmers.

It was time to seek out the mental distraction of my court jester, Jerry Zimmerman.

Jerome Zimmerman had met my father long before he knew me. My father had traveled to a Long Island car dealership in the mid-1960s to visit a friend named Charlie Gerraci. Dad was at the top of his form then. He was widely regarded as the most feared Mob enforcer in New York.

Gerraci took him for a walk around the lot. The dealership owner spotted the gregarious Zimmerman up on a ladder, fixing the dealership's promotional sign. Gerraci signaled for his partner to climb down.

"Hey, Spaghetti, what's doin', man?" Zimmerman shouted.

"What did he say?" my father asked, the muscles in his bull neck tightening.

"What's happening, Spaghetti my man?" Zimmerman repeated as he descended.

"Hey, what's this guy talkin' 'spaghetti,' " my father inquired of Gerraci.

By then, Zimmerman had reached them. "Jerry, I'd like you to meet a friend of mine, Sonny Franzese."

My father gave Jerry a look that nearly brought him to his knees.

"Ah ... uh ... glad to meet you. I'm ... I'm ... you know ... just a kidder. Me and Charlie, we're tight. We kid around all the time ... you know?"

My father understood, and what he understood he didn't like. He apparently wasn't too upset, though. Zimmerman survived.

I met Zimmerman during my Italian-American Civil Rights League days. He was friends with various Mob guys and supported Joe Colombo's misguided organization. After Colombo was hit, we stayed in touch. When my auto-leasing businesses began to prosper, I made Zimmerman one of my managers. When I was inducted into La Cosa Nostra, Zimmerman held his ground and worked himself into my inner circle.

I never trusted Jerry, and suspected him of pocketing payoffs and ripping me off for petty sums in countless ways. Regardless, the big Jewish man was a world-class con artist whose crazy schemes were wildly amusing. Despite his flaws, I allowed him to get close.

Zimmerman moved to California in late 1979 and acted as an advance scout. He started a used-car dealership, and I frequently shipped him cars that had a higher value on the West Coast than on Long Island. More importantly, Zimmerman's operation gave me an excuse to travel to Los Angeles. I loved the sunny skies and casual lifestyle—and especially loved the fact that California was three thousand miles away from Brooklyn.

Zimmerman also frequented Las Vegas, where he would run various scams on the big casino-hotels. If one was going particularly well, he'd call and ask me to catch a plane.

On one memorable occasion, Zimmerman conned the management of the Sands into believing that fat, dumpy Peter "Apollo" Frappolo, one of my underlings, was the don of the "powerful Franzese crime family in Long Island." He told the Sands that the family was moving its operation to Vegas and was going to dump millions into a hotel. The Sands responded by giving Frappolo and Zimmerman the hotel's best suite and surrounding them with all the trappings of luxury. When I arrived and walked into the place, I couldn't believe my eyes. Frappolo was perched in a thronelike chair and had two beautiful women attending him hand and foot. I approached. Frappolo waved me off and picked up the telephone receiver.

"Excuse me, Michael, I need to make a call."

"Excuse me?" I said, burning a hole through my underling. Zimmerman swept me into a nearby room.

"He believes it!" Zimmerman said, rolling on the bed laughing. "The guy really think's he's Don Corleone."

When we returned, the two women were feeding Frappolo strawberries. Zimmerman and I had to duck back into the bedroom to hide our laughter.

When we composed ourselves enough to make a third pass at the "don," he was being feted by the hotel's manager. "Mr. Apollo, I want to remind you that you have an appointment for a haircut and manicure in fifteen minutes, if that's okay?" the manager asked.

Frappolo indicated it was. When I tried to talk to him a few moments later, Frappolo interrupted. "Michael, I have a haircut and manicure scheduled."

I calmly asked the manager and the strawberry twins to leave the suite and give us some privacy.

"Pete, snap out of it!" I ordered. "Get your ass out of that chair. I've got to figure out how to bail you two out of this mess when they catch on."

Zimmerman explained they were being comped on everything, and had a $70,000 line of credit at the casino, which they planned to cash in. I advised them not to play the scam out too long. We hung around a few more days, then left with the money.

Aside from his amusement value, Zimmerman performed another valuable function. He was the one who introduced me to the movie business.

During one of my Los Angeles visits in early 1980, I found my con-man friend especially upbeat. "Michael, I want to do a movie!"

"What do you know about doing movies?"

"It's easy. Listen …"

Zimmerman laid it out. He had gotten his hands on a script for a horror movie called *Mausoleum*. He said the total budget would be a mere $250,000, and he already had two people willing to put up a third each. If I kicked in the final third, about $83,000, Zimmerman promised me the title of executive producer.

It sounded good. At that point, eighty-two grand was pocket change. I agreed, and Zimmerman set it in motion. From the start, the project was beset with the woes of amateurs. The two other financiers never materialized, socking me with the entire $250,000 initial budget. That sum was swallowed up before we were half finished. About $1.2 million later—$900,000 of which was my money—we had two film cans full of a hodgepodge of a movie ready to distribute.

Mausoleum promptly bombed. The only people the movie terrified were the financiers.

During the filming, Zimmerman had his hooks into an older man from the Midwest named Jim Kimball, a legitimate businessman, who was interested in getting into the motion-picture business. After being drained for a few hundred thousand, the guy shut off the tap. Kimball was in Zimmerman's office on Ventura Boulevard one afternoon checking out his investment when in walks Lenny Montana, the burly actor who played Corleone family enforcer Lucca Brazzi in *The Godfather*— the guy who got the knife through his hand at the bar. Montana, a real-life crook, screamed at Zimmerman, claiming he was owed a considerable sum of money. Zimmerman pleaded for time. The argument grew nasty. Suddenly, Montana pulled out a gun and shot Zimmerman in the upper body. Blood splattered everywhere as the big man dropped to the floor, gasping for breath.

Kimball, scared out of his wits, pleaded with Montana not to finish Zimmerman off. He promised to pay the $50,000 debt. Montana, apparently satisfied, put away the gun. Some of Zimmerman's associates dragged their bleeding boss to a car to rush him to a hospital.

Left alone in the office, the shaken investor called me. "Lenny shot Jerry!" he screamed. "Michael, Lenny shot Jerry!"

I put my hand over the phone and laughed. It never even occurred to me that the shooting might have been for real. I composed myself and continued the conversation.

"I'm going to pay!" Kimball reiterated. "I'm going to give him the money, okay? I'll make it good! You don't have to kill Jerry!"

I said that would be satisfactory. When I hung up, I dialed Zimmerman's home. He answered.

"I just received an interesting call. I understand you've been shot?"

"You should have seen the guy's face!" Zimmerman howled. "You should have been there!"

"You guys are insane."

Kimball coughed up the $50,000, which Zimmerman and Montana pocketed. Kimball then pushed to visit Zimmerman in the hospital to make sure he was okay. They held him off as long as they could, then went to a local hospital and rented a room under the guise of needing it for a scene in the movie. They bandaged Zimmerman and laid him in the hospital bed. Kimball visited for a half hour. Zimmerman moaned and groaned and never once cracked a smile.

The final coup came a few weeks later after Zimmerman had "recovered." I called Zimmerman, Montana, and Kimball into my office. I reamed out Zimmerman and Montana for the shooting and told them they'd better toe the line or they'd both be whacked. Kimball's hands trembled as he witnessed a real-life gangster laying down the law. After Kimball left, the three of us rolled with laughter.

That was the highlight of *Mausoleum.* I never recovered a dime of my $900,000 investment. Not only that, but Zimmerman had raised some of the budget by banking on my name and reputation, promoting me as a rich New York mobster with a bottomless pit of cash. That resulted in a grand jury investigation headed by a California Organized Crime Strike Force attorney named Bruce Kelton. Kimball was called as a witness and made no mention of the shooting incident. Despite losing his money, he testified that everything was on the up-and-up. The grand-jury investigation came up as empty as the *Mausoleum* box-office cash drawers.

Despite the financial horror of the experience, and the close call with the feds, I was bitten by the movie bug. I quickly saw that the money in movies wasn't in the production but in the distribution end. I invested another half-million in a legitimate distribution firm headed by a man named John Chambliss. The company distributed B- and C-grade movies regionally and made a solid profit. I leased a condominium in exclusive Marina Del Rey and looked forward to spending time in the California sun.

As always, I registered my dealings with the Colombo family. They approved of my efforts, pleased to get a foothold in Hollywood. However, instead of extolling the wonders of Los Angeles, I made sure I always bad-mouthed the city and the surrounding area. I didn't want any of my Mob associates moving in on my territory. "The place is horrible," I'd report to the bosses in Brooklyn after a long West Coast visit. "The pollution is so bad you can't breathe. The city is dirty and stinks. You guys are so lucky to be able to stay here in beautiful Brooklyn."

It was absurd, but the old-time Mob bosses were so infatuated with Brooklyn they reveled in the comparisons. I played the same game with Florida, describing it as a steamy swamp infested with blood-sucking insects and assaulted by staggering heat and humidity. "Florida's not fit for human life," I warned.

Meanwhile, I starting shifting my operation to the two "dreaded" locations.

In 1982, I took a stab at producing another film. This one was entitled *Savage Streets.* It boasted a semi-star, Linda Blair from the horror blockbuster *The Exorcist. Savage Streets* was a vigilante movie in the

Death Wish tradition. Blair was shown exacting her revenge on a gang of street criminals who had raped her sister. Smartening up on the ways of motion-picture financing, I financed nearly all of the $2.3 million budget through a loan from Michigan National Bank and a bond from Union Indemnity Insurance of New York. Although considerably better than *Mausoleum, Savage Streets* suffered from poor distribution and also bombed. Whatever money it made went back to the Michigan bank. By then, the insurance company had far bigger problems: it never recovered from the staggering loss it suffered in November 1980 when one of its clients, the MGM Grand Hotel in Las Vegas, burned down.

My third foray into the movie business was picking up an Italian horror film, re-editing it, changing its name to *Gates of Hell,* and sending it to the masses. The masses didn't like that one any better than the others, but the costs were so low the film turned a profit.

A better investment once again came from the distribution end. I worked a $3 million, eight-picture deal with Vestron Video, an aggressive company that delved into all aspects of the movie business, including the new trade of supplying video cassettes to the rapidly expanding home VCR market. I made money by picking up various foreign and domestic films for about $70,000, re-editing them and changing their titles if needed, then reselling the video, domestic, and foreign rights for $350,000.

As the action picked up in California, the agony continued in New York. In early May 1983, I returned from Los Angeles tan and refreshed, only to be informed that Carmine Persico's son Alphonse and Anthony "Tony the Gawk" Augello had been indicted on a narcotics charge. That caught everyone's attention. Persico was young and from another generation, so the drug charge against him wasn't that surprising. The Gawk's role was mystifying. A big, bearish man with huge hands, he was an old-timer who had come up with my father and Persico. He was schooled in the traditional ways of the Mob; for him to get involved in drugs was a direct breach of his oath.

I knew the Gawk well. Like many of the Colombo soldiers, he had spent so much time at our house he was like an uncle. Among my "uncles," I held a special feeling for the affable, smartly dressed Gawk. The big man had often attended my junior-high and high-school football games with my father, loudly cheering from the sidelines every time I ran the ball.

Following the arrest, the Gawk paid me a visit at Rumplik Chevrolet. He pulled up in his trademark bright green El Dorado. "I've got a good shot at beating this," the Gawk said, as much to convince himself as me. "It's all bullshit. Man, I hope the guys don't think I'm involved in drugs."

"If it ain't true, it ain't true," I said.

Although the Gawk's words were confident, his body language was screaming something else. He was fidgeting and trembling. His hands were shaking so much his diamond pinky ring sparkled like a mirrored disco ball in the sunlight. I had never seen the big man act like that before.

"It'll be all right," I assured him. "No one blames you."

"Yeah, yeah—how can anybody blame me? I mean, it's the boss's son, right? The boss's son. Right, Michael?"

"I don't think you have anything to worry about."

After he left, a chill washed over me. The Gawk wasn't handling this well.

Two days later, I received a call from one of my men. "The Gawk just blew his brains out in a phone booth on Broadway. He called his wife, told her he loved her, then ate his gun. Can you believe that? Blew his teeth clean outta his head!"

I shut the door of my office and turned off the light. I sat quietly for more than an hour. The trouble was, I *could* believe. That's what was so unnerving. The Gawk had been one of the few real tough guys I had known. He would have confronted ten armed men and bravely fought to his death for the family. He would have walked fearlessly through a wall of cops. But the Gawk couldn't live with his own fear. He couldn't live with the wait, not knowing which one of his thirty-year blood brothers was going to take him for a ride and put a bullet in his head. He couldn't live waiting to be called into that final meeting where you never come out. The Gawk had done it to others. He knew how it went.

I thought of how the previous week must have gone for the Gawk. The tension was no doubt unbearable, tearing at his mind and body. Whom could he trust? Who would his killer be? When would the call come? Why don't they just get it over with?

To relieve the paralyzing agony, the Gawk became his own assassin. He determined that death was better than living with the torment he had created.

The drug case against the younger Persico lingered, was transferred to another district, then was dropped.

The Gawk hit himself for nothing.

On May 27, 1983, my thirty-second birthday—eighteen days after the Gawk's suicide and a week after Larry Carrozza's murder—something happened that would forever change my life. Appropriately, it was another death, capping off a brutal month. This time, however, the cause was natural. Jerry Zimmerman's son Ira died of leukemia.

Ira's passing threw him into a depression. Zimmerman always had huge mood swings, and this time it looked like he was down for the count.

I wasn't in great shape myself. I was haunted by the specter of the still-unknown joint task force, and was emotionally rocked by the Gawk's suicide and Larry Carrozza's murder. To deal with it, I focused my energy on trying to cheer up Zimmerman. When nothing worked, I decided to make another movie—solely to snap Zimmerman out of his depression. Although Jerry had introduced me to the movie business, albeit with the terrible *Mausoleum,* he wasn't able to mesh with Chambliss and had faded from the subsequent movies.

I called Zimmerman from my home in Delray Beach and told him I needed to see him in Florida immediately. I didn't say why.

When Zimmerman arrived the next day, he was still depressed. "What's up?"

"I want to make a movie here in Florida, and I want you to produce it with me," I said.

His face lit up. The depression lifted.

"What kind?"

"I don't know," I said. "I like music. Let's do a musical this time."

"Sounds great!" Zimmerman gushed.

We had no cast, crew, director, or even a script, just a vague idea and my desire to help a friend shake the blues. I solved those problems with a few phone calls. The first was to a Hollywood agent named David Wilder. I instructed Wilder to put out an order around town for a musical script. Wilder responded a few months later with a screenplay entitled *Never Say Die,* written by Leon Isaac Kennedy, a suavely handsome black actor known for the *Penitentiary* boxing films and the Chuck Norris hit *Lone Wolf McQuade*. He was also known as the former husband of Jayne Kennedy, the onetime NFL football announcer. Leon Kennedy had weaved an energetic, interracial love story around a street gang, a rock band, and the fad of break dancing.

The project presented an intriguing casting dilemma. Instead of searching Beverly Hills for Hollywood's A-list, we'd have to cull the cast of such a movie from the squalid black ghettos of Miami and the gang-infested Latin barrios of Southern California.

III

CAMMY

CHAPTER 14

I first saw her lifting herself from the Marina Bay Club's pool in Fort Lauderdale. Her long, coffee-colored hair was wet and slicked back, accentuating her face and huge brown eyes. Her firm dancer's body appeared to be exploding out of her bikini. Her wet skin shimmered in the sunlight.

I felt a strange sensation in my chest that made me gulp for air. She had literally taken my breath away. She was, without a doubt, the most beautiful, sexy, and exotic woman I had ever seen.

"Will you look at that!" Frankie Cestaro said, as struck by the dancer as I was.

"I noticed," I said. "That girl's young, innocent, and awesome. She could be a lot of trouble for me. I've got to stay away from her."

"I think I'll give it a shot," Cestaro said.

"Be my guest. I don't want to get near her."

I had too much on my mind to be distracted by a poolside siren. My whim to film a movie in South Florida had quickly grown into a master plan of building a major independent motion-picture company there. I wanted to produce a series of big-budget, Hollywood-quality movies in Florida, and had arranged with First American Bank in Fort Lauderdale to kick in $10 million to help with the initial financing. Not that money was a problem. With the capital coming in from the gas business, I was able to be my own financier. The $2 million budget for Leon Kennedy's movie, renamed *Cry of the City* during the shooting and *Knights of the City* when it was released, was coming out of my pocket.

The movie, and my grandiose plans, had made me the darling of the local media and of Florida's state, city, and county politicians—none of whom bothered to check me out. The Florida Film Commission bent over backwards granting me permits to film at various locations. Miami Beach Mayor Malcolm Fromberg awarded me the key to the city and promised that the tourist town would donate prime land and help finance the building of an immense motion-picture sound stage. Fort Lauderdale Mayor Bob Dressler tried to present me with a plaque but was unable to pin me down for the presentation. The Broward County Sheriff's Department made me an honorary police commissioner.

A second reason for the open-arms welcome was the filming of *Knights of the City* itself. We held open auditions and encouraged disadvantaged youth to try out as dancers. The auditions were in both Broward (Fort Lauderdale) and Dade (Miami) counties and attracted two thousand youths per session. We selected 116 dancers and 250 extras, fed them and paid them well. I also made it a condition that those chosen would have to prove they were maintaining good grades in school.

The glitter of the movies, the jobs for low-income youths, and the good-grades requirement further ingratiated me with the media and public. And despite my background, I opened the movie set to the press, a move that initially resulted in added waves of positive publicity.

In addition, I was able to avoid a problem that frequently chases away potential filmmakers from South Florida. Although Florida is a right-to-work state with few unions, the Teamsters' South Florida branch is notoriously tough to deal with. The union specifically targets movie companies and demands that all its equipment trucks, including the trailers for the stars, be driven by Teamsters truck drivers. The drivers are paid $1,500 a week, even if they do nothing but stand by an idle truck or trailer for weeks at a time. This payoff bleeds the limited budgets of independent films.

Shortly after *Knights of the City* opened a production office, a big, burly Teamsters representative paid Jerry Zimmerman a visit. "This is a Teamsters film, or there won't *be* a film," he announced.

Zimmerman smiled. "You'll have to talk to my boss."

A meeting was set for the following day at the second-story office of Houston Holdings, the gas-company branch office in Fort Lauderdale. The union rep marched in and tried to bully his way around. "I told your partner, there will be no film without the Teamsters."

"Sounds like a threat," I said.

"No threat—just a fact. No Teamsters, no film."

"You see this window behind me," I said, pointing to the office's large picture window. "If I ever see your face in here again, you're going out that window."

"I don't think you understand what you're doing," he said, storming out.

Two days later, I received a call. "Mr. Franzese, I am sorry we got off on the wrong foot," the Teamsters man said, apologizing. "Whatever you want, you got it. If there's anything we can do for you, just name it."

"Okay, here's what I'll do," I said. "I'll take one Teamsters driver so it doesn't get around that we busted you out. My guys will handle the rest of the trucks."

As I stared at the young dancer by the pool, all the hassles of making the movie and running the gas operation appeared insignificant. I fought with myself over whether to give in to my desire or stay away and keep my mind fixed on business. There were plenty of available women around the set. Uncomplicated women. I didn't need this Mexican beauty.

Only I couldn't keep my eyes off her. When a cast member passing out T-shirts around the pool skipped her, I found myself doing what I swore I wouldn't. I ordered one of my men to get a box of shirts out of the trunk of his car and bring them to me. I used the T-shirts as an excuse to check her out.

Agent David Wilder was sitting near her by the pool and made the introduction. "Michael, this is Cammy Garcia, the girl we sent for in L.A."

"Hi—nice to meet you," she said, briefly glancing up, then shyly diverting her eyes.

Up close, she was even more beautiful than from across the pool. What struck me the most, however, was that she was both innocent and wildly sexy.

It was a troubling sensation. I didn't drink, take drugs, or fall in love for the same reason: I always wanted to maintain control. As I walked away, I again vowed to steel myself against the weakening effect of the woman. But there was something about her name, something about the strange way Wilder had introduced her that nagged at me. What was it?

It wasn't until I was back in my room that it came to me. Cammy Garcia—Camille Garcia. Cammy—Camille. It had to be the same girl. A week before, I was in my office when I received a call from a man demanding to speak to the movie's producer. The man said he was the father of one of the dancers and was worried about his daughter. He wanted to be assured everything was on the up-and-up. He said that she was young, innocent, and inexperienced and had never been that far away from home. In the world of movies and professional dancers, such a faux pas could have doomed the young woman's chances. Movie sets can be wild and sinful gatherings, and nosy parents are a major hindrance. Instead of being upset, I found the father's concern endearing. I promised him I would personally watch out for his daughter and make sure she was safe. After hanging up, I called choreographer Jeff Kutash and ordered him to give dancer Camille Garcia a private room to keep her from getting a wild roommate, and to boost her salary to $500 per week with $235 per-diem expenses, the top scale we were giving. Kutash didn't say anything. I guess he felt if I wanted to give special treatment to a particular dancer, he wasn't going to ask why.

It turned out that Kutash was baffled because although she was a member of his L.A. dance troupe, he hadn't selected her to be in the movie. She had lied to her parents and had come to Florida with a one-way ticket purchased with piggy-bank savings and borrowed money, hoping to somehow crash her way onto the set and get her career going.

When Kutash spotted her at the kickoff party, he was surprised and relieved. "Blueberry Muffin!" he said, calling her by the nickname he had given her. "What are you doing here?"

She swallowed hard and tried to play it cool. "I heard something about a dance movie in Florida. My friends have a part and invited me down."

"Don't worry," Kutash said, no doubt remembering his conversation with me. "I'll get you in. I'll get you a part."

In no time, the happy but confused young woman found herself with a private room at the Marina Bay Club with a view of the glittering bay, and a top-scale dancer's contract. The weekly $235 per-diem payment alone was more money than she had ever made in a week in any of her prior jobs. She was confused by it all, how fast and how easy it had come, but was smart enough to stay quiet.

I smiled as I thought about the weird set of circumstances that had enabled the dancer to crash the movie. When Wilder introduced her as "the girl we sent for in L.A.," he was just putting his own spin on her unusual arrival. It was now clear why she seemed so timid and afraid when we met, glancing up and then quickly looking away. With her tenuous position, she certainly didn't want to attract the attention of the movie's producer. She must have thought I was staring at her because I couldn't figure out who she was and why she was on the set. A veteran performer would have jumped at the opportunity to get close to the producer to snatch a bigger part. This young woman just wanted to hold on to what she had.

And she barely had that. When she tried out for his dance troupe in

Los Angeles, Kutash could tell she was unschooled and probably came from an underprivileged family. He also could see that she possessed creativity and natural talent and made a striking appearance on stage, an ethereal quality some of the most professionally skilled dancers never possess. His group was big enough to embrace some dancers purely on potential. It was a close call, but he decided to take a chance on the dark-haired teenager with the angelic face.

She had spunk, that's for sure. It attracted me to her even more. A woman like that can crash her way into a man's heart the same way she intended to push her way into the movie. A woman like that, especially a beautiful woman like that, could be trouble. I definitely had to stay away.

The close, familylike atmosphere of a movie crew on location made that plan impossible. I kept bumping into her in the hotel lobby or around the set. Every time I caught a glimpse of her it stopped me dead. Each new sighting burned another image into my mind. Cammy in her bikini. Cammy in her T-shirt. Cammy in shorts. Cammy in knickers that exposed her calves. Especially that. She wore high heels that accented her firmly developed calf muscles. I had never paid attention to a woman's calves before. Now the mere sight of this woman's lower legs was making me crazy.

Late one afternoon the following week, I spotted her in the lobby. She was wearing cut-offs, a white T-shirt, and sandals, and her hair was still wet. She looked incredibly sexy. I noticed she was carrying an envelope in her hand and was heading toward the mail slot near the front desk.

Just before she slipped it in, I grabbed her wrist. "You don't want to mail that," I said.

She was doubly startled, first that someone had snuck up on her, and second that it was the producer. The letter, as I guessed, was to her boyfriend in California.

"Why not?"

"Who's it to?" I asked.

"A friend."

"What's his name?"

Her eyes flashed and she smiled coyly. "How do you know it's a he?"

"You don't want to mail that," I repeated, affecting my best smile. "Why don't you throw it away."

"Isn't that your girlfriend over there?" she said, pointing to a woman with long brown hair I'd been speaking with earlier.

"No, she's the girlfriend of a friend. He called and I gave her a part."
I looked at her intently.

"I've got to go. See you around," I said.

I tried to keep my mind on business, but her image kept intruding. I remember an old Italian wives' tale about Italian men being "hit by a thunderbolt" at least once in their lives by a particular woman. There was no explanation, it just happened. I'd laughed about it before, but now I suspected it was true. My thunderbolt had come.

When a group from the cast and crew got together to see the movie *Breakin'*, Cammy was among them. Although we sat apart, I spent more time watching the blue light from the movie screen dance upon her face than I did looking at the movie.

The following evening, I saw her alone in the lobby. She appeared upset. I approached.

"You don't look too happy. What's the matter?"

She looked up at me. Her eyes misted. Her lips trembled. "I'm going to go home," she said. "These aren't my type of people. I'm just trying to mind my own business."

"Why?"

"There's a rumor going around that I'm sleeping with you."

I was so moved by her little girl's reaction to the typical movie-location gossip that I could hardly speak. What started as purely a physical attraction had, at that moment, turned into something far more terrifying. I was on the verge of falling in love.

"That's funny," I said. "This is just the second time we've spoken. Every time I try to talk to you, you're gone. Are you hiding from me?"

She brushed away a tear and briefly smiled. She must have been confused. I was the problem to begin with, and instead of combating the rumormongers, I was providing them with more ammunition.

"Meet me after the cast meeting and we'll talk and have a drink," I said, trying to convince her to stay in Florida without revealing why it mattered so much to me.

"I don't drink."

"I don't either. We'll have some milk," I offered.

She laughed and promised to wait.

I saw her walk into the meeting, then exit a few minutes later. When the meeting ended, she was nowhere to be found.

Although she had consumed my thoughts from the moment I first saw her, I had yet to realize her room was diagonally across the hall from mine. After that, I made no pretenses about staying away. There was no fighting the Italian thunderbolt. Only trouble was, the bolt apparently didn't strike both ways. Every time I bumped into her for the next week, I made her promise to drop by my room to visit me that evening. She'd say "Okay, okay," then never show. I was disappointed, but I found it amusing. Her no-shows only heightened my desire.

I had to go to New York for three weeks on business and found myself agonizing over her the whole time. The pain of such intense desire, such intense *unrequited* desire, was new to me. I hardly knew her, but it didn't matter. The separation did nothing to heal what I had almost begun to view as some kind of strange illness that had overtaken me. I hated New York more than ever, and wanted nothing but to return to Florida, return to her.

Any chance of making another feeble attempt at forgetting her was dashed when I flew back and paid a visit to the skating rink I had rented for the dancers. Seeing her in a hot-pink leotard blew me away.

The following evening, I threw a pizza party in my suite and made arrangements to show the pay-per-view Thomas "Hit Man" Hearns–Roberto Durán boxing match. A big, noisy crowd gathered, and the commotion attracted Cammy. She wandered in, fresh out of the shower again with her hair wet and sexy, and she was wearing an oversized orange shirt buttoned up the front. She looked unbelievably beautiful. I wanted to rush over and welcome her to the party, but I was trapped. I was sitting in the center of the room with my hair wet and a sheet tied around my neck. The movie's hairdresser was giving me a haircut.

Before I could get myself free, she was gone.

Fortunately, she returned twenty minutes later, just as Hearns was knocking Durán senseless with a thunderous combination.

"You came back," I said, not wanting to miss the second opportunity.

"I'm just looking for my friend Katie Lauren. I don't think she's here," she said, turning to leave.

I grabbed her hand. "Camille, before next Tuesday at midnight, you must come to my room and talk to me."

The deadline was arbitrary. It just popped into my head. She promised to come.

Tuesday came and went. She never appeared.

"I'm not going to his door in a negligee and high heels and say 'Here I am'!" she confided to a friend.

On Wednesday, Jeff Kutash invited me to watch the dancers practice in a local studio. I cleared my schedule to attend—only I wasn't going just to check out the progress of the movie's choreography. My interest in the dark-haired dancer was now apparent to everyone.

During a break, one of the other dancers, "Mister X," rushed over to Cammy backstage. "The producer has the hots for you!"

"Who?" she said.

"Michael! Haven't you noticed? He's been burning a hole through you the whole time."

After the rehearsal, a group of the dancers and crew members were chatting about where they were going that evening. The consensus was Shooters, a popular Fort Lauderdale nightclub. Someone asked me to join them. I said I was exhausted.

"If you want, you can bring a date," a cast member piped in, figuring I had a more private evening ahead of me.

"He doesn't need a date," Cammy said, edging in beside me and putting her arms around my waist. "He's with me."

The instant she touched me I felt like my body was on fire.

"That's right," I stammered. "I'm with Camille."

Everyone laughed. Cammy hung on for a few moments, then darted off and left me standing, still dazed by the brief hug.

"Looks like you have a date," Frankie Cestaro said, snapping me out of my fog.

"Yeah—little Cammy's coming out of her shell. Wake me up at about eleven and I'll go."

When Frankie called, I was in a deep sleep at my home in Delray Beach. I had been getting up at dawn each day both to oversee my business interests in New York and to handle everything concerning the filming of the movie.

"Is she there?" I mumbled.

"She's here," Frankie confirmed, "and she's wearing a red tank top. Man, does she look sensational!"

The description popped my eyes open like a burst of caffeine. I shot out of bed, quickly dressed, and drove to Shooters. When I arrived, an associate from New York, Peter Napolitano, was sitting next to Cammy. "Let me sit here," I whispered to him.

"Michael, I'm doing good here," he said, nodding Cammy's way.

"Pete, get outta there," I ordered, far firmer than he expected. He got the message and bolted.

"Well, here we are," I said. "We've finally gotten together."

She smiled.

"What made you put your arm around me today?"

"I don't know."

"Well, it worked. It got me out of bed."

We talked for the next couple of hours. It was as if we were the only ones there. We chatted about the movie and her dancing and her life. She told me she had grown up poor in the barrios southeast of Los Angeles and knew what it was like to go to bed without dinner, not because she was being punished but because there was no food in the house. She also knew what it was like to walk barefoot through the grass, not because she wanted to feel the sensation but because she had no choice. Her father, Seferino Garcia, was a radical Chicano rights activist who had been arrested eight times during the turbulent 1970s, mostly during protests of one kind or another. Some of the arrests included violent confrontations with the Norwalk, California police. He was roughed up pretty badly a few times.

In a strange way, her upbringing had been similar to mine. We had both grown up viewing the police as the enemy.

She was the oldest of seven children and had it pretty tough most of her life. She was determined to make something of herself, and that desire often did nothing but increase her problems. When she tried out to be a cheerleader in the seventh grade and made the squad, her friends from the barrio taunted her and called her a "Coconut"—someone brown on the outside and white on the inside. It's the Latin equivalent of a black being called an Uncle Tom, though not quite as severe. Apparently, her more radical Chicano friends felt that by becoming a cheerleader, she was succumbing to the conventions of a biased white society that had banished them and their parents to the barrios and treated them so harshly. The taunts led to a bloody fight with a gang of girls in front of her house.

What her friends didn't understand was that her father had filled her with a fierce pride. He made her feel that despite being poor and Mexican, she never had to hang her head, ride in the back of the bus, or defer to anyone. He made her believe she could be anything she wanted to be, including a cheerleader.

Another time, someone fire-bombed her small home and nearly killed the entire family. The culprits were never caught. They were rumored to be either local drug dealers her father had tried to chase from the neighborhood or off-duty police officers who hated her father because of his politics.

Cammy also told me she was a born-again Christian, a religious belief I knew virtually nothing about. She said her mother was a Christian and that she had become "born again" when she was in junior high. She had relied heavily upon her faith to get her through the hard times. I found myself wishing my own faith in God had been that strong when I was young. It would have helped.

I was fascinated by her story. After learning about who she was and what she had experienced, I liked her even more. I didn't think she was going to be too shocked when she found out who and what I was. Of course, I had no intention of telling her, at least not then.

We left Shooters and hit another place, a glitzy Fort Lauderdale disco called Faces. When Cammy excused herself to go to the ladies' room, a guy started hassling her on the way. One of my men, a muscular, 270-pound brute named William Ferrante, saw what was going on and came over. "You want me to take care of him, chief?"

I shook my head no. It was too soon for that kind of thing. Cammy had already begun to notice the unusual allegiance I commanded. I was half the size of the "shadows" that were always hovering around me. She figured it was just because I was the producer, and I wanted to keep her thinking that way.

The dance music was so loud it made conversation impossible. I reacted by merely staring at her, taking in her innocent beauty. This time, she stared back. We looked at each other for what seemed like an eternity. Finally, she took a half-step closer, stood on her tiptoes, and kissed me on the cheek. It sent a charge through my body.

I was falling in love, and falling hard.

CHAPTER 15

The sun was breaking in the eastern sky by the time we returned to the hotel. We walked to her door and I gently kissed her.

"Good night," she said.

I didn't move.

She squirmed. "Good night," she repeated.

I stood firm. I could sense how uncomfortable she was. Her father was right: she wasn't used to this kind of thing. She was so innocent it strained belief. I smiled and mussed her hair as if she were a puppy.

"Good night, Camille," I said, walking away.

We were inseparable after that, having lunch and dinner together every day. I enjoyed taking her to expensive restaurants and showering her with gifts. It was all so new, the smallest thing excited her. I was making so much money that it had lost its thrill. But a hundred-dollar lunch made Cammy rush to a phone to tell her mother. Through her, the thrill of the money had returned.

The relationship was progressing rapidly in every area but the bedroom. That didn't bother me in the least. In fact, I was relieved. I knew that she was a virgin. I knew I was in love with her. I knew that the moment we made love, there would be no turning back. I would be with her forever, and she would change my life.

"I want you to know you are very special to me," I told her at dinner one evening. "We don't have to rush anything. If it takes a week, a month, a year, it doesn't matter to me. Whenever you're ready."

I knew before we made love I would have to tell her the truth, at least about some things. I figured that she would be more interested in my marital status than in my occupation. My marriage, by then, had all but faded away. Maria had told me six months before that it was over. She had initiated the conversation based upon my long absences. I believe she had finally come to accept that we were close friends but not lovers. We would remain friends and do what was right for the children. However, I anticipated that explaining this to Cammy wasn't going to be easy.

I drove her to a beautiful spot on the ocean in Fort Lauderdale. The top was down on the Eldorado and the sun was just beginning to set. A light summer breeze was blowing. I told Cammy I loved her. It was the kind of opening that screams of a stunning "but" to follow. She, as usual, missed all the warning signs. By the time I got to the crux of the confession, I had softened the blow the best I could. I told her I was married and had three children. I said the marriage was in name only and had essentially ended years earlier. I was hardly ever home. When I was, I stayed in my son's room, which was the truth. I never had any reason before to legally end the marriage, but promised that I now did, and would.

She accepted every explanation. She believed me without question. The revelation didn't dampen her spirits in the least. I learned later that at that moment she started a personal policy that would carry her through the difficult years ahead. My other life simply didn't exist. Everything that came before was of no consequence. She wasn't going to let anything stand in the way of our future.

Although my confession had gone far easier than expected, I still wasn't inclined to drop the other shoe. I figured that would happen eventually, so why push it? There were hints. A new movie had just been released that I wanted to see. I took Cammy. The movie was *Once Upon a Time in America,* a Mob film starring Robert De Niro.

In her room later that evening, her friend Katie asked her how the date had gone. Cammy mentioned that we saw a movie.

"What film?" Katie asked.

"*Once Upon a Time in America,*" Cammy answered.

"It figures," Katie said.

Nothing registered.

Another time, Cammy was talking with *Knights of the City* director Dominic Orlando by the Marina Bay swimming pool. He was telling her about his future projects. "I'd like to do a Mafia movie," he said. "There's a lot of good material available."

"I like movies like that," she piped. "I find the men so attractive. They're really men. They have this powerful aura around them."

Orlando looked at her, startled for a moment, then laughed a big, hearty laugh. "You might be closer to that than you think!"

She figured he was referring to himself.

At that point, many of the cast and crew knew, or at least had heard the rumors, about their producer's "sinister" background. Cammy was probably the last to hear them. When she did, she pushed it out of her mind. After all, the rumors had been wrong about her sleeping with me, even if they were prophetic. She decided these new rumors were nonsense as well. In her eyes, it was unthinkable that I could be a criminal.

Although Cammy knew next to nothing about me, she too was placing a lot of faith in the month-old relationship.

A telephone call late one afternoon forced her to make a major decision. "Cammy!" an excited voice said. "You've got a shot! Can you catch the next flight out?"

She had been taking an afternoon nap when the phone woke her. She tried to clear her mind and sort out what she was hearing. The voice on the other end belonged to Cooly Jackson, a dancer on the syndicated television program "Solid Gold." He was calling from Los Angeles. Cammy had auditioned for a position with the program's dance troupe a few months before. There were more than a hundred hopefuls vying for a few open positions, and she'd made it to the final cut. Now, apparently, one of the dancers had been injured or quit or got married or something, and one of the to-kill-for positions was again available.

"Do I have to come now?"

"We need someone right away," Cooly explained. "There's a private audition. It's between you and two other dancers. It's now or never, Cammy. This is the chance of a lifetime!"

She begged for time to decide. Cooly told her to call him within the hour. She anguished over what to do, pacing the hotel room and carefully weighing her options. "Solid Gold" was indeed the chance of a lifetime. What more could a dancer want? The Solid Gold Dancers were probably the highest-profile dancers around at the time. The international television exposure would lead to a succession of jobs, a career's worth. The experience would light up her resume like—solid gold.

But what about me? She felt our embryonic love was too fragile to disturb. If she abruptly left Florida to begin a demanding, time-consuming career, it could kill our rapidly blossoming relationship.

Then again, the "Solid Gold" audition was a reality. I was definitely a gamble—in more ways than she could ever imagine.

By fate, I chose that moment to call her.

"Hi, Cam. I just wanted to tell you again how much I enjoyed our date last night," I said. "I'll see you at eight for dinner."

She gently placed the receiver down, then quickly lifted it and dialed Cooly Jackson. She thanked him and told him she couldn't make it.

The filming continued to go well. Aside from Leon Isaac Kennedy, the movie starred Stoney Jackson, "Diamonds" star Nicholas Campbell, soap opera actress Janine Turner, and veteran actor Michael Ansara. I even signed Sammy Davis, Jr., and Smokey Robinson to play cameos, though Davis's part was later edited out. Cammy was penciled in as one of "Jasmine's Bad Girls" and had to prepare for a climactic dance scene near the end of the movie. (Jasmine was played by Wendy Barry.)[*]

Despite the excitement of filming a movie, most of my attention was focused on Cammy. It was like we had burrowed ourselves inside a novel. Every date was magic, every day a thrill. Cammy saved the napkins and matches from every restaurant where we dined, every nightclub where we partied. A thousand little moments were etched in our memories forever. A thousand hints of a troubled future were banished from our minds.

"I love you, Michael," she said, snuggling close as we drove from Delray Beach one evening.

"I love you too," I said. "It sounds really crazy, Camille. I've only known you a few weeks. But I'm really in love with you."

"Michael, someday you're going to marry me. Someday soon," she said.

For the last few weeks of shooting, I moved the cast and crew to the Konover Hotel, an oceanfront concrete tower on Miami Beach. A Konover showroom had been rented for the talent-contest sequence, and it was more economical to move the entire production there. I took the liberty of moving Cammy's growing bounty of personal belongings into my master suite.

When she discovered what I had done, she threw a fit. Although we had shared many evenings together and had vowed our undying love in

---

[*]Both Michael and Cammy appear in the dance-contest segment hosted by Smokey Robinson near the end of *Knights of the City*, which is available in most video stores. Michael is standing with Robinson when the singer is introduced. Cammy is one of Jasmine's backup dancers; she's wearing a turquoise Spandex outfit, with her dark hair in a ponytail jutting from the top of her head.

an array of tropical settings, we had yet to consummate the relationship.

"I can't move in here with you!" she exclaimed.

"You can stay in the other room," I countered, motioning to the second bedroom in the suite.

"What happens if my mother and father call? And the operator says, 'Oh, that must be the young lady staying in Mr. Franzese's suite'? They'll kill me!"

She had a point. After all, I had promised her father I would look out for her. I had certainly done that, far more diligently than Mr. Garcia had intended.

I picked up the phone and reserved another room.

As our affair began sweeping beyond rumor into reality, Cammy felt the heat of the other dancers' jealousies. "He's just using you," one sour-faced woman said. "He'll dump you when this is all over," added another. "You're going to get your little heart broken," chided a third. "This happens on every movie. It never lasts," jabbed the first dancer again. "What are you going to do, be his mistress? The guy's married."

The taunts stung. She ran to her room in tears. Joanna Tea, the brown-haired woman she originally thought was my girlfriend, witnessed what happened and followed. They sat together on her bed. "Don't listen to them, Cammy," she said. "The girls are so jealous because it's so obvious to everyone that he really loves you. Don't worry about what anybody says. Gossip is part of this business. You're going to have to get used to it. Just be happy and enjoy yourself. If they bother you, just tell them to go fuck off and die!"

Intermingled with the sniping were encouraging reports from my associates. "You know something, I think my friend's in love with you," Frankie Cestaro told Cammy one evening. "I've known Michael a long time. I've never seen him like this."

"I sat with Michael during your rehearsal today," reported Emily La Rosa, the makeup woman. "All he did was talk about you. He's like a schoolboy in love. 'Look at her hair!' he said. 'Look at her beautiful eyes! Look at the way she moves!' If you handle this right, I think you'll really have a good thing going."

As the weeks progressed, my love continued to build. We sat together in Miami's Little Havana and watched Orlando and Kutash direct the big Busby Berkeley–style dance number. It began to rain. She made a move to leave. I pulled her back.

"You look so beautiful in the rain," I said. "The way your hair is curling...I've never seen you more beautiful."

"Would you please just get in the car—it's pouring!" She laughed.

Despite the gossip on the set, we headed into our second celibate month. Cammy was moving in that direction at a snaillike pace. The first night we spent together, she came to bed wearing sweat pants, a sweatshirt, leg warmers, and sweat socks.

"Where are you going—skiing?" I said, realizing the ice wasn't about to break anytime soon.

"I'm just cold."

"In Miami, in July?"

"The air conditioning is cold."

"I'm not going to attack you!"

"No, really. I'm chilly."

After that breakthrough, she spent the next night in the adjacent room with the door locked. Another trussed night with me followed; then she returned to her room downstairs. "You're totally leaving the suite tonight?" I said, amused by it all.

When her part-time roommate, Carol Gun, expressed an equal surprise at her preference, Cammy admitted her odd behavior. "He must think I'm crazy."

The moment we finally made love came without warning. We were lying on the couch together as the sun dipped behind my Delray Beach home. The light was diffused and deep yellow. I sensed that it was time.

"Come on," I said, taking her hand. "Let's go."

I led her from the living room to the bedroom. Her body was tense. She glanced at the room, then felt a stab of fear as her eyes fell upon the bed. She didn't know what to do, how to please me. Like a nervous newlywed from another time, she retreated into the safety of the master bathroom to brush her teeth, comb her hair, change into one of my blue-and-white Christian Dior shirts, stall, and try to prepare herself mentally for the first sexual experience of her life.

After folding her clothes and placing them on the counter, she put on some perfume, took a deep breath, and looked at herself in the mirror. She slowly walked toward the door, paused, took another breath, and stared down at the doorknob. She mustered the courage to turn it.

I waited for her on the bed clad in a pair of light blue shorts. She

emerged from the bathroom bathed in the soft summer light of a glorious Florida sunset. I was blown away. Her nervousness and anxiety
carried over to me. I knew it was her first time, and I wanted to make it
special. That added to the tension and made me equally nervous. She
edged forward. I gently pulled her down on top of me and kissed her
softly.

"Don't be afraid, Cammy," I said, breathing in the almond smell of
her hair. "It's going to be beautiful."

Her shirt opened and her dark brown hair fell across my face. She
looked at me with the huge, frightened eyes of a fawn. "Will you teach
me how to make love to you?" she whispered.

As our passion peaked, I felt as if my soul had shaken loose and had
been jettisoned into her body. I wanted that. I wanted her love, her
caresses, her body and her being. I wanted it all. I wanted her, and only
her, forever.

We remained in a tight, loving embrace as we cooled down.

"Are you okay? Are you hurt?" I asked, nervous over her long
silence.

"I'm okay," she answered.

"Are you sure you're all right?" I repeated, kissing her and running
my fingers through her hair. "You're not hurt or anything?"

"I'm fine, Michael, really."

She paused. Her insecurities returned. "Was it...was I...was it
okay?" she asked plaintively.

"Yeah, it was okay," I said, laughing. "It was more than okay."

After that night, I loved her with an obsession that was limitless.
Nothing would be more important than her, than being with her. All
vows and promises and alliances I had made up to that point were no
longer binding. Anything that might come between us was to be blotted
from our lives.

That vow had barely been spoken when it was immediately tested.
The movie set started humming with the juiciest gossip yet. Cammy's
boyfriend, a painter named Eddie Chacon, had appeared unannounced
from California. "And he's got a gun!" everyone was saying.

The word spread through the production: "Eddie's got a gun!"

The young man had deduced from the increasingly impersonal tone
of Cammy's few letters that something bad was happening in South

Florida. Checking with her mother, he learned why. Crushed, he decided he had to try to win his girlfriend back.

He located her on the set by the bandstand. She nearly fainted when she saw him.

"I missed you, Cammy," he said. "I haven't seen you in so long."

"I've got to rehearse," she said, darting off. "We'll talk later."

My men had also heard the gossip and were taking it seriously. They warned me of the potentially dangerous situation. "You want us to take care of him?"

The question hung in the humid South Florida air like an angry wasp. Eddie Chacon's life hung with it. One word from me and Cammy's boyfriend would be shot in the head, bound, driven out into the Everglades, and dropped to the bottom of a stagnant canal.

"He's just a kid," I said.

"They say he's got a gun. We can't risk it," the eager associates pressed.

"I don't think he has a gun. Leave him alone," I ordered.

Fortunately, I was secure in Cammy's feelings for me. But I was so consumed by love, I don't know what I would have done had I felt threatened. I might very well have used the life-or-death power I commanded against a perceived rival for Cammy's affections. In saner moments, it was just such a potent mixture of passion and power that unnerved me. There had to be a balance. Until then, I had successfully juggled the influence of La Cosa Nostra with the unprecedented amount of money I was making. Suddenly, my all-encompassing love for a nineteen-year-old Mexican girl had upset that critical balance. My emotions were on fire. I knew I had to be extremely careful.

My men obeyed my hands-off order but stuck close. When Eddie came walking toward my car later that afternoon, everyone tensed. I signaled for my crew to remain calm. My men eased their hands under their jackets.

"Hi, I'm Eddie, Cammy's friend," he said, extending a hand.

I shook it.

"Really nice meeting you, Michael."

The youth promptly turned and left.

"He's just a kid," I repeated, shrugging.

That evening, Eddie and Cammy met in her room. As nicely as she could, she explained that their year-long relationship was over.

"I kind of figured that when I didn't hear from you. You were never in your room when I called. You never returned my calls."

"I'm sorry," she said. "I didn't plan this. It just happened. I'm sorry you had to come so far."

"That's okay," he said, offering a weak smile. "I always wanted to see Miami."

Neither said a word for the longest time.

"Are you sure, Cammy?"

She nodded.

"Can we see each other when you come back?"

She shook her head no.

"I guess I always figured I wasn't enough for you. You're a good girl, Cammy. You deserve the best. Just be careful. If it doesn't work out, come home and call me. I'll be there."

She fought to hold back her tears. Eddie just stood there. The damp air inside the room was infused with grief. Finally, he left.

She was weeping softly in her room when the phone rang. It was Eddie. He was calling from the airport. "Are you sure you want me to go?" he said, making one last-ditch effort at winning back his girlfriend.

"I'm sure, Eddie."

Cammy was still crying when I picked her up for dinner that evening.

"Don't worry, he'll get over it," I said. "He's young."

The banishment of Eddie Chacon was a crossroad that bonded us even tighter. She cut her ties with her past. I added possessiveness and jealousy to the cauldron of uncontrollable emotions that were sweeping over me. I could never let her go, to anyone, or for any reason.

We were emotionally intertwined on a fairy-tale level, deeply in love, but in reality we knew little about each other. She certainly didn't know about me. And I quickly learned about the hot temper that resides inside even the sweetest of Latin women.

Michael Markowitz had flown in to discuss the joint purchase of a Miami restaurant called Martha's. We arranged to meet the owners of the bistro after it closed at midnight. We spent three hours eating, talking, sipping wine, and negotiating the purchase. When I returned to the Konover, it was after four A.M.

Cammy had been waiting for me, growing more furious with each passing minute. She figured I was out with another woman. By two A.M.

she had made her airline reservations to leave later that morning. By three A.M., she was packed and ready to go. When I returned, I found her door bolted tight. She refused to listen to any explanation.

Later that morning, I tried again. This time she let me in. She sat upright on her bed, clutching a pillow and pouting like an angry child. I tried to explain that I had been working.

"Working? You don't work at night," she said.

"I don't have normal business hours," I responded in a classic understatement. "I do things at night. I work at night."

I explained that I had to meet with the owners after the restaurant closed so we wouldn't be interrupted. She wasn't buying it. As she dropped the pillow a little, I noticed she was wearing an ice-blue negligee.

"You bought that for me, didn't you?" I teased.

"No I didn't," she lied.

"Come on, Cam, I know you bought that for me."

"I did not. I bought it for myself."

"Yeah, right."

We argued for a few moments until she dropped both her angry facade and the pillow.

"The only reason I'm still here is that you have all my paychecks in your briefcase," she said as I placed my hands under the sheer negligee and slipped it over her head. "Otherwise, I'd have been just a memory!"

"No way, Cam," I said, a chilling edge of seriousness cutting through as I nuzzled her breasts. "I can never let you go."

CHAPTER 16

Michael had come to Florida in part to escape the troubles that were mounting in New York. Cammy provided that escape in ways he had never imagined. Still, the turbulence in New York refused to give him peace. The joint task force continued to slave away, fueled by Roy Rogers hamburgers, unlimited federal resources, and skilled manpower. But they had become almost too effective. Their ambitious scope combined with Michael's vast operation to leave them with handfuls of dangling threads.

"The biggest problem we encountered was that every time we met, there were ten new crimes to report and dozens of new accomplices to add to our lists," prosecutor Ray Jermyn said. "Michael had so much going on—car dealerships, bank loans, money laundering, unions, gas taxes, gas terminals, insurance fraud, counterfeit bonds, loan-shark operations, construction businesses, movies, credit-card scams, the Russians, you name it. One week he'd be in California making a movie, the next week he'd be in Florida getting the key to the city, which really blew us away. Here we are hunting this guy who's a Mafia captain involved in dozens of criminal activities, and the mayor of Miami Beach gives him the key to the city and puts his police force at his disposal. Incredible."

In April 1984, an unrelated incident worked to renew the task force's vigor and link some of the disconnected fragments of its case. Larry Iorizzo was tried on past charges relating to Vantage Petroleum and was convicted of grand larceny, tax evasion, and mail and wire fraud. His sentencing was set for June.

The conviction of a close criminal partner is always a bad omen, especially when the partner is the less desirable target. I was uneasy when Iorizzo went down, but I trusted him like a brother. In the ensuing months, he repeatedly told me not to worry; he insisted he'd find a way out of the mess.

As the sentencing hearing approached, his attitude changed. "I don't want to go to jail, Michael," he confided. "It doesn't make sense. With all my money, why should I be in jail? I've got solid connections in Panama."

In addition to registering his companies in Panama and hiding his money there, Iorizzo owned a large estate in the Central American country. One of the reasons he had chosen Panama was because the country did not have an extradition treaty with the United States. Iorizzo told me that he had been paying millions to an acne-scarred Panamanian general named Manuel Noriega in return for banking connections, personal security, and other services. "I'm not going to stick around for the sentencing," he announced. "I can run the operation from Panama. I've got it all set."

"That's insane, Larry," I advised. "Once you run, you become a fugitive. That's a whole new hell. You should stay and fight for bail. Your lawyer says you have a good shot at beating the charges on appeal. I'd stick around."

Iorizzo wouldn't listen. "I'm leaving the night before the hearing," he said.

In June, the day before the hearing, Iorizzo showed up at my home in Delray Beach. Frankie Cestaro, Louie Fenza, and assorted other associates were there. Iorizzo had everything worked out. He was taking the Lear jet with Wife Number II, the "girlfriend" wife, who apparently had been designated his official fugitive wife. The pilot had prepared a phony itinerary that had them hopping around various Caribbean islands, including Port-au-Prince, Haiti, to muddy the trail. Cestaro provided Iorizzo with a phony passport under the name Salvatore Carlino. Iorizzo gave him $5,000 for his troubles.

That evening, we shared an emotional farewell dinner at Iorizzo's nearby mansion in Boca Raton. I invited Cammy. The multimillion-dollar oceanfront home was the largest she had ever entered. Touring the house, she spotted one of Iorizzo's belts hanging over a chair. She was drawn to it like the serpent drew Eve. She couldn't believe its length. It looked like a bullwhip!

At the end of the evening, Iorizzo and I embraced and offered warm goodbyes. We had not only made millions together, I had grown to consider him one of my closest friends.

When I walked out the door, it marked the last time I saw him as a free man—or as a friend.

Iorizzo's plan of running Galion Holdings out of Panama worked for the next two months. He was not a smart fugitive, however. He called the United States daily, leaving himself open to phone traces. He flew around the world "as if he had a license to be a fugitive," as one associate put it. He began setting up an operation to steal gas-tax money in Austria. He tried to entice me to join him in the foreign operation: "The tax on gas in Europe is two dollars a gallon. Can you imagine the money we could make?" he said, giddy with excitement.

"I'm not committing any crimes in Austria," I said. "For all I know, they probably shoot you there. If I get in trouble, you think Uncle Sam is going to help me? He'll probably say 'Keep 'im. Shoot 'im. We don't want 'im.'"

Iorizzo's arrogance as a fugitive was limitless. He scheduled his daughter's wedding in Austria and made arrangements to charter a jetliner to carry three hundred guests from New York. A flood of wedding invitations announced the gala.

That was the last straw. In October, the feds negotiated an agreement with the double-dealing Noriega to flush out Iorizzo. A team of Noriega's soldiers swept in and dragged him from his fortress. He was tossed into a stone dungeon without a bed. He languished there for three days until the FBI "rescued" him.

Iorizzo was flown to Miami and stashed in a wretched prison overflowing with crazed Latin drug dealers and a swarm of additional Cuban and Central and South American psychos and criminals. Within weeks of the arrest, word was out that Iorizzo had cracked and was going to turn.

A relative of Iorizzo personally delivered a disturbing message to me. "Larry's always considered you his ticket out if he got into trouble," the man explained. "He has a file on you six inches thick. He's kept every clipping that appeared in the newspapers, and kept records of every illegal transaction you and he ever made. Watch yourself. This could be big trouble."

I refused to believe it; we had been so close. But as more information filtered back from Miami, the unthinkable began to look more and more thinkable. Prison is a hard place for a 450-pound man. He couldn't sleep on the narrow prison beds. The food was killing him, and his fellow inmates were torturing him. There were reports that the guards had stripped him and forced him to walk down the corridors as the inmates jeered.

I met with Iorizzo's son, Larry Jr., at the Howard Johnson's on the Jericho Turnpike. I assured the young man that I was doing everything in my power to help with his father's case. Delicately questioning the twenty-year-old, I could sense that the stories about Iorizzo's rough prison stay were true.

Shortly before Iorizzo was scheduled to be transported to New York, an associate paid me a visit. "Larry's been driving me crazy with his calls," he said. "He has a plan. He begged me to present it to you."

The way he reported it, Iorizzo figured that there would be two U.S. marshals who would escort him to the Eastern District courthouse at the corner of Cadman Plaza East and Tillary Street in Brooklyn. Iorizzo's plan was for me to have a car waiting when he arrived. I was to dispatch a hit squad to kill the marshals on the steps of the courthouse and free him.

If I refused to go along with the plan, then it was understood that Iorizzo had no alternative but to roll over on me.

The consequences either way were severe. Iorizzo's testimony could put me in prison for the rest of my life. On the other hand, murdering two U.S. marshals was not an acceptable alternative.

"Is he out of his mind?" I asked. "This guy is cracking up."

The scheme was the last contact I had with my partner and friend. The word was that Iorizzo was singing his lungs out, and I was the lyric.

Still, I rejected it. I had heard rumors of people testifying against me in the past. When they took the stand, they copped out on the prosecutors. In my heart, I felt Iorizzo would do the same.

Cammy knew nothing about any of this, and I didn't want her to. She was my salve, my pressure release. When I was with her, it was like New York never existed. The stress lifted from my neck and shoulders. Cammy was a porthole to another world. I wanted to enter that world and never come back.

Michael sent Cammy home for a short visit near the end of film-
ing. Back in Los Angeles, and back to reality, the glow of Florida

began wearing off. Distancing herself from the romance that had intoxicated her, she could see that what happened in Fort Lauderdale was wrong, morally and religiously.

Her mood alternated between elation and remorse. She wondered about Michael's children. If he was rarely home, as he said, they must miss him terribly. And if it did work out and she and Michael became serious, she would be taking him from his children. They might blame her for the loss of their father.

She hadn't acted like much of a Christian in Florida. She was swept away by a married man and had her religious and moral beliefs trampled. She hadn't lost them; but she had suppressed them so she could enjoy an affair that flew in the face of everything she believed.

She rationalized it all by telling herself that it was a special love, and that God not only approved but had sent her to Michael because He wanted them together. But was that really God's will, or just her own glossy coating?

She fell to her knees by her bed, as she had done as a child. Tears streamed down her cheeks as she prayed. "Dear God, what should I do? I love Michael so much, but I don't want to offend you. I believe you brought us together, but I know what I'm doing is wrong. Please tell me what to do."

Insecurity tormented her as well. Michael wanted her, but why return and get hurt? The taunts from the dancers still stung: "not serious," "happens all the time," "love ends when the movie ends," and, the worst one of all, the word she hated most, "mistress."

Michael didn't give her much time to let the dark thoughts fester. He called every few hours, every day they were apart. "I love you," he said. "I don't ever want to be without you."

The words sounded wonderful. The attention was comforting. Still, she was afraid and unsure. When she was fourteen, she had made a vow never to marry a man who had been married before. Of all her father's twenty-two brothers and sisters, only one was divorced. That's the way it should be, she thought. She'd also vowed never to marry a man with children.

Michael failed on both counts.

"I'm doing exactly what I said I'd never, ever do," she sighed to herself.

She fished around in a small suitcase and removed an envelope. Inside were eight checks for $500 each. In typical poor-girl fashion, she had saved all her paychecks while in Miami, cashing only her per-diem checks to get her through the week. Looking at the check on top, she examined the swirled signature of the person who authorized them.

Michael Franzese.

It wasn't a fantasy. Everything he ever said came true. Every promise he had made to her he kept. She had to trust him. She had to keep believing it would work out.

She cashed her stack of checks and treated her family to dinner. It felt good. She could wine and dine them and delight them with stories about Fort Lauderdale and Miami Beach and her new boyfriend. But she couldn't tell them the whole truth. If she did, they'd never let her return.

The *Knights of the City* wrap party was the apex of my life. All the forces that had molded my past, and those that would direct my future, converged during the glittery event staged at a Fort Lauderdale skating rink.

Although the $2 million, independently produced movie was small by Hollywood standards, the wrap party was first-rate. I was still new to the movie business, but I was a pro at throwing parties. I spent more than $150,000 on food, spotlights, liquor, and decorations. The local media were invited to the all-night event and turned out in force, blinding everyone in the bright lights of the television cameras and flash photography. To add to the festive atmosphere, the big dance numbers from the movie were displayed on giant screens around the room throughout the evening.

Also present were most of my crew, including Michael Markowitz and a contingent of his Russian army. The combination Hollywood/Cosa Nostra/Russian affair made for some unusual scenes. Not only was I fawned over by the movie's cast and crew and all the wannabees who had conned invitations, but for the first time in Florida, I was openly honored in Cosa Nostra fashion by a squadron of men greeting me with the traditional kiss on the cheek. Any cognizant person observing this should have immediately noticed that something was out of kilter. Few, if any, did. Movie parties are strange affairs under normal circumstances.

Cammy had returned to Miami earlier that afternoon. I picked her up at the airport and drove to my home in Delray Beach. She changed into one of her favorite dresses, a traditional Mexican style of some kind with lots of colorful layers, and said she felt like Cinderella going to the royal ball. Inside, she bumped into a large, graceful man who turned and smiled. It was Muhammad Ali. Across the room, she spotted Emmanuel Lewis, the little fellow who starred in TV's "Webster." She spent half the night talking with her dancer friends, and the other half by my side. She was too immersed in her Cammy-in-Wonderland dream to notice anything out of the ordinary.

Several local politicians gave speeches. Archdiocese of Miami Auxiliary Bishop Agustin Roman presented me with a Bible signed by Pope John Paul II, praising me for offering jobs and hope to disadvantaged youth. Bishop Roman had arranged for the signing when he read about the movie in the *Miami Herald*.

Early in the morning, about four o'clock, a substitute publicist informed me that a crew from the Miami NBC affiliate, WSVN, had waited all night for a chance to interview me. I had been cautious about doing interviews that evening because my regular publicist, Richard Frisch, was out sick. Frisch was under strict orders to screen the requests to weed out the knowledgeable New York media along with any nonentertainment journalists who might snoop around. The substitute publicist pleaded the case for the patient WSVN crew, and I relented. I grabbed Zimmerman and we were both wired for sound and placed under the bright lights. We expected to field some fluff questions pertaining to the movie.

Only the crew wasn't from the local NBC affiliate—they were top guns from NBC News. Instead of a puff-piece entertainment reporter, the correspondent was Brian Ross, a tough network investigative journalist.

After a few polite questions, Ross zeroed in. "Michael, isn't it true that you are the stepson of Sonny Franzese, an underboss in the Colombo crime family, and that you yourself are a capo in that family?"

"What?"

"And isn't it true that you are financing this movie with stolen gas-tax money?"

I fought to stay cool; I knew my reaction was being taped.

"And Jerry," Ross said, turning to Zimmerman, "isn't it true that you are a convicted felon, convicted of perjury—"

"I'm not taking this," Zimmerman snarled, losing his composure. The big man stood up, unclipped the microphone from his shirt, and walked away.

Ross turned his attention back to me. "The FBI says you are a member of the Colombo Mafia family."

"The FBI can allege and say whatever they like. They've been doing it for many, many years," I responded.

When Ross tried to continue, I gently cut him off. "Mr. Ross, it's very late and it's been a long night," I said. "If you would like to continue this interview at another time, I'll be happy to accommodate you."

Ross ordered the cameras to follow me walking away. As he did, a late-arriving underling greeted me with a kiss. I cursed the bad timing. When the television lights shut off, I located the publicist and chewed him out. I then scolded my inner circle for allowing a network bulldog to walk in undetected.

Cammy had observed what had happened from across the room, but she wasn't close enough to hear Ross's revealing questions. Judging from my reaction, she feared it was something terrible and wanted to go back to the Konover immediately. I had Louie Fenza drive her. When I arrived about an hour later, she didn't ask me for details. I didn't volunteer anything, nor did I warn her what it meant. Ross was obviously being fed information by a New York prosecutor, probably Rudolph Giuliani or one of Giuliani's assistants. He had come to Florida to prepare a report on a pending indictment.

I instructed my attorney to contact NBC and arrange another interview. I wanted to have my say, but more importantly, I wanted to know what Ross knew. Ross interviewed me for an hour at my Houston Holdings office. I denied that I was a Mob captain and said the movie was being legitimately financed. I also denied that my father was in the Mob. Ross deleted all my comments when the damning segment aired on NBC News a few weeks later. It was the first of a half-dozen network news reports about me that would be broadcast over the next twelve months.

The walls were starting to crack.

●　　●　　●

When the film wrapped, I felt unusually vulnerable and wanted Cammy to remain close. I encouraged her to stay with me in Delray Beach longer than she had planned. When she was around, I was able to forget, at least temporarily, the serious charges I knew were hanging over me.

Early on the third morning, we were awakened by the howling wind and heavy rain from a summer thunderstorm pounding on the roof of the house. I got up, walked to the porch, and looked out at the dock. My $25,000 Chris-Craft had vanished. Looking closer, I could see its mooring lines pulled taut and heading downward. I returned to the bedroom.

"What happened?" Cammy asked.

"My boat sank," I said, climbing back in bed.

"What are you going to do?"

"Go back to sleep."

"But Michael, it's brand new!"

"It's raining."

A sunken boat was the least of my worries.

After a few weeks, Cammy went back to California and I returned to New York. I felt tense and agitated, and I was being followed everywhere I went. I decided to go to California to see Cammy. California was even farther from New York than Florida, and that was an added advantage. I checked into the Westwood Marquis Hotel, called Cammy, and asked her to meet me at six. She arrived with her brother Dino and a friend of Dino's named Matt Amador. Amador had a small truck, and that was the only transportation Cammy could arrange to get to the hotel.

I had some visitors when she arrived and told her to wait for me in the bedroom of the suite. Dino and Matt got bored and left.

When I ended my meeting, I rushed into the bedroom to see her. She wasn't there.

"In here," a voice echoed from the bath.

I laughed when I saw her standing in the dry bathtub, marveling at its huge size. It was the biggest bathtub she had ever seen. I jumped in and hugged her tightly.

"I missed you so much!" I said, kissing her all over her beautiful face. "What have you done to me? What have you done to my life? I can't think. I can't work. What have you done to me?"

I withdrew from the embrace long enough to lead her out of the tub over to the dresser. I removed a long, black felt box and handed it to her. Inside was a gold necklace with the word "Michael's" spelled out in fat diamonds, including the apostrophe. She nearly fainted.

"For me?"

I suspected from the start that Cammy didn't live in Beverly Hills. Still, when I parked my green Jaguar sedan in front of her house in Anaheim, I had to look around a few times before leaving the car. The neighborhoods had steadily declined as she directed me through Anaheim, where her family had moved from Norwalk. For Cammy, the perspective was entirely different: it could have been a lot worse. She could have been taking me to one of her former homes in the Norwalk barrios.

Her house was small and overflowing with people. There were nine members of her immediate family, plus a swarm of friends and relatives. Her brothers and their friends were break-dancing in the garage. Although it was crowded, it was a lively, happy place that had obviously become the center of the neighborhood. After meeting her parents and various brothers and sisters, I took her aside.

"Cammy, where do you sleep?"

She shrugged. "It's not so bad."

I met her parents and took them out to dinner that night at a spruced-up Black Angus in Anaheim. I spent a great deal of time talking with her father. He told me that when he was a teenager, he lost five teeth and was shot in the leg when a gang of Mexican-born drug pushers ambushed him and his friend Alex Moreno after a New Year's Eve party in San Diego in 1959. His face was slashed with a straight razor, and his chest was gashed with a flattened can opener. His teeth were dislodged by a gang member wielding a lead horseshoe stake. The drugged sociopath was about to crush his skull when Moreno whipped out a .22 pistol and shot him in the stomach. Moreno shot a second pusher in the groin before the gang scattered. Moreno, a 150-pound fifteen-year-old, lifted Seferino's bleeding, 160-pound body from the pavement and carried him six blocks through a thick fog to Seferino's sister Eva's house. The teenager hid his gun in the toilet tank, along with the .38 Seferino had never gotten out of his belt.

Moreno had saved Seferino's life, but the police weren't impressed.

He ended up doing eighteen months in a tough youth prison for his heroics.

Seferino told me he'd ducked the police by traveling across the border to Tijuana, and giving a horse doctor a few pesos to carve the bullet from his leg sans anesthesia while he screamed in pain. He told the veterinarian he'd been shot by the border patrol. He returned to San Diego and was brought to Paradise Valley Hospital, where doctors mended his face, mouth, and chest with 160 stitches. He told the American doctors he had gotten into a fight while in Mexico.

After he healed, Seferino said, he plotted his revenge. He hunted the remaining gang members like an urban terrorist. He and a friend cornered one in the lights of his friend's 1955 Chevy, knocked him down, then ran over his legs, crushing them. Tipped that another gang member had been arrested and was going through heroin withdrawal at the San Diego jail, Seferino had himself brought in and jailed on a minor charge, located the sick and emaciated drug addict, and beat him nearly to death.

It was some story, and Cammy's father had the scars on his face and leg to back it up. After hearing it, I was even more convinced that when the truth came out about who I was, it wasn't going to faze him.

After dessert, I floored everyone by making a little speech. "I want to thank you for allowing Cammy to come to Florida. I love your daughter very much and I intend to marry her," I said.

Cammy nearly dropped her fork. The first chance she got, she confronted me.

"You didn't tell me you were going to say that, Michael!"

"I didn't intend to. It just came out. Now I really have to marry you," I joked. "Remember when you said that someday I would marry you? Well, I was just confirming what you said."

After visiting her cramped home, I decided she needed her own apartment. We spent the rest of the week looking at condominiums around West Los Angeles. Every one looked perfect to her, but I was more exacting. Finally, I chose a $160,000 unit in Brentwood.

With that done, it was time to bring Cammy to New York so she could be with me while I took care of things there. I put her up at a hotel in Garden City, Long Island. The first morning, I left her a note along with an envelope. The note encouraged her to amuse herself shopping while I worked. Inside the envelope were twenty one-hundred-dollar bills.

"Shopping?" she told me later. "I could buy a store! I could *live* on this!"

I rented a small, one-bedroom unit in the Fairhaven Apartment complex in Woodbury, Long Island, and moved her in. I explained the coziness by telling her, "When I'm in the living room, I want to be able to see you in every room."

Soon afterward, I came home with an American Express card with her name on it. She had once said that her dream was to one day have a credit card. "This is for you," I said. "Buy whatever you want."

Just touching the cool green plastic seemed to send a charge through her body. She couldn't believe it had her name on it, but there it was in raised plastic.

I was a little afraid that Cammy was going to get the financial bends. We were heading into our third month, and she had a condo in Brentwood, an apartment on each coast, along with a magical American Express card that no matter how much she bought, the bills seemed to vanish into the stratosphere. But I couldn't help myself. It made me feel so good to buy her things. I wanted to give her everything, fulfill her every dream.

CHAPTER 17

After spending a few weeks at the condo in Brentwood, I was at the Los Angeles airport preparing to fly to New York when I phoned my secretary. She told me that two men I knew, financier Mel Cooper and Dr. Jesse Hyman, had been arrested with half a dozen others for loan-sharking and racketeering. Included among the others was a rabbi, Chaim Gerlitz, fifty-three, a cantor and teacher at Temple Israel in Great Neck, Long Island.

"That's too bad," I said.

When I arrived at Kennedy International Airport in New York, Frankie Cestaro was there to pick me up. Two men approached us the instant we left the terminal.

"Michael Franzese, you are under arrest."

"Who are you?"

"FBI."

Within seconds, a dozen more agents materialized and surrounded me. I emptied my pockets of my wallet, money, and keys and gave them to Frankie.

"Call Cammy. Tell her I've been arrested and I'll talk to her later tonight. Tell her not to worry."

A three-car FBI caravan ushered me from the airport. The cars headed toward Manhattan instead of Brooklyn or Long Island, where I was normally arrested (and where the joint task force operated).

"What's this all about?" I asked.

"We're arresting you in the Jesse Hyman case," the lead agent said.

"Are you kidding?" I said. "What have I got to do with that?"

The agent didn't answer.

When I learned of the charges, I was amazed. I was hit with seven counts of loan-sharking and racketeering based upon a Lake Success, Long Island operation run by Cooper, Hyman, and the rabbi. It almost made me laugh. I was reportedly stealing $100 million a month in gas taxes, and all Rudolph Giuliani and his Southern District forces could do was try and toss me into somebody else's loan-shark indictment. Actually, it was more complicated than I realized. The Southern District was apparently trying to jump the gun on the Michael Franzese Task Force, the investigative army that I still wasn't aware of.

Cammy was at her parents' in Anaheim when Frankie called.

"Cammy, Michael's been arrested. He's in jail."

"Why? What for?"

"He'll explain when he bails out. He's okay. He just doesn't want you to worry."

She initially took the call in stride. Her father had been arrested eight times in his life. Some of her uncles had been arrested and jailed. With that background, it wasn't a shock to get a call saying her fiancé had been arrested. She viewed it as she viewed everything having to do with me: I'd take care of it, and everything would be perfect again.

I put up my Brookville home, where Maria and our three children were living, to cover the $350,000 bail bond they slapped on me. I was released within hours of the arrest. I called Cammy and was surprised at how well she was taking it. It wasn't until later that I realized that she figured my arrest would be like those of her father and uncles—they'd go to jail for a day or so, and that would be the end of it.

To the contrary, my trial was certain to be long, grueling, and stressful.

When I called again later, Cammy was more upset. She was late. As the day wore on, the two crises began to intertwine. Her fiancé had been arrested for crimes unknown, and she believed she was pregnant. She was worrying herself sick.

"I'm going to die. My parents will kill me," she told me over the phone.

"Don't worry about it," I said. "Everything will be all right. However it turns out, we'll make it right."

She caught a jet to New York the next day. On the plane, the pregnancy issue cleared up.

"Guess what," she said, entering the apartment in New York. "I'm not pregnant."

I hugged her, then backed off.

"What's the matter?"

"When I thought you were pregnant, I was happy. I knew you

weren't prepared, but if you ever are, I'm ready to stand with you."

After dealing with that, I sat her down and tried to explain why I was arrested. She didn't understand what either racketeering or loan-sharking meant. I explained that racketeering was a pattern of at least two criminal acts committed within a ten-year period. Loan-sharking, I said, was lending out money at high rates. I passed both off as "white collar" charges that businessmen often get slapped with, and assured her that they were false.

My first move in my defense was to take a shot at trying to talk my way out of the still-pending indictment. I had been arrested on "an information," a legal maneuver that allows the police and prosecutors to round up and process suspects prior to the actual indictment, a policy that gives the police the critical element of surprise. The twenty-one-day gap between arrest and indictment offered me room to operate. I contacted my attorney, Harold Borg, and had him schedule an appointment with prosecutors Bruce Baird and Aaron Marcu and FBI agent Stanley Nye. At the meeting, Borg and I spoke for two hours trying to convince our adversaries that I was innocent and shouldn't be indicted. The agent and prosecutors listened attentively and took notes.

While awaiting the prosecutors' decision, I received a call from infamous attorney and fixer Roy Cohn. Cohn said he could help and invited me to his Manhattan office. With dramatic flourish, Cohn assured me he could get the indictment dropped. "I'm good friends with Ed Meese," he said, strutting about and dropping the name of the attorney general. "I have contacts everywhere. It'll be a snap.

"I'll need $50,000 cash up front, then $200,000 when the indictment is dropped," Cohn said.

"I'll tell you what," I countered. "I'll give you $500,000 if you can get the indictment dropped. But you get nothing up front."

Cohn demanded the advance. Suspecting it was nothing but a cheap hustle, I held firm.

"I'm offering you twice what you wanted," I reiterated. "All you have to do is wait a few weeks. If you can do what you claim, that should be acceptable."

I never heard from Cohn again.

Neither Cohn's alleged connections nor my arguments had any effect. I was indicted along with the others.

When I read the indictment, I was surprised to discover that I was portrayed as Mr. Big again—just like when I was in college. I was accused of providing most of the money—more than a million dollars— and the muscle for the loan-shark operation. The seriousness of the charges was not to be underestimated. Regardless of my innocence, I faced 140 years in prison. As I studied the names of my co-defendants, the confusion started to lift. There appeared to be two separate groups involved. The first was a band of eight men, headed by four Jews. The second group was a disconnected mix of seven Italians. From what I could tell, the Jewish group, including the rabbi, had the greatest exposure. It was their operation. The Italians, which included several made men and associates from four of the five New York Cosa Nostra families, were probably innocent, or at least well-insulated. I guessed that the Italians had been swept in at random for their publicity value. Indict four Jews and the media yawns. Salt the proceedings with seven Italian gangsters and the press goes wild.

Despite the arrest, or maybe because of it, my whirlwind romance continued unabated. I took Cammy to Las Vegas at the end of August to celebrate her twentieth birthday. We stayed at the Sands Hotel. I told her to pick out anything she wanted at the gift shop and I'd win the money to buy it. She chose a molded metal sculpture of a circus wagon with various animals pulling it. The price was $1,000. Twenty minutes and a few dozen blackjack hands later, I had the grand and she had her memento.

Later that evening, as we looked at the stars from our penthouse suite, an unusual series of patterned lights hovered high in the distant sky. The UFO attracted the attention of the local newspaper and everyone who could pull himself away from the gaming tables. "I had it fly by just for your birthday," I joked as we watched the unearthly phenomenon.

Back in New York, I worked feverishly on my case, often arriving home late in the evening. Cammy invited her younger sister Sabrina to fly to New York to keep her company. My late evenings and frequently delayed dinners began to grate on the sisters. I promised to make it up to them by cooking a special pasta dish. When I arrived home, two hours later than promised, Cammy coldly told me not to bother. I had a rare loss of cool.

"Don't you realize I'm fighting for my life? If I don't win this case, I'll be gone for twenty to forty years! If I don't win, you and I will never be together!"

My words knocked down the locked doors in her mind. She had blocked out my problems the way she blocked out so many negative things about our unusual relationship. She was unable to sleep that night. She lay in bed crying, staring at me while I slept.

I felt her eyes on me and awakened. She was sitting up in bed, tears rolling down her cheeks.

"What are you doing? It's five A.M."

"I can't sleep," she sobbed. "I'm afraid."

"I didn't mean to scare you. I just wanted you to know I'm not out messing around. If I could be with you, I would—every minute. But I've got to put everything I have into fighting this case."

She cried off and on for the next few days. She steeled herself for the worst, promising to wait for me until she was twenty-six, maybe even twenty-seven, if I went to jail. For her, that seemed like an eternity.

After that, the good times mixed with the bad like an ever-spinning yo-yo. From the Halloween night I was sworn in as a member of La Cosa Nostra, I knew that one day I'd have to do time. I accepted it as part of the price I paid for my underworld membership. We all do. I had visited my father enough to know that prison could be survived. I wasn't looking forward to it, but neither did I fear it.

But that was before I met Cammy. Now, the thought of being locked up and kept from her tortured my mind. It was one of the reasons I never wanted to fall in love. Love makes a man dread prison.

I decided to channel my nervous energy into fighting the case with all my resources. The first step was to change lawyers. Howard Borg was good for what he did—make deals, set meetings, handle appeals, negotiate, and push for parole. A federal court trial was something else. I needed a young, aggressive courtroom fighter who had worked as a prosecutor in the same courts where the legal battle would be fought. I wanted someone who knew all the players on a personal level. I also didn't want to use an attorney like Barry Slotnick who was known for defending mobsters. The attorney I selected was John Jacobs, a former assistant U.S. attorney in the Eastern District of New York. Jacobs fit the criteria.

I also wanted a nontraditional private investigator. My experience with my father had soured me on the breed, most of whom I felt were worthless. Instead, I hired a former IRS agent named Don Taylor, then working for a record company in Atlanta. Taylor was a whiz at paperwork.

My team assembled, I began the difficult task of building a defense. A guilty man knows where he'll be attacked. An innocent man is in the dark. I didn't have a clue what the prosecutors had, nor did I know how they intended to link me to the loan-shark operation. I had to fight blind.

In September, I went to my dentist in Long Island to have a filling replaced. Before I could enter the office, I was swarmed by Nassau County detectives.

"Michael Franzese, you're under arrest."

"What's the charge this time?"

"Aiding and abetting assault."

"What the hell is that?"

The unusual charge stemmed from a four-year-old incident in which the landlord of my Mazda dealership, Thomas Trimboli, was beaten with a ballpeen hammer by a tough one of my men, Frank "Frankie Gangster" Castagnaro, had recruited. Castagnaro, a short, rough guy, earned his nickname because he loved being a gangster. (Trimboli told prosecutors that the only reason he survived was that his thick gray-and-brown toupee cushioned the blows to his skull.) I knew little about the conflict beyond the fact that Frankie G. heard that I had had some heated words with Trimboli a few months earlier, and enlisted the guy to score points with me. My only involvement was posting bond for the assailant as a favor to Frankie G. The hammer man, William Reese, was convicted and did nearly four years. For some reason, Nassau County had decided to resurrect the stale case and pin it on me. I felt it was nothing more than an opportunity for the Nassau County prosecutors to wrestle some headlines from their counterparts in Manhattan.

I also felt there was a disturbing wave of prosecutorial jealousy sweeping New York. Because I operated in such a wide territory, I had become the target of both the Nassau County and Suffolk County prosecutors, along with prosecutors in two of New York's most powerful districts, Giuliani's Southern District (which had declined sending a representative to the Michael Franzese Task Force) and Raymond Dearie's Eastern District. Whenever one made an indictment, it appeared to infuriate the others and prompt an intensification of their investigations. In this case, the Southern District's indictment lit a fire under Edward

McDonald and the joint task force meeting in Uniondale. McDonald's Organized Crime Strike Force assistant, Jerry Bernstein, was so determined to put me behind bars he delayed his scheduled move into private practice for three years. With Iorizzo in the fold, Bernstein and friends were certain to come up with something stronger than "aiding and abetting assault."

I dealt with it by plunging deeper and deeper into the sheltered world I created with Cammy.

In late December, a few weeks before the scheduled beginning of the trial, we went to Peppone, a romantic Italian restaurant in Brentwood. After dinner, I ordered a bottle of Taittinger Rose champagne, clutched her hand, and took a deep breath.

"I love you, Cammy. You've changed my whole life. I want us to be married."

I told her to close her eyes. When I instructed her to open them, she looked down and was surprised to see the soft light sparking off a three-carat, emerald-cut diamond ring perched in a black felt box.

"Do you like it?"

She didn't answer.

The waiter spotted the jewel and spread the news about the happy occasion. A parade of diners dropped by our table to scrutinize the ring and wish us their best.

I told her I wanted to get married before the trial. Then I changed it to during the trial. Finally, I took the more sensible approach and decided to wait until the verdict.

Hovering like a storm cloud over the pending marriage were the *New York Times* and *Newsday* stories and NBC television reports that portrayed me as a vicious criminal. They were disturbing, but she refused to accept them. She had the same reaction that my mother had decades before: the man in the newspapers and on television was not the man she knew. It had to be a mistake.

I did something without thinking one evening that forced her to re-evaluate her view. She was in the Woodbury apartment when I called and said I would be home late. I was having some business problems, and I must have sounded jumpy. The agitation in my voice made her worry. She tossed and turned on the bed, peering at the clock on the nightstand. It was one A.M., then two A.M., then three A.M., and still I hadn't returned.

She thought I was dead.

Shortly after 3:30 A.M., she heard the pounding footsteps of someone running up the stairway into the apartment. I burst into the bedroom, threw down my coat, and began frantically tossing things around. I reached under the bed and pulled out a black handgun. I opened up the chamber, checked to see if it was loaded, snapped it back in place, then stuck the gun into my belt.

She couldn't believe what she was witnessing. It must have seemed as if the man she knew was gone and the stranger in the newspapers had suddenly appeared in the room.

"Michael, what is this?" she said in a panic. "What are you doing?"

"Don't worry. Everything's okay," I said.

"Don't go," she said, crying.

"Got to," I said, grabbing my coat.

"Take me with you. Don't leave me."

I flashed her a brief "you must be kidding" look, gave her a quick hug, and kissed her forehead.

"I've got to run, baby. Everything's okay."

"Call me!" she screamed as I disappeared out the door.

She dialed my beeper number about twenty-five times over the next three hours. I had to shut the damn thing off. She paced the room, then sat on her bed and squeezed a large stuffed monkey. She cried and drank shots of NyQuil in a fruitless attempt to knock herself out. A hundred different scenarios passed through her mind. The peculiarities of our relationship crystallized. There wasn't a single person she could call to check on me. She couldn't call the police. She hadn't even met my parents. If something happened to me, she'd have to read about it in the newspapers.

And what about those newspapers? She opened a drawer in her nightstand and pulled out an article she had saved. She stared down at my photograph and the word "mobster" in the headline. She wondered for the first time if what they were writing was true. I told her I was charged with white-collar crimes, harmless paper crimes. She refused to believe I was involved in violence, gambling, murder, and prostitution like the stereotypical gangsters in the newspapers and movies. But that illusion had been shattered. I had a look in my eyes she had never seen before. I had brushed her aside and rushed out into the night, packing a pistol.

I returned home at 6:30 A.M. It turned out to be a false alarm, an uneventful night. But not for Cammy. I found her sitting on the floor in the corner, trembling and clutching the monkey. Her eyes were bloodshot from crying, her face swollen.

She was relieved when she saw me, then quickly became furious. She glared at me and refused to talk. When I finally prodded her enough to speak, she exploded.

"You ask what's wrong?" she said, incredulous. "You come in at 3:30 A.M. like a maniac, looking like you are about to strangle someone. Then you take out a gun and count the bullets right in front of me. You don't explain, you just run off. You don't call. You don't answer when I beep you. I don't know if I should wait, pack up and go home, or what! I don't know who to call to ask about you—to ask 'Do you know where Michael is? Do you know if he's killed someone? Do you know if he's still alive?'!

"How could you do this to me?" she said.

"I'm sorry. I couldn't get to a phone."

"Where did you go? Why did you need a gun?"

"It was just a raccoon wandering around outside," I said, shooting her a grin. "I didn't want it to get into the trash."

I fawned over her the rest of the day, buying her roses and stuffed rabbits and teddy bears. I never explained what had happened that night. She didn't ask. I took her in my arms and promised that nothing like that would ever happen again. She believed me. The man she loved had returned. The memory of the chilling look in my eyes faded away as if it never had happened.

But it had. Hidden in the house among the flowers, the cheerful stuffed animals, and the piles of cash was a weapon that gave off a faint odor of fresh gunpowder. Three spent shell casings were lodged in its chamber. The missing ends of the deadly projectiles had not been used to scare off a pesky raccoon.

As 1984 ended, the prosecutors scored another major victory. New York indicted Michael Markowitz on fourteen counts of tax evasion. The Rumanian promptly rolled over—although "flopped around" may be a better description. Double-talking, selling old news, and veiling himself behind a feigned lack of understanding of the English language, Markowitz gave his captors fits. He also played both ends and alerted me to the state and federal prosecutors' moves. How much of a threat the crazy Rumanian posed to me was impossible to determine.

What wasn't hard to determine was the effect this was having on the gas business. There was apprehension on the street about where the operation was going and who would be going down with it. With both Markowitz and Iorizzo rumored to be singing, and my indictment, the cash pipeline began to shrink.

I kept all of this from Cammy. She continued to be my respite from the growing nightmare. When we were together, nothing else seemed to matter. My only fear was that the looming troubles might cause me to lose her. I was torn over how to handle it. If we married before the verdict, it would lessen the odds of losing her if I was convicted. On the other hand, if I was given a long sentence, a marriage would damn her to a miserable life.

The loan-shark trial began January 7, 1985, on a cold and overcast morning, and lasted through the winter and into the spring. For the first seven weeks, I sat like a spectator as the prosecutors built their case against the Jewish defendants and their cohorts. My name was never mentioned. When they did get around to bringing me in, the connection was weak. To bolster their case, they brought in their literal and figurative big gun, the massive Lawrence Iorizzo. While I sat stunned, my best friend gave a rambling testimony that included charges that I had forced him to hide out in Panama and had tried to kill his son Lawrence, Jr. The dramatic accusations had nothing to do with the loan-shark indictment, but they did spice up the tedious proceedings.

Iorizzo refused to look at me while he spewed his lies. He wasn't so shy about scrutinizing the courtroom gallery. When Frankie Gangster walked in during his testimony, the fat man freaked. He no doubt had a flashback of Frankie G holding the gun to his head and threatening to kill him if he ever hurt me. Iorizzo's reaction was so extreme the trial was interrupted and Frankie G was escorted from the courtroom.

From Cammy's perspective, the four-month court trial was a revealing experience. Her father had regarded the police and prosecutors as the enemy for most of his life, and this attitude had been ingrained in her. But as she matured, it had faded. Now, watching me on trial, it returned.

She was allowed to attend only a few sessions; Jacobs felt that her presence, and her silver fox coat, would have an unfavorable affect upon the jurors. The sessions she did attend were enough to make her believe me when I claimed my innocence. After testifying about numerous illegal deals, a witness was asked to point to me in the courtroom. He pointed to co-defendant Mel Cooper, the financier. The prosecutor quickly regrouped and asked the witness to try to identify me again. This time he pointed to a man sitting in the front row of the audience. The prosecutor had to virtually stand behind me and wave his hands before my alleged "business partner" got it right. The same witness later testified that he beat his wife only "when she needed it," a statement that infuriated Cammy and most of the people in the courtroom, including the jurors.

Another state's witness, a loan-shark victim, saw mobsters under every rock. He testified that he knew Catholic priests in the Mob. When asked how many people he owed money, the witness responded, "Everybody."

As with most long trials, there were ups and downs. After a bad day in court, I came home in as dark a mood as Cammy had ever seen.

"I'm worried about you, Cammy. I'm afraid for you. I don't know how this is going to come out. If I'm convicted, what then? Sometimes I think I should let you go. I'll take care of you. I'll give you a good start on a new life. I just don't want to hurt you."

"Please don't make me go home," Cammy begged. "I don't care what happens. I'm not going to leave you. I don't care what you say. If you have to go away, we'll survive. Just give me a child. I want to have something of you to remember for the rest of my life, something to keep with me. Just give me a child and I'll wait for you forever."

Her spontaneous sentiments flew in the face of everything we had decided before; she had been so fearful of being pregnant when I was first arrested. Now, in the darkest moment of our lives, she wanted a baby.

I resisted. Why ruin her life? Why drag a beautiful young woman down with me?

She was unbending.

"I want to marry you, but not with all this hanging over our heads," I said. "But if you really want a child, we'll try."

I hardly had time to weigh the ramifications of her request before she made the point moot by becoming pregnant. When I saw a pair of baby shoes in a little box on my bed—Cammy's way of announcing her pregnancy—all my doubts vanished. I also wanted something lasting to spring from our love.

I decided to have the official engagement party a few weeks before the verdict. The rationale was that if I was convicted, I'd at least have one last happy memory in my life. The event was scheduled for April 6 at the Hotel Bel Air in Los Angeles.

Complicating matters was Cammy's rough pregnancy. The severe stress of the trial was tearing her up inside and making her hemorrhage. Her doctors feared she'd lose the child.

On the morning of the engagement party, we woke to find the bed covered with blood. She phoned a doctor and made an appointment for eleven A.M. On the way to the doctor's office, we stopped to have breakfast with Frankie Cestaro at the Bel Air Sands Hotel. After we finished, I handed Cammy a crumpled paper lunch bag and said, "Don't lose it." She suspected it held the money to pay for the party, but didn't give it much thought. Bags of cash were typical of the way I operated. In fact, Cammy thought so little about it that she left the bag, and the $10,000 it contained, on the toilet-paper dispenser in the hotel lobby's restroom. She didn't remember until nearly an hour later.

"Michael," she said in a panic at the doctor's office, "I left that bag you gave me in the bathroom!"

I told her not to worry. I called Cestaro and ordered him to search for the cash. He boldly entered the ladies' restroom and inspected the stalls.

"No way, chief. That money's history," Frankie reported.

I turned to Cammy, who was waiting nervously by the phone. "You're in luck," I lied. "Frankie found it, just where you left it."

She was elated. I was relieved that she went for it. I figured if I told her it was gone, she'd cancel the party, or stress out even worse and endanger the baby. Besides, I could empathize. I had once left $130,000 in a suitcase at the Island Inn in Westbury, Long Island. It was still there when I returned three hours later.

Cammy's luck, at least the way I partially designed it, was with her that morning. The doctor said that despite the hemorrhaging, the baby was unharmed. If she took it easy, she'd make it.

That evening, as two hundred people mingled at the Hotel Bel Air and paid their respects, she stayed in her seat. Despite the energetic music and the exhilaration of the event, she fought the urge to dance.

I put up a solid front, never letting on to Cammy how much I was dying inside. I wanted it to be a memorable event for her, especially if it was going to be our last. I knew her emotions rode with mine. If I let my defenses down and displayed my nervousness over the verdict, her shields would dissolve and she might suffer a miscarriage. I had to keep smiling, keep confident. I had to continue to make her believe that I was invincible.

Behind my smiling mask, I was hurting. I had developed two ulcers from the stress of the trial combined with the fear of losing Cammy. As I feared all along, I chose the worst possible time to fall in love, and I was suffering for it. The future appeared darker than ever. If I was convicted on any one of the seven counts in the loan-sharking/racketeering case, I was going away for thirty years. They had been after me for too long for me to expect a reasonable sentence. Even if I was acquitted, the Eastern District/Michael Franzese Task Force indictment was sure to follow. And there was now no longer any doubt that Iorizzo had turned. Not only was the fat man ratting, he was lying. They had marched him out during the loan-shark trial as a practice run for his future appearances.

I was also deeply worried about my children. I knew what it was like to lose a father to prison, how traumatic it is for children. The last thing I wanted to do was leave my kids without a father.

Something happened before the end of the trial that, for a few harrowing hours, made the pending verdict, Cammy's pregnancy, the Mob, and everything else insignificant. It caused me, for the first time in my life, to openly challenge my father and had a profound effect on our future relationship. It started with a call from Jimmy Angellino.

"The Boss wants you to come in for a meet at nine P.M."

"What's this about?"

"The Boss wants you in."

Angellino's voice was as lifeless as it had been on the day he told me they were going to hit Larry Carrozza. I immediately called my father, who was again out on parole. As I expected, he had just received a similar call, only his sit-down was scheduled for 7:30 P.M.

"We need to talk, Dad," I said. "I'll be right over."

"No, I'll come there," he said.

As I waited for my father, I thought about what had gone wrong. My operation was generating an immense amount of money, which in turn resulted in a rapid expansion of my crew. That brought unwanted notoriety. Those elements combined to make my Mob associates uncomfortable. There was talk—inflamed by the federal government and a local television news report—that I had broken away from the Colombos and had become the head of my own family. At the heart of these rumors was the mistaken belief that I was making more money than I was telling the bosses in Brooklyn and was holding back millions of dollars.

Complicating this were the actions of my parents. Although my father applauded my success, my mother was unable to accept the changing of the guard. She resented the fact that my life-style, and that of my wife, had surpassed hers, and that we had created our own identities. From her perspective, when my father was jailed, her status had also fallen. She hounded Dad about this, demanding to know why he wasn't in charge of my operation, and why they weren't reaping the wealth that I now possessed. She was relentless and drove him to question my men about the amount of money we were making. He even quizzed Markowitz and the Russians, who were terrified of him. They reported back to me, and I confronted my father. I told him he was telegraphing to Brooklyn that there was a rift between us. Plus, if my own father suspected me of hiding money, what would the bosses think.

"Dad, what are you doing?" I demanded. "You can't do this. You're going to get us both killed."

He vehemently denied that he had confronted my men and said they misread his intentions. As much as I wanted to believe him, I knew he wasn't telling the truth.

Angellino's call confirmed my worst fears. My father and I were in serious trouble. I'd heard about those kinds of calls all my life. My father had experienced them on the other end. You walk into a meeting like that, and they carry you out.

My senses had suddenly become so sharp, so pumped with adrenaline, that the whole world looked different. Colors were brighter. Sounds and smells were more intense. I could see everything around me in greater detail. My entire body was powering up for a fight to the death. And that was my problem. Instead of Dad and me banding together and going out in a blaze of gunfire, I knew that he would want us to walk into that room at our scheduled times like lambs to the slaughter and passively accept whatever fate the Mob decreed. Of all the aspects of the Mob I had grown to despise, the legendary death summons was the worst. I had vowed never to willfully walk into a room where someone was waiting to take my life.

This was the conflict I faced with my father. We would engage in a verbal, life or death struggle that pitted the old Mob values of strict adherence to the code against the saner interpretation held by America's second generation of mobsters. I wondered what argument, beyond blind militarylike allegiance, my father could use to support his position. His way had brought nothing but two decades of grief, hardship, and heartache to himself and his family.

When he arrived, I ushered him to the driveway of my home in Brookville. It was late afternoon and the air was chilly. As the sun set, I was reminded of all those hours my father and I had bounced that rubber ball off my grandfather's chimney, each of us fiercely determined to win our makeshift game. We had a different battle that evening, but this time, the stakes were our lives.

"I have a bad feeling about this, Dad. I don't like it, 'you in first and then me' stuff. This isn't right."

"Michael, this is our life. We have been given an order. We must obey."

"Dad, do you hear what you're saying? Do you understand? We have families. We both have wives and children to support. There are things that are more important than the Mob's self-serving oath. All this is over money. Greed and money. We've given them enough. We've given them more than anyone's ever given. Everything was going great. Then you started asking questions. I know why. I know it was Mom. But you started asking questions, planting seeds of doubt. And that caused them to start asking questions. And suddenly, the millions I was turning over weren't enough because the rumors were that I was making billions. Suddenly, they felt cheated. And on top of that, you've revealed to outsiders that we've broken our father/son bond. That's the worst betrayal of all. So now, they're calling us in. You know what's going to happen."

"I don't think so," he said.

"Neither one of us is sure. So why should we do this? Why risk our lives?"

"This is our way. Whatever happens tonight, happens."

"Don't give me that shit!" I screamed. I'd never taken that tone with my father. He just stood there like a rock, saying nothing, feeling nothing, determined to live by the code right to the end.

"Okay, Dad. Okay. I know how you are. I know this is your life and you believe in it. I know that you can't change. I know what the oath says—If they call us, we have to drop everything and go. Okay. But let's go together. Me and you, together. We shouldn't let anyone separate us."

"We can't. That's not how they want it. We can't change it. We can't show fear."

"Fear? Is that what this is about? Showing fear? You're going to walk in there and let them stick a gun to the back of your head and blow your brains out so you won't be accused by some punk of showing fear? You're going to let them kill me, your son, just because you don't want to show fear?"

"This is the life we chose," he repeated.

"Dad, you know, I always envisioned it would be me and you, side by side, machine guns in each hand, taking on the world. Me and you, back to back, going down like warriors. If we're going to die tonight, let's do it that way. Give me that respect. Give yourself that respect. Let's go out together, fighting."

He looked down and stared at the pavement. I grabbed him by the shoulders and forced him to look at me. I could feel the power in his body, but I couldn't feel the will anymore. The will was gone.

"Dad. Let me die fighting. Let me die with dignity!"

"That's not our way, Michael. We will go separately, the way they asked. Whatever happens, happens."

He walked to his car and opened the door.

"It's the right thing, Michael," he said. "We are sworn to obey. The oath and the life is more important than any two individuals. I'm going to go. And you must follow. You must!"

He entered the car and disappeared into the night.

I paced the driveway, then walked around the grounds of my home. My senses were even more intense than before. But now my mind began to rationalize, desperately trying to mask with intellect the primal signals my body was sending. Maybe I was overreacting. Maybe my father was so bravely following his beliefs because he knew something I didn't. Or maybe he knew that he wasn't the one on the spot, that he could disavow any detailed knowledge of my operation. That would be easy. I had specifically kept him distanced to protect him from being violated and having to go back to prison. Now he could use that to his advantage.

The time drew near. If I didn't show, it would reflect upon my father. If he had escaped his meeting, and I didn't show, I could be sentencing him to death. I got into my car and drove into Brooklyn. I parked on the

street and walked to the lunchonette where Jimmy Angellino was scheduled to pick me up. That was telling. Instead of being told where the
meeting would take place and driving there myself, I was to be driven to
an unknown location.

Jimmy was cold and distant as we drove. We had been made together and were close friends. I felt shaky and empty inside, but fought the
urge to question him. We drove in silence for about ten minutes. Jimmy
pulled up to a large, dark house in Brooklyn that I had never seen
before. It was a perfect place for a hit. I expected the meeting would be
downstairs in a soundproof basement. At that point, I would face two
possibilities. If I opened the door and found the room empty, I was
dead. I'd be clocked before I could turn my head. If there were people
in the room, that meant they were giving me the respect of a hearing
first. In that situation, I expected acting boss Andrew Russo—Persico
was in jail—and the entire family hierarchy to be sitting around a table.
There would be a single, empty chair to Russo's right. At the end of the
table would be a young soldier, a man who didn't belong at such a high-
level meeting. He would be stationed on my side, but set back so I
couldn't see him if he got up. This person would be my assassin.

I walked down a narrow stairway, took a deep breath, and opened
the door. There were people in the room. I found everything exactly as I
envisioned in my second scenario. It was as if I had seen that table, those
men—and my death—in forgotten dreams buried in my subconscious.
The assassin was just as I had imagined, a young, hard-looking man sitting alone at the end of the table on my side. I saw a bead of sweat on his
temple. His hands trembled. I knew Russo—my first captain when I was
a recruit—would give the signal. And I knew that whatever it was, no
matter how secret or cloaked the acting boss tried to make it, I would
recognize it as clear as a flashing billboard. It would be my last thought.

"We want to ask you about your business," Russo opened as I sat
down in the chair to his right.

"Go ahead," I said. For the next two hours, Russo and the family
grilled me on my operation. I answered them firmly in a strong, unwa-
vering voice. I had decided that if I couldn't go out shooting, at least I
could wage this war with my wits.

"Ask me all your questions. I've held nothing back. If you think I'm
making more than I've said, show me the facts and figures. Bring in my
accusers and let me confront them. You're attacking me with specula-

tion, rumors and conjecture. I've given you the exact percentage I promised. I've generated this money myself, and I've generously shared. You're listening to bullshit and reading stories in newspapers. You're taking Larry Iorizzo's wild statements on their face. He's exaggerating the income to build up his importance as a government witness. It's a routine move by someone desperate to stay out of prison."

Russo grilled me hard about Iorizzo. The fat man had rolled, and he was my responsibility. If Iorizzo fingered a single made man aside from myself, it would cost me my life.

"I've sheltered everyone in the family from Iorizzo," I continued. "He's my responsibility and he won't be able to take down anyone but me. I doubt he can even do that. I followed the rules. I've kept my oath. I've protected the family."

"But your father said ..."

I knew that move. Like a trial attorney or a homicide detective, Russo was trying to trap me with something I said that didn't match my father's story. And he and his associates were going to put words into my father's mouth to see if they could get me to falter or stumble.

"Don't tell me what my father said. Don't play that game with me," I countered. "Don't put me in that position. I'm not going to go for that bullshit. You should never have gotten my father involved in this. He doesn't know my operation. I've protected him for his own good. I've kept him clean. I fought all my life to get him out of jail, and I'm fighting now to keep him out. If you wanted to speak to us, you should have brought us in here together. If he's going to say something, let him say it in front of me. My father and I are together on this. We've always been together. Don't believe anyone who tells you differently. If you have questions, you ask me. You don't ask him."

The tenseness in the room eased. Russo gave a signal, but it wasn't the one I'd expected. He motioned for someone to serve the wine. I turned and subtly glanced at the assassin. He looked relieved. They had accepted my explanation—for now.

The wine tasted sharp and bitter. My body had been on such a razor's edge that it had altered my internal chemistry. My "brothers" walked around the room, chatted with me and talked among themselves, but I couldn't concentrate on their words. They tried to act like everything was back to normal. But it wasn't. Just moments before, they were going to sentence me to death. I could never forgive them. It would never be the same again. Not with this family, or my own.

"Jimmy, if they were going to whack me, would you have told me?" I asked as he drove me back to my car.

"What would you expect?"

"Hell yeah, I'd expect you to tell me!" As I said it, the truth drained from the words. Jimmy picked up on it.

"If they were going to whack me, would you tell me, Michael?"

"No," I said. "That's sick, isn't it Jimmy? What kind of friends are we? What kind of life is this?"

"It's our life, Michael. The life we chose. We knew what we were getting into. You especially. You've lived with it from the day you were born."

That was true. Who better than me to understand the life. My father had acted just as anyone would have predicted—absolute, blind adherence to the code.

"I tell ya something, Michael," Angellino said. "You got some balls. If I were in your shoes, I don't know if I could have taken it. You were ice. Man, you were ice. You sat in this car like you were going to dinner."

"Don't think my heart wasn't pounding," I admitted. Before I got out, Jimmy made a rare and unexpected confession.

"I wouldn't have told you if it was a whack, but I can tell you now, you had a serious problem. Both you and your dad. You somehow talked your way out of it. Brilliant performance. But I'll tell you something. And this is between me and you. It goes to the grave with us. Your father, he didn't help you in there tonight."

"I can't believe that," I said.

"Believe it," Angellino insisted.

I knew Jimmy wasn't lying. And I knew what my father had done. He played dumb. It was the right move to make in that situation. In fact, I set it up that way. But still, it hurt. He could have taken a stronger stand and told them that everything between us was okay, that everything else was bullshit.

But that wasn't his way. It wasn't the Mob's way.

My father went to sleep feeling proud that night. He had obeyed his oath under the most trying circumstances. He had faced death without showing fear. He had done his duty. I wished I could have viewed it that way. Instead, I felt like a sap, like I was the ultimate sucker. I should never have gone to that house. I should never have risked the future of my children and my new life with Cammy by playing this insane, deadly game. I had violated my own vow by willingly marching into a death chamber. For what? To show a few mobsters in Brooklyn that I had balls? To justify my life to them?

In Dad's own way, there was a measure of courage in what he did. But our family, the bond between him and me, should have come first. He should not have asked his son to go into that house. Because of that, I felt a tremendous sense of loss. Although we had escaped with our lives, something did die that night. An insecure little boy had lost the blind hero-worship of his father.

The one positive thing I did take from that evening is the knowledge that I could face death without succumbing to fear. I could maintain my composure enough to survive on my intellect. But the next time, if I did confront death again, I would damn well go out fighting.

A sweetly ironic epitaph to this is that a few years later, the tables would be turned on Andrew Russo, my chief interrogator. Russo's brother-in-law turned undercover informant and rolled on eight of the top Colombo bosses, including Russo, Carmine Persico, Young Allie Boy Persico, and Jerry Langella—sending them all to prison. When Russo is released from prison sometime in the mid 1990s, he'll be called into a room—probably an empty room.

By the time the jury began its deliberations, the snow had melted and the breezes turned from bitter to warm. On the morning of the verdict, Friday, April 19, I stared at Cammy for hours while she slept and continued to stare after she awakened. I wanted to burn her image into my brain so I would never forget. I wanted to memorize every fleck of color in her eyes, every crease in her lips, every contour of her smooth skin. I felt that the visual information I stored that morning might have to carry me through the rest of my life—a bleak, depressing life locked behind bars.

The jury had been deliberating since the previous Monday. I told Cammy they wouldn't come back with a verdict until the following week. That was a ruse. I suspected they would reach their decision on Friday. Jurors don't like to be held over the weekend.

I flew Cammy's mother to New York earlier in the week to be with her just in case the news was bad.

Driving to the courthouse that morning, I talked with her over the car phone the entire way. "I love you, Cammy, don't ever forget that."

As I sat in the courtroom, awaiting the verdict, all I could do was think of her. I replayed the still-fresh memories of Florida, from the moment I saw her at the pool to the first time we made love.

"Count one, Franzese, not guilty."

It was a good start, but by no means was the battle won. It was a twenty-eight-count indictment, and my last charge was count twenty-seven. The verdicts were read in order and applied to each of the fifteen defendants. I had to listen for an agonizing thirty-five minutes to make sure I was cleared on all the counts. As the other defendants' "guilty"s began mixing with the "not guilty"s, the stress and pressure became like a vise tightening on my head.

"Count twenty-seven, Franzese, not guilty."

I had escaped again.

I rushed to a telephone. "Baby, it's over," I said. "Not guilty!"

"What?"

"Not guilty! Not guilty! Can you believe it? All the Italians were found not guilty!"

She screamed for joy and hugged her mother. They both bounced up and down on the bed. Her hemorrhaging ended the moment she heard the words "not guilty."

When the scorecards were tallied, the result was a split decision. All of the Jewish defendants and their associates were convicted. All the alleged Mob guys were found innocent. For once, I felt the system had worked perfectly. The jury had somehow managed to wade through the government's bull and separate the guilty from the innocent.

U.S. District Judge Leonard B. Sand handed down stiff sentences. Hyman and Cooper were each given thirty years and fined $160,000. Hyman rolled over and entered the witness protection program. Cooper, interestingly enough, escaped. The financier spent nearly two years on the lam before he was captured in Florida.

There was one notable exception to the tough prison terms. Judge Sand went easy on the rabbi and gave him five years' probation and two hundred hours of community service.

As I drove home to Cammy, the tension that had built up inside me was released in a burst of laughter. It was the rabbi's money that helped float the operation.

The singing rabbi was Mr. Big.

CHAPTER 18

In June 1984, while I was busy falling in love and filming *Knights of the City*, in that order, my father completed his two-year parole-violation sentence and was released. I interrupted my activities to present him with a new Mercedes to celebrate the occasion.

I had long given up hope that my father would return to his 1960s stature. It didn't matter much anymore anyway. I had enough money to make kings out of ten thousand fathers. I just wanted him to live out his life in comfort and dignity.

He wasn't free long before his other family decided to undermine the second part of my master plan. In a rare decree, Carmine "the Snake" Persico demoted my father from captain to soldier. The Colombo boss said the move was intended to take pressure off my father by easing him into retirement and decreasing the chance that his parole would be violated again. Few believed it. Persico could have allowed him to lay low with his title intact. Most saw the demotion as a direct message to me that regardless of how many millions I was making on Long Island, and how large my army was growing, Persico was still the boss.

I was furious. I viewed it as a continuation of the insults heaped upon my father by the "brotherhood" he had sacrificed half his life to protect. He could have made a dozen different deals with the feds to wipe away his conviction, but he had always followed the oath and stayed silent.

"Aw, let it go, Michael. Let it go," he told me. "What can you do?"

It was another broken strand in the fraying rope that bound me to New York, and to the Mob. My life was now Cammy and California, sunny skies, warmth, and the Pacific Ocean. I stored the disrespect shown to my father in the ever-fattening file I kept in my mind detailing the Mob's hypocrisy.

• • •

Free from the burden of the trial, I quickly got back to the business of settling my life. I worked out a divorce settlement with Maria, giving her the million-dollar Brookville home along with a million-dollar interest-bearing account that paid $7,500 a month living expenses. We settled the matter ourselves without attorneys.

I didn't, however, tell Maria about Cammy. Nor did I tell my mother, whom I feared would run to Maria and complicate matters.

Shortly afterward, I arrived at the condo in Brentwood carting a dozen yellow roses, a bottle of Taittinger, and a big smile.

"My divorce is final," I told Cammy. "Now we can get married. Start planning."

I uncorked the champagne, poured us each a glass, and made a toast.

"To you and me, forever."

Cammy scouted the best hotels in the Los Angeles area for the celebration. She decided upon the Beverly Hilton because of the stunning ballroom and the professional manner of Linda Kent, the Hilton's director of party planning. She consulted with Dr. Myron Taylor at Westwood Hills Christian Church and determined that July 27, 1985, would be the best date.

During the second week of May, Cammy, her mother, and her five-year-old sister, Raquel, traveled to Las Vegas to visit her grandfather. I met them on the third day of their stay and joined them at Caesar's Palace. The following day, we took Raquel to Circus Circus, the giant casino-hotel that features a lively indoor circus and circular carnival arcade. As we walked to the arcade, Cammy's mother spotted the Chapel of the Fountain, the hotel's blue-bathed wedding chapel.

"Why don't you two get married now?" she said.

Cammy and I joked that we were both too chicken. Her mother persisted, no doubt motivated by the advancing state of her daughter's six-week pregnancy and the always volatile status of my life.

"You two are in love, so why wait?" she pressed. "You should make it right."

"Okay," I said.

"Okay," Cammy said.

We approached the chapel and looked inside. It was tiny but attractive. It looked like a pocket church.

"Wait a second," I said. "Let's go back to the hotel and think this over."

At the hotel, we teased and goaded each other some more. Finally, I picked up the phone and made the appointment.

"It's set for tomorrow at three-thirty."

As the hour approached, we eased our nervousness by continuing our strange game of marital chicken.

"I'm getting ready—are you getting ready?" I said, searching the closet for my clothes.

"I'm getting ready—are you?" Cammy parroted.

We repeated the banter with each item of clothing.

"I'm putting my socks on."

"I'm putting on my stockings."

Once dressed—me in black pants and a black-and-gray plaid shirt, Cammy in a white dress with blue flowers—we gathered up Mrs. Garcia and Raquel and went to the chapel. My palms became clammy and my knees buckled a little the moment I entered. Cammy stayed cool until she started walking down the fifteen-foot aisle.

Much to Mrs. Garcia's delight and Raquel's boredom, we made it to the altar and were married. We celebrated by seeing Bill Cosby and Sammy Davis, Jr., perform that evening at Caesar's Palace.

After the show, Cammy called her father to give him the good news. He wasn't pleased.

"Why didn't you tell me? I could have flown down!" Seferino was so angry at being left out that he hung up.

"Don't worry about him," Mrs. Garcia said. "He'll get over it."

The one-hundred-dollar Circus Circus marriage in Las Vegas was so quick and offbeat it didn't seem real. I knew how nervous Cammy's mother was about her daughter's pregnancy, and understood Mrs. Garcia's impatience with the July ceremony. I did it more for Mrs. Garcia than for Cammy. I wanted to assure everyone that my intentions were honorable.

While the Vegas wedding was legal in the eyes of the law, the July wedding at Westwood Hills Christian Church would be a union in the eyes of God. That aspect of the ceremony was troubling me. I hadn't thought much about God in the past decade. When I was younger, I had relied upon the Catholic Church and parochial schools to handle that part of my life. After two decades of Masses, communions, confessions,

Lents, ashes on the forehead, priests, nuns, sacraments, dashboard saints, Hail Marys, and rosaries, nothing had taken root. When my schooling ended and my father stopped driving me to church, my religion faded. Stealing tax money and being a good Mob soldier became my prime considerations. Neither jibed with what I had learned in Catholic school.

Cammy began watering whatever dormant religious seed I had in my soul. She outlined her beliefs and gently pressed me to join her as a born-again Christian. I went to church with her at Westwood Hills Christian Church and read the Bible for the first time. I focused on the four Gospels—Matthew, Mark, Luke and John—that chronicle the life and death of Jesus. I was moved by Jesus' story and the persecution He suffered.

The pending church wedding pushed the born-again issue to a head. We were going to be married in a church that revolved around being a born-again Christian. If I was going to be married there, if I was going to take part in their ceremony, then I felt I should be a born-again Christian like my wife.

In late May, I was sitting on the bedroom rug next to our bed at eleven P.M. reading from John's Gospel while Cammy slept. I came across a verse I remembered seeing on the banners near the end zones at professional football games. Usually when one team kicked an extra point, there would be someone in the crowd behind the goal posts waving a sheet that said "John 3:16." I had wondered about it, but was never curious enough to track down a Bible and look it up. Now I had stumbled upon it by chance:

"For God loved the world so much that he gave his only Son so that anyone who believes in him shall not perish but have eternal life."

I read the verse over five times. It was clear why, of all the verses in the Bible, the football-stadium Christians had chosen that one to flash into the nation's consciousness. The verse was a summation and a confirmation of everything Cammy had been telling me.

I turned, looked across the bed, reached out my hand, and gently shook my wife awake.

"Cammy, I want to be a Christian. Help me say the prayer."

"What?" she mumbled.

"Help me say the prayer."

She leaped off the bed and knelt down beside me before I could change my mind. She clutched my left hand in her right and bowed her head.

"Dear God, thank you for listening to my prayers and putting this desire in Michael's heart."

She then led me through the short prayer that she'd told me makes one a born-again Christian. I said it out loud as I squeezed her hand:

"Dear God, I know I'm a sinner and only Jesus can save me. I'm willing to turn away from my sin and submit to your will. I believe that you sent your son Jesus to die on the cross and shed His blood to pay the price for my sins, and that He arose again. I ask you, dear God, to come into my heart and save me. I ask that Jesus Christ become the Lord of my life. Amen."

"Oh, Michael, now you're saved!" Cammy said, hugging me and crying. "Now if anything happens, you'll go to heaven and we can be together there forever."

"Are you sure that's it?" I said. "That's all I have to do?"

"That's it."

"Are you sure it's that easy?"

"It's that easy!"

I climbed onto the bed and thought about what I had done. I couldn't help comparing it to the other oath I had taken, the other time I had been "born again." That oath was shrouded in ceremony. There was a half-circle of men, dim lights, blood and fire. Many wiseguys had waited twenty to twenty-five years for a chance to be inducted. Now my wife was telling me that my name had been written into the Book of Life and I would live forever in heaven because of a simple prayer I said while kneeling on a lavender rug by a king-sized bed. And it didn't matter what I had done in the past or how much money I'd stolen.

It was hard to believe.

I reached for the remote control and flicked on the television. I scanned the cable channels until I saw John Travolta walking down a New York street swinging a can of paint as Barry Gibb's falsetto energized the scene. I locked onto the channel as I always did when the movie was on. The story of the Brooklyn kid trying to disco-dance his way out of his mundane life was one of my favorite movies.

I spent the first two hours of my new life as a born-again Christian watching *Saturday Night Fever* on Home Box Office for the twentieth time.

• • •

The church wedding and gala reception were solely for Cammy and her family. I invited only a few people from New York, including a brother and a sister, neither of whom showed. The reason for the New York blackout was again my mother. I still didn't feel comfortable about telling her, nor was I confident that she wouldn't do something to aggravate me or interfere with the proceedings. And I didn't want it thrown in Maria's face. I did tell my father, and he understood. Since I wasn't inviting my mother, I couldn't invite many others from back East lest my mother find out. So, like everything else in New York aside from my children, I just blotted it out. I was starting a new life in California. No need to spoil the moment with any reminders of past and future troubles in New York. If people would later feel insulted and betrayed, I'd deal with it.

For Cammy, the wedding started out as an emotional wringer. The night before the ceremony, her maid of honor, Rosita Soto, and three of her eleven bridesmaids didn't have finished dresses. The seamstress, a relative of the Garcias, said not to worry. She promised to rise early and whip them up in time for the two o'clock ceremony. The next morning, when the young ladies went to retrieve the dresses, the shop was closed. Peering through the window, they saw that the cobalt-blue dresses had been cut and partially stitched but weren't finished. They called Cammy and she burst into tears. Her dressless cohorts tracked down the seamstress at her home. She was sleeping blissfully. They roused her out of bed and all but hog-tied her and dragged her to the shop. Cammy alternated between murderous waves of anger and wails of despair as her bridesmaids reported on the progress. By the time they made it to the church, the bridesmaids had to augment their dresses with pins to keep the hastily sewn garments from falling apart.

I wasn't faring too well either. Although I had already married Cammy in Vegas, I was extremely nervous before the ceremony. I wiped the sweat from my brow and paced up and down the church hallways. The fact that I had no relatives and few friends of my own to talk with added to my anxiety. Unlike Vegas, this was a church. This was a real marriage, a binding that was certain to shake up my life. How, I wasn't sure. All I knew is that I wanted this young woman more than I had ever wanted anything else, more than I ever thought I could want anything.

The ceremony went without a hitch. The moment the music started, Cammy forgot about the problems with the dresses. She floated down the aisle in a five-thousand-dollar white wedding dress made of lace, satin, and silk and dotted with pearls. A ten-foot train trailed behind her like a snowstorm. A pearl and sequined headpiece, specially ordered from Italy, was woven into her long, dark hair.

The seamstress's daughter sang "Endless Love" while her mother watched from the audience with the rest of the overflowing Garcia clan.

The reception at the Beverly Hilton's grand ballroom featured caviar, escargots, and separate walls of Italian and Mexican food set under each country's flag. The name of every guest was displayed in Swiss chocolate at the tables, while a basket spilling over with an assortment of rich chocolate served as the centerpiece. The master of ceremonies was Leon Isaac Kennedy. Prince and Michael Jackson impersonators performed, as did a full orchestra. Later in the evening, a disc jockey played dance music as Cammy's brothers and friends entertained the crowd by break-dancing. During the dollar dance, a Mexican tradition, guests pinned dollars to Cammy's dress and danced with her. Female guests similarly paid me a dollar for a dance.

The tension of the dress problems combined with Cammy's pregnancy and the weight of her dress to drain her energy. Midway through the festivities, she teetered and felt faint. She retreated to her room in the hotel, escaped from the heavy gown, and rested on the bed for twenty-five minutes. She then climbed back into the dress and returned to the party.

Late in the evening, she bumped into her first boyfriend, a young man named Rudy Chavarria she'd known in the seventh grade. She thought it especially meaningful that "my first boyfriend and my last" were at the wedding. After kissing her on the cheek, Chavarria offered the comment of the night: "You definitely have come a long way from Norwalk."

We honeymooned in Hawaii at the Hilton on Maui. The island paradise reminded us of our halcyon days in Fort Lauderdale and Miami. We shopped, swam, danced, ate, made love, and watched glorious sunsets. Even losing a race with a wicked tropical thunderstorm in an open jeep failed to dampen our spirits.

Returning home to California, we were greeted by a court summons. It was from the seamstress. She sued, claiming she hadn't been paid enough for her services.

The seamstress won by default. By the time the case reached court, I had to be in a higher court on another coast.

• • •

During the next three months, I split my time between New York and Los Angeles. Despite my hectic, bicoastal schedule, I managed to attend the Thursday-night Lamaze natural-childbirth classes with Cammy for six straight weeks without missing a session. Sometimes I'd fly in from New York just for the evening class, then leave that same night on the red-eye.

While I was practicing breathing exercises with Cammy, the Michael Franzese Task Force continued its basement meetings in Uniondale, Long Island, intensifying its efforts to put me away for good. By then I knew that Ed McDonald of the Eastern District was on my trail, but I still didn't know about the interagency-task-force muscle he had behind him.

To get closer to its prey, some of the task-force meetings were held at the IRS criminal investigations office in Smithtown, Long Island, a few blocks from Peter Raneri's restaurant, where some of my crew, including Iorizzo, Markowitz, and the Russians, frequently ate. Agents mounted video cameras in the trees around the restaurant to monitor their activities.

McDonald's investigation was so intense I could feel the heat all the way to California. Most of my energy was directed at preparing for the next indictment. I began constructing my defense long before the arrest. And although I was 5–0 in trials, I knew my luck was bound to run out. I liquidated all my property, including my boats, jet, and helicopter. I placed double and triple mortgages upon my real estate holdings; if the government seized them, they'd have to deal with the banks.

I instructed John Jacobs to assure all the investigating bodies that I would voluntarily surrender when the indictments were announced. This included notifying the prosecutors who were investigating me in Florida. There was no need, I had Jacobs explain, to send the storm troopers to ambush me. I wanted to spare my wife and our California neighbors from the sudden police invasions that had marred my life when I was growing up.

During one of my New York trips, Frankie Cestaro met me at the airport and said there was an important meeting we needed to attend at Shelly Levine's office on Long Island. Gathered were Levine, Joe Galizia, Michael Markowitz (free on bail), David Bogatin, and several others in the gas business.

I sensed something was wrong the moment I entered the building. It felt like a trap, which it was. Cestaro was unaware that the Long Island Organized Crime Oil Industry Task Force had wired Levine's office for sound and rigged the building's entrance for video. In a battle of espionage and counterespionage technology, the task force had planted state-of-the-art miniature audio receivers in the office that could not be detected by the weekly electronic bug sweeps performed by a retired police detective Levine had hired, and were not affected by the white-noise emitters installed in the office to jam listening devices.

Instead of going to Levine's office, I anchored myself at a table in the coffee shop downstairs and ordered Cestaro to tell anyone who wanted to see me to meet me there. I advised my associate to return immediately after delivering the message.

Police detectives and prosecutors, including oil task force spearhead Ray Jermyn, head of the Suffolk County Organized Crime Bureau and a member of the joint task force, listened to the entire meeting. Jermyn dispatched teams of detectives into the building to find out where the hell I was. They spotted me in the coffee shop. Jermyn kept sending in fresh teams to see if I was making any movement toward joining my associates upstairs. The investigators reported back that I was reading the stock-market listings in the *Wall Street Journal*.

By the time the meeting ended, everyone in the room upstairs had made damning admissions of criminal activity. Included among the self-incriminated was Frankie Cestaro, who had lingered in Levine's office for more than an hour instead of returning as I had ordered.

As rumors of an indictment swirled, my men began to panic. Two came to me one afternoon on Long Island with a request to hit James Feynman, the operator of the Babylon Cove Marina. Feynman had testified against me in the loan-shark case and was expected to give further testimony about a credit-card scheme in the pending case.

"We can get to him—we know where he is. Just give the word and it'll be one less problem for us."

I thought of the prayer I'd said with Cammy back in May. I was a born-again Christian now. It was an oath I took seriously, just as I had my previous oath. I figured God could understand lapses and failures in smaller areas as I tried to escape my old life, but ordering someone's death? I had avoided doing that before I was a Christian. Feynman was certain to hurt me, but there was no way I could order the man killed.

"No," I said, shaking my head. "That's never been my way. We can't start killing all the witnesses. That'll just get us in more trouble."

•　•　•

Back in California, my first child with Cammy, Miquelle, was born on November 25, 1985, at Cedars Sinai Hospital in Beverly Hills. It was a difficult birth. Cammy was in labor for twenty-two hours, gritting her teeth and sucking on ice cubes and lemon drops. She taped pictures of our wedding on the wall by her bed to provide inspiration and take her mind off the pain. At one point, the agony was so great she began clawing at her beautiful face. I rushed over and offered my body as a human scratching pole. She grabbed me and dug in.

When the child finally arrived, I was allowed to cut the umbilical cord. That evening, I slept in the hospital in a bed next to my wife. The next morning, I awoke deathly pale with my head about to explode from a pounding headache. I had stayed by Cammy's side without eating or drinking for nearly a day, and it caught up with me. I rushed down to the hospital's pharmacy, grabbed a bottle of Excedrin and a carton of orange juice, ripped each open, and swallowed four tablets before paying.

Two days later, on Thanksgiving, I cooked the turkey for my wife and infant child. I slaved in the kitchen with a towel draped around my waist. At one point, I caught a glimpse of myself in the bathroom mirror, holding a large spoon and knife and wearing my makeshift apron.

"Do you understand who I am?" I said to Cammy. "Can you believe this?"

Cammy, who still really didn't have a clue, merely laughed. The following day, when Frankie Cestaro called, Cammy explained that I was busy vacuuming.

"Don't tell them that!" I scolded.

"Why? It's the truth," she countered.

The Long Island don had become California's Mr. Mom.

CHAPTER 19

On December 16, 1985, Paul Castellano, boss of the Gambino family, was gunned down in what was believed to be a power play for family leadership. My flea-market rival John Gotti ascended to the Gambino family throne. The New York media ran with the story. It would mark a banner week for Mob news.

Three days after Castellano's bloody death, I was awakened at 5:30 A.M. by a call from Frankie Cestaro.

"I have friends at my home."

The "friends" were FBI agents. The joint task force's dime had been dropped, and they would be coming for me any minute. I quickly dressed and left the house. Calling New York from a pay phone, I learned that an army of twenty agents, along with an NBC television crew, had swarmed my Brookville home before dawn looking for me. Maria told them that I no longer lived there. They accepted her explanation and left.

The feds obviously had ignored my request to come in on my own. They were bent on staging an arrest, preferably in view of network television. I called John Jacobs and told him to tell everyone I would surrender on January 2, after the holidays. Jacobs argued that the feds weren't about to wait and advised me to come in and post bond. I told my attorney it wasn't going to be that easy this time. I had heard about investigations concerning old charges, including my alleged death threat against my father's probation officer. I was certain that the prosecutors were building a case to paint me as "a danger to society" in order to keep me in jail without bond up to and throughout the trial. I knew that the prosecutors were weary of my past success at ramrodding my defense, and that they wanted me locked up so I couldn't mount another winning effort. Jacobs disagreed, assuring me I would make bond.

Cammy met me that afternoon for lunch. I was cheerful and acted like nothing was wrong. She had an appointment at a local beauty salon to get her hair trimmed. I offered to drive her. On the way, the phone beeped in my white Mercedes.

Cammy's heart sank when she heard my end of the conversation. "Who else was arrested?" I said without thinking.

When I finished, she forced herself to ask what happened, hoping what she suspected wasn't true.

"The fireworks went off in New York," I said. "Everyone's been arrested. They want me to turn myself in."

"Now?"

"Now."

"Not again," she said, bursting into tears.

The phone rang a second time. It was Cammy's sister Sabrina. She said FBI agents had surrounded our Brentwood condo. That scared Cammy even more. Policemen she understood. FBI agents? That had to mean I had done something really bad.

"Is this the way it's going to be the rest of our lives?" she said through her tears. "Every six months, FBI agents are going to come to our home?"

The FBI agents grilled Sabrina. She clammed up, pretending to be a baby-sitter. I circled the area and explained to my wife that I had decided to surrender in Florida. I told her the feds were acting like asses, so I would steal their thunder by giving up to the state authorities in Fort Lauderdale. I dropped Cammy a block away from our home and told her I was going to the Bel Air Sands Hotel. "Don't try to come. You'll just lead the FBI to me," I explained.

Two agents met Cammy at the door. She told them I had already left for New York. They asked if they could come inside the apartment and she said sure. The agents questioned her about herself, her marriage, the baby, and anything else they could think of. Cammy played the part of the totally ignorant wife, which wasn't that difficult since I still hadn't told her much about my life. The agents left but continued to stake out the building.

When I called, I was mad that she'd let the agents in. "You never, *ever* let them inside the house," I said. "You meet them at the door and leave them out there."

Meanwhile, Sabrina was standing on the balcony of the first-floor condominium chatting with a handsome Italian FBI agent. He asked the pretty, tousled-haired teenager if she was an actress or a model, and was a few smiles away from asking her for a date when Cammy ordered her inside. Sabrina held firm. Cammy had to go out and get her.

"I'm sorry we have to do this, Mrs. Franzese," the agent said. "We're just doing our job."

"Yeah, great job," Cammy snapped, pulling Sabrina inside.

"These guys are here to put my husband in jail, and now they're scamming on my sister! I can't believe it," she exclaimed.

I drove to the Gap clothing store in Westwood and bought a pair of jeans and a striped shirt for the trip to Florida. While I was shopping, Cammy made a test run to Ralph's supermarket on Wilshire Boulevard to see if she would be followed. She was. She noticed that the agents waited outside in the parking lot instead of going into the store. The wheels spun in her mind. She could drive to a mall, go in one end, come out the other, and catch a taxi to get to me. Despite my instructions to the contrary, she felt she had to see me. Like me, she had a premonition that this time I wouldn't be coming back.

Returning home, Cammy packed some of my clothes and stuffed them in a garment bag. As the hours wore on, the number of agents surrounding the building dwindled. The randy Italian outside the balcony had departed. Cammy sent Sabrina out for a walk to survey the situation. Sabrina reported that the remaining agents were staking out the apartment's entrance.

Cammy went to the balcony, dropped the garment bag to the grass, then climbed down the balcony wall. She braced her feet on a garden-hose reel, then jumped to the grass. She picked up the garment bag, ducked into the parking garage, hopped into the midnight-blue Nissan 300 ZX I had bought her for Thanksgiving, and sped out of the building. She drove around the next hour, darting in and out of traffic, stopping to get gas, and weaving across parking lots to determine if she had a tail. Far as she could tell, there was none. She drove to the Bel Air Sands, slipped into the elevator as unobtrusively as possible, and found my room. She tapped on the door.

The knock nearly sent me through the roof. "Who is it?" I said.

"Me."

"Are you alone?"

"Yes."

"Are you sure?"

"Yes, Michael. Yes. Let me in."

I opened the door and looked sternly at my impetuous wife. "Why did you take the chance?"

"I don't care. I had to see you."

I waved her in, locked the door, and squeezed her tightly.

"I couldn't find a flight to Miami," I said. "I tried to charter a jet, but none were available."

She picked up on my apprehension about New York. Florida seemed less menacing. It was sunny, and that's where we met. There was no logic to it, but this was no time for logic. We were grasping onto anything positive or pleasant. She grabbed the phone in one hand and the Yellow Pages in the other and began calling every airline. She found an Eastern flight that could get me to Fort Lauderdale with two stops. She made the reservation in the name of her younger brother Cuauhtemoc Garcia, a name I couldn't even pronounce.

We ordered room service, shared a solemn dinner, then lay on the bed for two hours hugging and crying.

"Who's going to take care of me if you go away?" Cammy whimpered. I hadn't even left and she already felt terribly lonely and afraid.

I brushed the tears off her cheek and looked into her huge, frightened eyes. She was just a baby, a scared child.

"We'll get through this," I promised. "Just try to be strong. I'll call you as soon as I can. Have your family stay with you. I don't want you to be alone—not for one night."

She cried the whole way to the airport. It tore me up to see her in such anguish. As I drove, tears ran from under my glasses and down my cheeks. "Don't cry," I said, ignoring my own tears. "Everything will be okay."

At the departure ramp, I gathered my things, said goodbye, and walked away. I stopped, turned, and gave Cammy a wink.

While I headed toward Florida, the feds searched the airline listings to try and intercept me. They stationed agents at the airports in Miami and Fort Lauderdale. They were looking for Michael Franzese, not Cuauhtemoc Garcia, and Cammy's quick thinking helped me foil their plans. During a stopover in Dallas, I passed by a row of newspaper boxes and was struck by a headline in *The New York Times* announcing my indictment. I fished in my pocket for some coins, dropped them into the slot, and removed a paper. As I flew to Fort Lauderdale, I read about the mounting troubles of a young Cosa Nostra capo. The weariness of the all-night flight made the words of the story intermingle with scenes from my life. It was such a contrast. I found it difficult to comprehend that I was the hunted criminal being written about on the front page of *The New York Times.*

Arriving in Fort Lauderdale, I hid my face as I walked through the terminal. I flagged a cab and directed the driver to a nearby McDonald's. Jacobs had arranged for me to meet a Broward County detective at the fast-food restaurant. The friendly detective led me to his car and drove directly into the garage area of the courthouse in order to dodge the FBI agents staking out the building. The agents were intent upon intercepting me on the courthouse steps, pulling rank on the local police, and shanghaiing me to New York. Since the local Florida police didn't like the FBI's Gestapo tactics any more than I did, we were allies.

Inside, I was charged with sixty-five counts of Florida's massive 177-count tax-evasion indictment. I posted 10 percent of a $124,000 bond and satisfied the state obligation.

"I know," I told the detectives after being symbolically released. "The feds are waiting downstairs."

A heavily armed band of grim-faced FBI agents took over from there. They started driving me to the Metropolitan Correction Center in Miami, a civilized federal facility, when a message squawked over the car radio: "Divert the prisoner to Dade County."

I sunk back into my seat. They were going to bring me to the same Miami hellhole that had cracked Iorizzo. I arrived at the North Dade Detention Center and was assigned a cell. I quickly began to understand why Iorizzo had turned. The place was filthy. The inmates were filthy. The food was terrible. And hardly anyone spoke English. It was like being in prison in a third-world country.

All weekend long, the television blaring in the county jail broadcasted news reports of my arrest, in English and Spanish. My fellow Florida inmates had never seen a real-life mobster before. Loony as they were, they were impressed. They treated me like a celebrity. Many asked in broken English how they could join "the famous American Mafia."

Upon Jacobs's advice, I waived extradition to New York. My attorney wanted to have my federal bond hearing in New York instead of Florida. In retrospect, it was a questionable decision. They hardly knew me in

Florida so I'd probably have made bail. In New York, I was a certified, second-generation, blue-blood gangster. They'd fight to keep me locked up.

Three long, miserable days after I arrived in South Florida, two task force members, Suffolk County police detective Frank Morro and U.S. Postal Service agent John LaPerla, flew to Miami. They came to escort the "Long Island don," as the United States Congress had all but dubbed me, to New York. Morro and LaPerla were decent and didn't bother to handcuff me until we arrived at Islip Airport in Long Island. Even then, the handcuffs were a show for the crowd of reporters waiting to record my arrival. The reporters aimed their cameras and shouted questions at me as I was taken to a waiting car. I was driven to the federal courthouse in Uniondale, Long Island, and taken to a courtroom a few floors above the same basement conference room where the Michael Franzese Task Force had sealed my fate.

By some stroke of demented bad luck, the judge assigned to the case was Jacob Mishler—the same Jacob Mishler who had presided over my father's cases and had sentenced him to fifty years in prison nearly two decades before. The same Judge Mishler who had overruled our appeals attempting to prove that my father had been framed. The same Judge Mishler whose daughter I was said to have planned to kidnap. The same Judge Jacob Mishler whom my mother once sarcastically applauded in open court, screamed insults at, and openly accused of being part of a vicious scheme to frame her husband.

I would enter that courtroom guilty, with no hope of being proven innocent.

John Jacobs immediately filed to have Mishler removed from the case, citing the judge's long, stormy history with the Franzese family. Despite the logic behind it, I wasn't in complete agreement with the motion. There was no question that Mishler would be tough during the trial and devastating during sentencing. I'd be lucky to get a "mere" fifty years like my father. But the judge had always been lenient in awarding bail. He had allowed my father to remain free on appeal for three years following the bank robbery conviction. More than anything else, I wanted to make bail. The way I saw it, we could motion to have Mishler bounced after the bond hearing.

Jacobs remained adamant that Mishler had to go without delay. He continued to push hard to have him ousted. Mishler countered that he hardly remembered my father's case or the threat against his daughter and could be fair with me. Jacobs continued to protest and demanded a speedy trial, a calculated move based upon the fact that Judge Mishler was scheduled to sit on the bench in South Florida as part of his rotating federal jurist duties. Mishler finally relented and gave up the case. It was reassigned to Judge Eugene Nickerson.

Judge Mishler's courtroom had been in the wide-open spaces of Uniondale, Long Island. Nickerson's courtroom was in Brooklyn. Despite my attempts to escape to the sun of Florida and California, I had come full circle.

In Brooklyn, I was finally able to read the twenty-eight-count racketeering indictment produced by the fourteen-agency joint task force headed by the Eastern District of New York. Indicted with me were most of my top associates: Louis Fenza, Frank "Frankie Gangster" Castagnaro, Frank Cestaro, Harold Sussman (my accountant), financier Gerard Nocera, Allied International Union boss Anthony Tomasso, union attorney Mitchell Goldblatt, and Walter Doner. Doner, my Rumplik Chevrolet partner, was a Catholic deacon and Little League baseball coach and was totally innocent. He had the misfortune of being caught in the drift net with the others.

Once again, I was astounded by the charges. I was accused of conspiracy, mail fraud, obstruction of justice, extortion, uttering a counterfeit security, violating federal antikickback laws, embezzlement, and wire fraud. The companies I was said to have defrauded of $5 million included such blue-chip corporations as Mobil Oil, Citicorp, General Motors, Mazda Motors of America, Merrill Lynch, Chemical Bank, Beneficial Commercial Corporation, and Allied International Union.

The bulk of the charges involved wild accusations of fraud and extortion in my auto dealerships and in my association with the security guards' union. There was even a charge for credit-card fraud based on a five-hundred-dollar rubber raft someone had given me as a gift. There was just a single count pertaining to the gas business, and only $3 million alleged stolen. Part of that was based upon Iorizzo inflating the figures on a financial statement filed for a fuel-tax bond. I was charged with knowing the statement was false, which I didn't. I rarely saw that kind of paperwork. Similarly, I had no idea the $100,000 treasury note that was put up as collateral for the $500,000 Rumplik floor-plan loan was counterfeit. I thought it was stolen. The last count was a "Kline conspiracy," a blanket accusation that every business I was ever involved with was created for the sole purpose of stealing taxes.

The indictment indicated that I owned twenty-one separate or related businesses spanning the construction, auto, and motion-picture industries, and traced the spending of millions of dollars.

The 177-count Florida indictment listed twenty-six co-defendants—including Austrian Duke Henri Alba-Teran d'Antin—and dealt solely with the gas business. I didn't know a dozen or more of the co-defendants, including the duke, and had no idea why they were indicted. Others I knew well. They included Frankie Cestaro, Vincent Aspromonte, William Ferrante, Sebastian "Buddy" Lombardo, Peter Raneri, Jerry Zimmerman, Michael Markowitz, David Bogatin, and Leo Persits.

My first thought upon reading the indictments was that I could beat them. The union embezzlement charges were imprecise and I was insulated from them. The rest of the charges were a mishmash of truth, fiction, other defendants' crimes, and routine business practices like falling behind on floor-plan loans. The accusations could easily be attacked. With all the millions I was stealing in gas taxes, it appeared that they were still mostly harassing me instead of building a solid case.

IV

MICHAEL AND CAMMY: QUITTING THE MOB

CHAPTER 20

I was among friends at the Metropolitan Correctional Center (MCC) in New York. Included among my fellow inmates on the ninth floor were family boss Carmine "the Snake" Persico, Jr., Colombo underboss Jerry Langella, and Genovese family boss Anthony "Fat Tony" Salerno, along with a band of Sicilian mobsters awaiting trial in the "Pizza Connection" drug case. My cellmate was a terrorist who was involved in a number of bombings in Chicago and New York. Although he explained his organization, motive, and cause at length, it now escapes me.

Cammy and I argued about whether she should fly to New York. I didn't want her to suffer through my ordeal; she wanted to be there with me. She won. Cammy, Sabrina, and the baby flew to Kennedy Airport the next day. John Jacobs booked her into the Lombardy Hotel, an old, stodgy structure that was nevertheless quite expensive. Cammy found it so gloomy she called around the next day for a brighter hotel and found three she liked. When I called, I vetoed them, saying they were too close to wretched Forty-second Street, a thoroughfare infested with pimps, prostitutes, muggers, street crazies, and aggressive panhandlers and winos. We finally agreed that she would stay at the Parker Meridien Hotel off Central Park.

That afternoon, she came to the Metropolitan Correctional Center to visit me. So began her own "imprisonment," which for spouses can be nearly as bad as for those inside. She stood in a long line out front with people from all walks of society. It was freezing and raining as she stood shivering.

Inside, she was roughly searched, had a hand-held metal detector run up and down her body, and was ordered to check her fur into a locker. She filled out some forms, squeezed herself into a packed elevator, got off at the ninth floor—the Mob floor—and was directed to a cramped visiting room overflowing with people. When I appeared, she rushed to me. I gave her a restrained hug and explained that emotional displays were frowned upon. She asked if I was okay. I said I was.

She remained in New York for the rest of December and all of January, as my bond hearing kept getting postponed and extended to accommodate Judge Nickerson's vacation and to enable the prosecutors to build a stronger case. She was allowed to visit me for an hour every Tuesday and Thursday. Her mood altered between enthusiastic optimism and days when she felt like jumping out of the hotel window. Most of the time, her mood reflected mine. When I was up, she was up; when I was down, it plunged her into despair.

The Garcia family took shifts staying with her. When Sabrina had to leave, Cammy's mother, father, and brothers flew in to take her place.

At MCC one afternoon, I watched a pair of Chinese Dragon gang members, in prison on murder charges, beat a bulky weight lifter bloody with a pair of broomsticks. The bodybuilder was a bully who threw his weight around, especially in the telephone area, and the Chinese guys had had enough. They were as quick and deadly as mongooses, and ended up breaking the bigger man's arm.

What was more alarming, however, was the fate of the other Mob guys. They kept going to trial, losing, and getting hammered with harsh sentences. Every other day it seemed someone was coming back with a thirty-, forty-, fifty-, seventy-, or hundred-year sentence. The city seemed to be engulfed in a wave of Mob hysteria, and the prosecutors were on a roll. That didn't bode well for me, especially when considering that it was the ringleaders who were being hit the hardest.

During my bond hearing, the prosecutors dredged up every damning incident from my past, including the alleged death threat on my father's probation officer. Iorizzo was hauled out to repeat his lies that I had tried to kill his son and had ordered him to hide in Panama. This time, he added that I had also threatened to kill him.

Taped conversations from various points of my life materialized as if by magic. I learned for the first time that Luigi Vizzini, one of the men who tried to entice me into offering a bribe to national parole board director Benjamin Malcolm, was an informant who had taped our conversations. Vizzini was later murdered. The prosecutor implied with his questions that I found out about the setup and killed Vizzini. It made for a nice story but wasn't true. I didn't know until that court proceeding that I had been set up, and I hadn't been aware that Vizzini was dead.

The prosecutors trotted it all out to try to convince the judge that the "Yuppie Don" was actually an old-fashioned blood-and-guts Mob killer who was a menace to society and unworthy of bail at any price. By calling witnesses who twisted the facts, they were doing a pretty good job of it. When the hearing ended, Judge Nickerson reserved his decision until an unspecified date.

It didn't surprise me when he ruled, a week or so later, that I was to be held without bond. Still, it really ticked me off. By comparison, John Gotti and a gang of his associates were, at the same time, awaiting trial in Nickerson's court for charges ranging from murder to drugs, and none of them had been remanded. Except for a few poorly supported extortion counts, I had been charged with white-collar crimes.

Cammy took it even harder than I did. When she found out that I wasn't going to be released, she collapsed onto the bed and sobbed uncontrollably. After soaking her pillow, she bolted upright, grabbed our baby, bundled her up, and threw on her coat.

She told me what happened from there during her next visit.

She called a car service and asked the driver to speed down to MCC. It began snowing as they made the trip downtown to the Lower East Side jail at 150 Park Row. She arrived a few minutes after seven P.M. Inside the hallway, a bulky black guard informed her that it was too late; visiting hours had ended at seven. She pleaded with him to give her a break, but he refused. She walked to the door of an adjacent room in an attempt to reach the phones. The guard blocked her way. He wouldn't let her call a taxi, nor would he allow her to sit down and catch her breath in the foyer.

"You're sending me out in the snow, with a newborn baby?" she screamed. "How could you!"

"You have to leave. That's the rules," the guard repeated, grasping her firmly by the arm and roughly pushing her out the door.

She found herself alone on a dark and deserted New York street. She put her back against the wall to shelter the infant from the snow that was falling in big, wet flakes upon her face. My wife cried and prayed for a miracle to get them out of there before some mugger came along and killed them. (She was unaware that New York City police headquarters were just around the corner.)

A light appeared down the road. It approached. It was her car-service driver. The Iranian refugee had gotten lost on Park Row and circled back. She frantically flagged him down.

"Thank God you're still here!" she said, sobbing.

"Why crying? Why crying?" the driver asked. He had driven her many times before and felt like he knew her. Because of her beauty and her expensive clothing, he thought she was an actress and that the twelve-story granite building he was taking her to was a theater. He had no idea of the true nature of the big beige building.

Cammy explained that she might not see me again for many years. She added that God had confused the driver and made him get lost so he could rescue her. He responded that he was always getting lost in the massive city and suspected Allah had a hand in it. She smiled. He was a nice man, a contrast to the heartless prison guard.

At the hotel, she retreated into the bathroom, fell to her hands and knees, and began throwing up. She banged her head against the toilet, crying out, "Why, God? Why? Why did this have to happen to us?" Her mother found her writhing on the floor, inches away from a total nervous breakdown. She hugged her and cried with her.

"You can't make yourself sick over this," Irma Garcia said. "Think about the baby. She needs you."

"Mom, I think I'm pregnant again," Cammy said.

"How can you be? You just had a baby. You're not supposed to have sex for six weeks."

"My husband was going to jail. I'm supposed to say no?"

They laughed through the tears.

Cammy lifted herself from the bathroom floor and fell on the bed. She prayed that it was a bad dream and she would wake up at the apartment in Brentwood with me beside her. But as she prayed, she was stung by the nagging thought that the pain was God's doing. Our marriage had been founded in adultery. A price had to be paid. Was this God's punishment for her sin? She drifted into a troubled sleep.

As Cammy slept, her mother sat by the window and watched the hustle and bustle of people on the busy New York street below. Her strength began to fade. She missed her children terribly, especially little Raquel. The gloom in the hotel room was so thick it swept over her, filling her mind with dark, irrational thoughts. She was certain she would never see her children again, that something awful would happen in New York or on the plane trip back. The tears fell harder as she struggled to muffle her sobs to keep Cammy from knowing her pain. After crying herself out, she too drifted into an uneasy sleep.

Irma awakened with a brighter outlook. The doom of the previous night was nothing more than stress and fatigue. "No matter how bad things may seem now, Michael's going to get out," she assured her daughter. "God's going to release him from his misery. Nobody has power over Michael but God. We've just got to let God pilot this ship or we're all going to crash."

With the morning came the news that Cammy wasn't pregnant, just sick. The bitter New York cold and the emotional stress had crippled her defenses. Baby Miquelle was also sick, and Cammy rushed her to a doctor. The baby had pneumonia, probably from being in the harsh elements after the prison guard threw her and her mother out onto the street.

After the first month, Cammy, Sabrina, Irma, and the baby moved to the Omni Hotel to find a more casual atmosphere befitting what was now to be a long, trying stay in Manhattan.

Cammy's ordeal pounded my predicament home even harder. It was exactly what I didn't want, exactly the kind of situation I had always avoided getting myself into. I wanted to do my inevitable jail time clean without screwing up anyone else's life. I had witnessed firsthand how my father's imprisonment devastated my mother and ruined the lives of my younger brothers and sisters. Here I was, doing the same thing to my families. I was confident that Maria would be strong and would be able to take care of her children. She was mature, steady, resourceful, and in control of her emotions. Cammy was something entirely different. Although she was street-tough and a fierce fighter, she was extremely emotional and empathetic. She would be dying each day I spent in prison.

I had to get out of jail, at least for the stressful time prior to and during the trial. There had to be a way. I figured all the angles. Another inmate told me about a new law that allowed prisoners with complicated cases to be released part of the day to work on their defense. Since my Florida indictment included twenty-seven co-conspirators, I figured I was a natural to test the law. Jacobs, my attorney, discouraged me, calling it a frivolous motion. I wrote most of the briefs myself and ordered Jacobs to present the request to the judge. Incredibly, the judge granted it. And not only did he grant it, he awarded me more time than I sought. I asked for six hours a day, five days a week; the judge gave me ten hours a day, six days a week. I would be transported from MCC to Jacob's office at 10 A.M., watched over by U.S. marshals, then returned to the jail around 8 P.M.

My first request during my initial ten hours of freedom was food. Louie Fenza, out on bail, raided a deli in Little Italy and delivered a feast of pasta, bread, cheese, and antipasto. Despite the array of delights, my stomach had shrunk so much from the prison diet that I was able to eat only a small portion.

After surveying the scene at Jacobs's office, I spied an inner office that was secluded from the others, especially when the firm cleared after 5 P.M. I motioned to Cammy and we ducked inside, away from the marshals and lingering attorneys, locked the door, and moved a chair from behind the desk. It felt great to embrace my wife again, to smell her perfume, touch her hair, and caress her body. We eased down on the soft carpet and made love.

John Jacobs's office was a prison of another kind, but it beat the total lockdown of MCC's ninth floor. I could eat better food, see my wife and child, sneak a moment or two of under-the-desk passion, and fight my case. It could have been a lot worse.

Studying all the charges, I began considering the possibility of working out a plea. One of my co-defendants, union boss Anthony Tomasso, had already rolled over. That was significant, because the union activities were an area where I was at risk. And even if I mounted an effective defense against Tomasso and Iorizzo, the current indictment was merely another in what appeared to be an endless string. Brooklyn's organized strike force chief, a sharp prosecutor named Laura Brevetti, was busy working on a gas-tax indictment. She was closing in on my most vulnerable area—the money we made stealing gasoline taxes—and that was the one indictment I feared.

By this point, Cammy was beginning, on her own, to understand the nature of my business. As her understanding grew, it struck me that I had made the same mistake I accused my father of making when I was a child. It upset me that when he was going through his legal problems, he never sat the family down and explained the newspaper stories, explained what was happening. I felt he should have told us what to expect and told us who and what he was. When it came my turn, I never sat my families down, either. I took the same silent route as my father. As close as I was to Cammy, I never admitted who I was or gave her a history of La Cosa Nostra.

What bothered her most was the savage cannibalism of the crime families themselves. From her perspective, she had more to fear from my friends than from the prosecutors. She had a point. Vincent Rotondo, a DeCavalcante capo she'd met when he was a co-defendant with me in the Hyman/Cooper loan-shark trial, was blown away in front of his Brooklyn house while his wife and children huddled inside. Rotondo's body was covered with fish he had purchased for dinner from a nearby deli. It is widely believed that he was killed because Jesse Hyman was his associate and he had introduced Hyman to other made men. When Hyman became a government witness, Rotondo was finished.

Veteran mobster Johnny Irish Matera, a close friend of my father's, arrived at Kennedy Airport one afternoon from North Miami and drove to a meeting in Brooklyn headed by Persico. He failed to notice that he had an FBI tail. Persico's parole was revoked for associating with felons. Johnny Irish paid for the mistake with his life.

My initiation-ceremony cohort, Jimmy Angellino, would later incur the Mob commission's wrath by trying to muscle in on the Gambino family's interests in New York's billion-dollar garment industry, which surrounds the Empire State Building. He was taken for a ride by his Colombo family brothers and hasn't been seen since.

Rotondo's death, and the murder of Gambino boss Paul Castellano, hit Cammy especially hard. She envisioned me going out the same way, in a puddle of blood in front of our home or on a dirty New York sidewalk outside an Italian restaurant. She decided that she'd rather have me in prison in California than free in New York.

That feeling, and her acceptance of my being in prison, made agreeing to a plea a great deal easier. I was concerned about her increasing fears and had decided that I never again wanted to come home and find my emotional wife on the bedroom floor, trembling, crying, and clutching a stuffed monkey. All else considered, I would have fought the indictments in court, where I had always won. But even if I dodged yet another bullet, I would merely doom Cammy to a life of tormenting anxiety that would age her and extinguish her beauty. And I'd be putting my children through the same hell my father's life-style had put us through.

For Cammy, I'd give up my criminal empire, go to jail, and attempt to do the impossible—quit the Mob.

With those private goals in mind, I concluded that my best position would be to offer an all-encompassing plea that settled everything, past and future. Over the next six weeks, I hammered away at the prosecutors until they accepted a deal we could all live with.

I agreed to plead guilty to two of the twenty-eight counts filed against me—federal racketeering and tax conspiracy. I was given a ten-year prison sentence, was forced to forfeit nearly $5 million in assets, and promised to give the government 20 percent of my future earnings—on top of my regular income taxes—until I had paid another $10 million in restitution.

As part of the deal, I also agreed to plead guilty to the sixty-five counts charged against me in Florida, which included racketeering, grand theft, conspiracy, theft of state funds, uttering a forged instrument, and failure to account for taxes collected. The nine-year Florida sentence would run concurrent with the ten-year federal sentence. A $3 million Florida restitution fee would come from the $15 million federal agreement.

In addition to the pleas, I privately promised to quit the Mob. Publicly, I sang a different tune, one in keeping with my oath. "I am absolutely 100 percent not a member of organized crime," I told the Associated Press. "It's because of that label that I've had all these problems. I'm willing to give the government a pound of flesh if this will be the end of it."

In return for my "pound of flesh," the slate would be wiped clean. The sentence would cover past crimes and future indictments, and clear me of everything I had ever done except murder and perjury.

The feeling among the multitude of prosecutors and law-enforcement officers who hunted me varies widely on the plea. Those who supported it felt it was a major victory over a criminal who had proven difficult to convict. I would go to jail, my billion-dollar operation would be shut down, and I would have to pay what they saw as an enormous restitution fee. Plus, they viewed my vow to quit the Mafia as the clincher. That was a death sentence.

"He's agreeing that he'll forever owe the federal government $14.7 million," Brooklyn strike force and joint task force prosecutor Jerry Bernstein told reporters. "That's very meaningful. He's a pretty resourceful individual in terms of making money."

"I'm very pleased with the disposition," added strike force and task force chief Ed McDonald. "We've convicted a major organized-crime figure and forced him to make a significant restitution."

The United States Department of Justice was also pleased. It awarded each member of the Michael Franzese Task Force a plaque commemorating his accomplishment.

In Florida, the official response was similar.

"We were lucky. We caught our problem early. In New York, they're saying $500 million may be missing," said Robert Dempsey, commissioner of the Florida Department of Law Enforcement (FDLE). "This is a tremendous departure point," agreed Rolando Bolanos, FDLE chief. "Normally, when the head of the organization falls, the backbone will follow."

Those who fought the plea bargain felt that I got off too easy. The detractors point to the deal made by junk-bond king Michael Milken in April 1990 as a comparison. Milken agreed to pay a staggering $600 million in restitution, then later received his own ten-year prison sentence. "And Milken stole less money than Franzese," noted one bitter prosecutor.

"He got the deal of the century," said Suffolk County district attorney and organized crime specialist Ray Jermyn, a key joint task force member. "The government was suckered just like he suckers everybody else. The guy's amazing. Everybody loves him. He smiles, steals them blind, and everybody still loves him."

I strongly disagree with that assessment. I felt the plea was fair. Not only did they fine me $15 million, they were taking four to ten years of my life, depending on my conduct in prison.

In simple terms, I lost and the government won. The score might have been closer than some wanted, but I still lost. The task force achieved its stated goal of destroying my organization and putting me behind bars. Never, in my most private moments, did I feel I suckered anybody.

CHAPTER 21

I was allowed to fly back to Los Angeles with Cammy and our baby after the plea agreement was signed. The only difficulty we encountered was getting her baggage home. She had come to New York in the dead of winter with little more than a sweater and parka to fight the cold. Her sister, mother, and brothers, all lifetime Californians, also lacked winter clothing. Cammy purchased so many bulky coats and sweaters during her sojourn that she had to hire two taxis to tote her bags to the airport. She ended up having to ship most of her belongings on a cargo airline.

During the flight, my U.S. marshal escorts let me sit with my wife and child. I hugged Cammy and played with Miquelle as we made the five-hour trip. When we arrived in Los Angeles, I spent the weekend at home before reporting to the U.S. marshal's office for phase one of my punishment.

Among the numerous riders I negotiated into my plea agreement was one that enabled me to spend the three months prior to my sentencing in a Los Angeles halfway house. Halfway houses are set up, in part, to prepare long-term inmates nearing the end of their prison stays to re-enter society. I took the position that I needed to prepare to *leave* society. I was assigned to the Suicide Prevention Center/Community Treatment Center on Menlo Avenue. I arranged it so I could be out from six A.M. to eleven P.M. each day. Basically, all I did was sleep at the place.

However, I wasn't totally free during the day. As per the agreement, U.S. marshals monitored my every move. But because of the imprecise language in the plea papers, I was able to dictate the terms of my watch. The agreement stated that I was to pay the salaries of the officers on the twenty-four-hour detail, a sum that amounted to $4,000 a week. This apparently led the U.S. marshal's office to view it as a sort of "rent-a-cop" situation. They asked me how it was supposed to work. I quickly laid out the least intrusive scenario. The marshals were to follow me in a separate vehicle on my daily rounds. They would park outside the buildings where I stopped but would not follow me inside.

In New York, the prosecutors were under the impression that the order meant I was to be bodily surrounded by marshals at all times. I was aware of this perception. Whenever any of the New York prosecutors came to California, I had the marshals stick by my side. When the prosecutors left, the marshals were sent back to the trail car.

My unusual arrangement with the U.S. marshal's office led to my becoming almost friends with my shadows. They were decent men who worked hard, and I liked them. I did my best to make their job easy, and let them know that I wasn't going to get out of line. I even alerted them in advance of my schedule so they could be properly attired.

"I'm going to the beach tomorrow, so bring your shorts," I advised them one afternoon. The marshals appeared the following morning dressed in swimsuits and carrying picnic gear.

"We're going to see the Dodgers tonight. I've got box seats for everyone," I announced a week later.

On one occasion, the officers became disoriented by the plethora of white Mercedeses in Los Angeles and followed the wrong car. I had to double back and hunt them down. Cammy and I chased them up Wilshire Boulevard.

"Hey, where you guys going?" I shouted at a stoplight. "I turned on Beverly Glen!"

When Miquelle was christened at Westwood Hills Christian Church, we invited the marshals and their wives to the event and to the party afterward.

Cammy was happy during the halfway-house experience. The only negative was the knowledge that the clock was ticking down with each day. Being unable to spend the night with her was unpleasant, but we adjusted. I'd arrive around 6:30 A.M. and slip into bed beside her so we could wake up together. Neither the missed evening hours nor a diaphragm was enough to prevent her from becoming pregnant again. This time, the news depressed her. She wanted only one baby at that time. And I was on my way to prison for up to ten years.

I didn't share her dismay. As the home pregnancy kit registered dark blue, a big grin formed on my face. "That's the bluest blue I've ever seen," I quipped. "I don't think there's any doubt."

We celebrated by moving from the condo in Brentwood to a half-million-dollar luxury apartment in the exclusive Mirabella building on Wilshire Boulevard in Westwood. I wanted a complex with security guards, and the Mirabella, with its elaborate closed-circuit-television security system, was deemed perfect.

One evening, as we huddled in our new bedroom, watching television, I flipped through the channels and caught the beginning of the classic movie *Spartacus*. I remembered having enjoyed it years before, and wanted my wife to watch it with me. For the next four hours, we sat mesmerized as Kirk Douglas and Jean Simmons played out the tragic love story of the former Thracian slave who led an uprising against the Roman Empire in 73 B.C. I was especially moved by a scene near the end where, prior to going to battle, the powerful gladiator/warrior Spartacus tells Varinia (Simmons) that his love for her has weakened him and made him feel fear for the first time in his life. Varinia responds that he is so strong he could be weak with her. Those lines really hit home. I had avoided falling in love all my life because I equated love with weakness—specifically, the loss of control and the fear of jail. I was now in the grip of a still-new love and weeks away from prison. Yet somehow I felt it would be all right. When the burdens facing me became too heavy to bear alone, I could let my guard down and tap into Cammy's strength. That didn't make me weak. It didn't make me any less a man. Jean Simmons had assured me of that. Like Spartacus, I was strong enough to be weak with Cammy.

As I watched the tortured Spartacus dying on a cross, and Varinia standing below him, crying, clutching his feet and lifting their baby son so the gladiator could see the child before he died, my mood shifted between the sorrow of the movie, the uncertainty of my own life, and the comfort that I didn't have to face the future alone.

"With you, Cammy, I can be a man and be weak," I told her, echoing Spartacus. "I can be strong, and I can cry. I never thought I could be that way with anybody."

When we moved to the Mirabella, I continued attending services with my wife at Westwood Hills Christian Church. As an infant Christian, I hungered for more knowledge about the beliefs I had accepted when I said the "born again" prayer Cammy had taught me. I was especially drawn by Westwood Hills pastor Dr. Myron Taylor, a dignified, fatherly man with white hair, a warm, caring face, and a talent for making his sermons both interesting and easy to follow. Whether speaking softly in his office like a learned professor or reaching a thunderous peak during one of his fire-and-brimstone Sunday sermons, Dr. Taylor got through. I sat in rapt attention each Sunday, taking in all the stories Dr. Taylor took from the Old Testament and the New, and following up with my own study of the Bible. I was drawn to sermons and chapters about the reluctant leader Moses, the hotheaded warrior Samson and his fall with Delilah, King David and his tragic relationship with his beloved son Absalom, and the life and crucifixion of Jesus Christ. I was especially heartened by the apostle Paul, a man who persecuted and murdered hundreds of Christians before Jesus selected him to be one of his top disciples. If God could forgive Paul, God could forgive me.

As I listened to Dr. Taylor Sunday after Sunday, I found myself admiring the preacher for his intense dedication to God and his conviction to do good. It was a stark contrast to my old feelings. I used to look up to men like Carmine Persico, Joe Colombo, and Jo Jo Vitacco, men the rest of the world viewed as evil incarnate. Now I was revering a man of the cloth. The backward thinking ingrained in me as a child was starting to reverse.

It wasn't an easy process. Despite Cammy's assurances, I couldn't shake the nagging doubt that I had to do more to become a Christian than say a simple prayer. One weekday morning, my insecurities brought me to Dr. Taylor's office inside his majestic church on LeConte Avenue. I originally intended to ask some questions about my salvation to make sure my wife knew her stuff. As we talked, I found myself overwhelmed by a need to confess—no doubt a throwback to my Catholic upbringing. I told Dr. Taylor who I was, what I had been, and where I was going—to prison. The pastor didn't flinch.

"God forgives everyone. It doesn't matter what you did in the past."

"But shouldn't it be harder than just saying a prayer?" I asked.

Dr. Taylor smiled. He knew from experience that people with troubled pasts who truly long to be forgiven find the promise of instant absolution difficult to accept.

"It sounds as if it should be harder, but God made it simple so that everyone can understand, and everyone who asks can have eternal life."

"If that's the case, then I want to make sure I got it right. I want to make sure I said the prayer right."

I repeated the prayer Cammy taught me, remembering it by the initials A-B-C: A for asking God to save me, and to come into my life as my Lord and Savior; B for believing that God sent his son Jesus Christ to die on the cross for my sins; and C for confessing that I'm a sinner and can be saved only by the grace of God.

Dr. Taylor said it was correct.

That helped, but I still felt something missing. I couldn't escape the need to do something ritualistic, to go through some official ceremony that would erase the oath I had sworn to the Mob the first time I had been "born again."

"Both you and Cammy should be baptized," Dr. Taylor suggested, sensing my longing.

As the pastor explained what a total-immersion baptism entailed, my mood lifted. That was it! A physical and spiritual cleansing of my body and soul in a formal and sacred setting steeped in biblical tradition. That would blot the memory of Halloween night, of the blood and the flash of fire in my cupped hand. Water dilutes blood and destroys fire. It's the stronger element. A baptism would break the blood oath.

I left the church free of the last ache I carried inside me, the one pain even Cammy couldn't deaden.

As I lay in bed with my wife the following morning, blackout shades darkening the bedroom, a bright beam of light flashed before us. I jumped up and searched for its origin. I couldn't locate it or even surmise how it was created.

I told Cammy it was a sign from God that everything would be okay.

The light buoyed our spirits for weeks. Whenever one of us became depressed, the other mentioned the light.

The halfway-house segment of the sentence was to last three months. My intention was to extend it for as long as possible, with the ultimate goal of spending my entire sentence that way. I argued that I couldn't earn the government its $10 million if I was in jail. Better I be given the freedom to make movies and build profitable new businesses, I reasoned.

Whether the feds intended to accept this or not, my limited freedom ended abruptly when Brian Ross and his NBC News crew flew to Los Angeles to update their viewers on "the Franzese story." Ross and company spotted me cruising down Wilshire Boulevard in a white Eldorado convertible all but singing Frank Sinatra's "Summer Wind." They videotaped me from a van, then later shot my marshal friends abandoning their post in front of my condominium to go on an extended coffee break. (I had told them I wasn't leaving the house anymore that day.) Ross and his producer, Ira Silverman, intercut my seemingly carefree L.A. life-style with scenes of shackled inmates in grimy federal prisons. When the segment aired, Ross pointed out the contrast between how most federal prisoners do time and how I was doing time.

The moment I saw the broadcast, I knew I was finished. The following day, I received a call to report to the U.S. marshal's office in Los Angeles. I told Cammy I might have to return to New York. I tried to hide my feelings, but she knew something was terribly wrong. I walked the long hallway of my condominium like I was going to the gallows. Cammy stood and watched me from the door. Just before entering the elevator, I turned and flashed her a weak smile.

"I'll be back."

I would keep my promise—three and a half years later.

At the marshal's office, I was cuffed, driven to the airport, and put on an American Airlines flight to New York.

"Relax, pal," I told a nervous American Airlines clerk at the gate. "I'm in for tax fraud—I'm not a murderer or anything." The passengers similarly gawked at my handcuffs as the marshals paraded me through the cabin to my seat in the back.

In New York, I was brought before a miffed Judge Nickerson, who had no doubt seen the NBC News report. The judge ended the halfway-house arrangement and ordered me to prison. I was bused to the Otisville federal corrections facility near Middletown, New York. My freedom had ended so fast that I was unable to schedule my baptism.

Otisville wasn't bad. It had a large exercise yard and reminded me somewhat of Hofstra University. Half the prisoners were Italian, and a good percentage were Mob guys or Mob associates. One of my crew members, Frankie G, was there. The Italians and the Chinese controlled the kitchen and took turns making lunch and dinner. The food was excellent.

The plea agreement stated that I would be allowed to serve my sentence in California. That was one area where the government hadn't been up front. Prosecutors could recommend where I was sent, but the final decision lay with the Federal Bureau of Prisons. The prison authorities aren't beholden to plea-bargain deals. Once they have a prisoner, they own him.

"I've got good news and bad news," I told Cammy over the phone.

"The good news is I'll be coming home. The bad news is I don't know when. It looks like it's going to take a while to get back to California."

"I'm coming there," she said.

"No, don't come."

"I want to see you. I'm coming," she insisted.

Cammy, Irma, and the baby flew to New York, then took a limousine to the upstate prison. She stayed a week at the Holiday Inn, eating her meals at Swensen's and Denny's.

The only negative at Otisville came near the end of my two-week stay. Just before I entered the visitors' area to see Cammy, a guard came over. "What are you doing with that ring?" he asked, pointing at my diamond wedding ring. "That's not on your personal-belongings list."

"They must have overlooked it," I said. "I'm only going to be here a few more days."

"You'll have to give it to me," he said.

"No way," I argued. "I'll give it to my wife in the visiting room."

"I've got to take it," he said. "You don't know what can happen. An expensive ring like that, another prisoner will cut off your finger while you're sleeping to get it."

"How?" I said. "Break through the bars? Have you forgotten where we are? Nobody's going to take my ring."

"I've got to have it," he insisted.

We argued for a few more minutes. He refused to allow me to just give it to Cammy, which really made me mad. Finally, I relented. Cammy was waiting and I thought the guard might cancel the visit if I didn't hand it over. That was the last I ever saw of the two-thousand-dollar ring.

After Cammy returned to California, I was transferred to a federal prison in Lewisburg, Pennsylvania, and was assigned to K-Dorm, a basement dungeon out of a Stephen King novel. The bottom floor at Lewisburg had previously been condemned, but was reopened after a riot at a nearby Washington, D.C. prison ended with the prisoners burning the place down. They shipped 250 of the 1,000-plus D.C. prisoners, all black, to Lewisburg and dumped them into the basement, which was nothing more than a large army-style barracks with exposed pipes and rows and rows of filthy bunks. There were no bars or individual cells. Everyone just wandered around, made noise, argued, picked fights, and got on each other's nerves. The food was so bad I ate only one meal a day. It was such a hellhole that I insisted that Cammy not visit me there.

I had some friends on the more civilized floors above. Among them were Tony West and James "Jimmy the Gent" Burke. West owned a bar and restaurant next to my brother-in-law's Italian restaurant, Trattoria Siciliana, on Second Avenue and Twenty-ninth Street in Manhattan. Burke is the Lucchese family associate Robert De Niro played in the movie *GoodFellas*. I'm not sure why West was in, but Burke had been convicted of murdering Richie Eaton, one of his partners in the infamous $6 million Lufthansa Airlines theft at Kennedy Airport in 1978. (Eaton was found frozen solid in a refrigeration truck.) Burke would place cigarettes, candy bars, books, or postage stamps in a small bag, tie a long string to it, drop it out an upstairs window, and lower it to me through a window in the shower room. I don't smoke, but cigarettes and candy are like money in prison. I traded them to other prisoners in exchange for their phone time.

K-Dorm was a holding area for prisoners being sent somewhere else. The flights out were every Tuesday and Thursday. The list of those scheduled to leave was posted after midnight that same morning. Everyone wanted to get out of there so badly that we all awoke after midnight on those mornings and trudged to the board to check if we were on the list. Finally, after three weeks, my name was posted. I took a two-hour bus ride to an airport somewhere, turned around, then took a two-hour ride right back to the prison. Apparently, the plane had broken down. We left the following day.

I was sent to El Reno, Oklahoma, another paradise. They put me in the hole (isolation) the entire week I was there. I passed the time reading a Bible.

Cammy surprised me by flying in from Los Angeles. When told I had a visitor, I thought it was a mistake. I was so grubby from my incarceration I jumped into a shower before appearing. My hair was long and unruly and my beard was dark and stubbled. I was wearing baggy pants with huge cuffs, black shoes with rubber soles, a khaki shirt, and had lost fifteen pounds.

"You look like a homeboy," she joked, using an inner-city expression for a friend from the neighborhood.

"You should have seen me before I took a shower," I said. "I wouldn't have come out."

Back East, things were looking grim. Undercover agents spotted my father having dinner at Laina's Restaurant in Jericho, Long Island, with a convicted gambler and loan shark named Joseph Caridi. According to Nassau County Assistant District Attorney Elaine Jackson Stack, Caridi interrupted his meal to collect a usurious loan payment from one of the agents. My father's parole was subsequently revoked for the second time, once again for associating with known felons. He was shipped to a federal pen in Petersburg, Virginia, for eight more years, beginning in April 1986.

My mother was beyond grief. For the first time, both her husband and her son were in prison. And the corrections officials made sure that my father and I were never at the same prison.

I felt helpless. Locked away myself, there was nothing I could do for my father. That hurt.

After my week in the hole at El Reno, I was transferred to a new prison facility in Phoenix, Arizona. That was as close to California as I was going to get for the next four months. Because of its newness, the Federal Correctional Institution in north Phoenix was sparkling clean.

"My mother could do time here," I joked to Cammy, trying to ease her mind.

The farther I got from New York, the more my Mob background seemed to affect people. The day I arrived, the prison's chief lieutenant summoned me to his office. "This is mah. prison," the beefy Texan drawled. "You ain't gonna come heah and take over."

"Hey, I don't recall sending you a resume for a job," I countered. "I'm just a prisoner. I'm not taking over anything. In fact, you can keep me in lockdown twenty-four hours if you want. I just want to do my time in peace."

After that, the guards and I got along fine.

Cammy flew in every weekend on America West Airlines and stayed at the Westcourt Hotel. Her visits were made doubly pleasant by the prison's outdoor patio area. As we enjoyed the sun and the beautiful Arizona winter, we amused ourselves by observing the domestic situation of one of my fellow inmates. The American Indian was married to twin sisters and had a girlfriend on the side. The three women visited him every weekend, sharing their time and presenting him with an assortment of children.

At Phoenix, I met and befriended Jeffrey MacDonald, the former Green Beret captain and military doctor convicted in 1979 of killing his twenty-four-year-old wife and two daughters, ages five and two, at their Fort Bragg, North Carolina home in 1970. I found the doctor to be a pleasant guy who frequently worked out in the prison's exercise yard and staunchly maintained his innocence despite a best-selling book, *Fatal Vision,* and television movie that said otherwise. Since Dr. MacDonald was more intelligent and educated than the average prisoner, we were able to converse on a wide range of subjects. For the most part, I believed MacDonald's claim of innocence. But every once in a while, when the setting sun hit the doctor's eyes, I detected a strange glint, an odd spark that made me wonder.

"Cammy, that man two tables over, to your right—that's Jeffrey Mac-Donald," I said during one visit.

Cammy, who had read *Fatal Vision,* shuddered as if a breath of frigid air had blown over her. "He gives me the chills," she said, oblivious to the irony that Dr. MacDonald could point me out to his visitors and they would probably get worse chills.

Despite the pleasant visiting circumstances and the almost college-campus atmosphere of Phoenix, the distance from Los Angeles made the trips wearing for Cammy. When she was eight months pregnant, her doctor ordered her to stay put. I told my attorneys to push harder to get me to Los Angeles. Finally, the order came through and I was sent to Terminal Island, a federal facility near San Pedro that was a forty-five-minute drive from the Mirabella.

"Baby, I'm home," I told my wife over the phone after I arrived.

"Home" was worse than Phoenix, but Terminal Island was better than most of the other prisons I'd been in and was survivable.

However, my new home turned out to be hell for Cammy. Visiting the overcrowded prison proved to be a nightmare. Because of the size of the facility and its proximity to metropolitan Los Angeles, visitors swarmed the place. Cammy had to wait two to three hours in an outdoor line before being allowed to see me. The wait strained everyone's nerves, and fights often broke out among the people in line. Cammy frequently brought her brothers, Dino, Cuauhtemoc, Joaquin, and Che—all former high-school football stars—along to help her deal with it, but they weren't always available. One time when she was alone, a pushy Mexican woman tried to cut into the line and then bumped Cammy hard a few times when she protested. "Why did she pick on me?" Cammy asked a con's wife she had befriended.

"You have the best car and nicest clothes. Sometimes I want to bump you also," her friend replied.

I chewed out the Mexican woman's boyfriend and told him if it happened again, he would suffer the consequences. It didn't happen again. When my wife continued to experience extreme aggravation in line, I paid a visit to the warden.

"If you don't take care of that line outside, I'm going to have some guys come here with my wife and they'll take care of it," I threatened. "Our wives and children are getting hurt out there."

The warden didn't take kindly to the threat, but after that, the line was policed by the guards.

After she'd waited for two and a half hours one afternoon, the guard at the door, a jerk who abused all the women, decreed that Cammy's silk blouse was see-through, and wouldn't let her in. She refused to leave. "It's not our fault you have this stupid job," she said. "It's not our fault you can't get any job but this miserable job."

After her outburst, the guy let her in. When I noticed she was upset, I asked what had happened. When she told me, I raised hell. The following day, the abusive guard was taken off the door assignment.

By the second week, Cammy realized that it had taken less time and stress to fly to Phoenix and take a cab to the prison than it did to see me at Terminal Island. However, after fighting so hard to get close to Los Angeles, it was too late for me to ask for a transfer. I wouldn't have anyway. Knowing Cammy was close compensated for the poor conditions.

I requested and was granted permission to attend the birth of my second child. Two days before Cammy went into labor, the New York prosecutors overruled the decision, deeming me a high-level organized-crime figure who shouldn't be afforded any privileges. Fortunately, this time Cammy didn't need her human scratching pole. She was in labor only four hours, and the birth was a breeze by comparison. We had a second Cammy-look-alike daughter, Amanda, born January 22, 1987.

"I hope you're not upset that it's not a boy," she said when I called.

"No, baby, I'm not upset at all."

Since Terminal Island was my long-term facility, I was given a job. After some basic training, I was designated a "psychiatric aide" and was assigned to B-Dorm, the prison's psychiatric ward. It was just like *One Flew Over the Cuckoo's Nest,* only worse. Every day I'd have to ride herd over the crazies. I'd assist the doctors, prevent the patients from attacking the nurses or each other, and do my best to keep things at a tolerably insane level. It wasn't easy.

The characters in B-Dorm were unbelievable. One guy had taken female hormones in preparation for a sex-change operation, then changed his mind at the last minute, and took male hormones to reverse the effect. The male hormones made him grow hair all over his body like a monkey. The seesaw act with his gender must have cooked his brain, because he was a mess. One minute he would be a woman, giggling and coming on to someone, then the next moment he'd be a macho man. He was in prison because he wrote a threatening letter to President Reagan. He didn't sign the letter; his boyfriend turned him in after an argument.

Another guy thought he *was* President Reagan and played the part pretty well. He was a mad-professor type with disheveled hair and clothes but talked intelligently about government and world affairs. It sounded like he'd once been a real politician. His main problem, however, was that he had this thing about stuffing trash into mailboxes. That's why he was in prison. He was caught dumping garbage into a blue postal box. In prison, he'd be espousing his presidential decrees, sounding good, then try to sneak off and dump junk down the prison's mail slot.

"Hey, Prez," I'd say. "What are you doing?"

He'd get this weird grin on his face and try to hide the garbage behind his back. "I'm carrying out my presidential duties."

"No you're not. You're stuffing trash in the mail slot again. Cut it out," I'd order. "That's how you got in trouble in the first place. What's with you and this garbage thing?"

He never explained.

For a while, the constant tension and anxiety of never knowing what some B-Dorm lunatic was going to do next made the time pass and helped get me through the long days. After about eight months, however, it had become so mentally and physically taxing that I requested a transfer out of there before I began stuffing trash down mail slots with the Prez.

More lasting was the friendship I forged with Kelly Hamilton, another psychiatric aide. Hamilton is better known in the Northwest as "the I-5 Bandit." The way he told it, he was watching the Steve McQueen–Ali MacGraw movie *The Getaway* one afternoon and decided to spice up his life by becoming a bank robber like McQueen. A bright guy, Hamilton successfully robbed a string of banks along Interstate 5 before being caught. He never used a weapon. He just handed the teller a note demanding cash, smiled, and made off with the money, usually just a few thousand—enough to get him to the next town. He was tried, convicted, and sentenced to twenty years. Character-wise, the I-5 Bandit was the most stand-up guy I met in prison. Our daily battles with the denizens of the psychiatric ward helped bond our friendship.

There were other prisoners at Terminal Island whom I wanted nothing to do with. One afternoon in the prison yard, I ran into someone who looked familiar. When he saw me, he nearly freaked. It wasn't until later that I realized it was Henry Hill, the lowlife Lucchese family associate from the book *Wiseguy* and the movie *GoodFellas*. I barely recognized him because he looked so old, broken, and haggard—he was no Ray Liotta, the actor who played him in the movie. Hill had wandered in and out of the witness protection program after ratting on everybody he knew, including my friends Paulie Vario and Jimmy Burke, and was now in jail for new crimes he'd committed while back on the street.

The prison's chief lieutenant, Henry Navarra, called me into his office. "Michael, Henry Hill spotted you in the yard and came in here white as a ghost."

"I thought I recognized that scumbag," I said.

"He demanded to be put into solitary. He's says you'll kill him."

"I'm not going to touch the guy," I said. "He's got nothing on me. He's not worth killing."

Hill remained so terrified they shipped him out within the week to another prison.

The officers and the guards at Terminal Island treated me well—sometimes too well. Some of the guards kept pestering me to take them out for a night on the town. They were actually going to sneak me in and out of the prison. I told them they were crazy. Their interest in me stemmed more from the fact that I was a movie producer than a mobster. The guards wanted me to put them in the movies. I played along, agreeing to do just that in order to get an extra visit, better food, a color television in my cell, access to the telephone, small things like that. Once, when the warden found out about my television, he had the guards confiscate it and then called me into the office to discipline me. While we were talking, another color television was being brought to my cell.

Another time, after being transferred from Terminal Island to the

Boron federal prison in Victorville, California, I was allowed to leave on an eight-hour pass. There was a mistake in the paperwork that said I was to return the following day instead of that same evening. When I returned eight hours later, I figured I was going to have trouble—prison guards don't like to do paperwork unless they have to.

"Franzese, get out of here," the guard at the gate said. "You're not due back until tomorrow. Nobody comes back early. You must be nuts."

"The return date is a mistake," I argued.

"If it says tomorrow, that's when you return. Go home," the guard ordered.

I thought of spending the night with Cammy at a hotel in nearby Silverlake, then thought better of it. Someone could have caught the mistake during the night and they'd have a fugitive warrant out for me by dawn. They could arrest me as an escaped felon and screw up my parole chances. I had to get back inside that prison. I argued with the guard some more. He wouldn't let me in. It appeared the only way I was getting in that jail was if I broke in—which would have been a twist. I convinced the guard to fetch the lieutenant. The lieutenant read my orders and told me to come back tomorrow.

"Look, you can put me in the hole," I offered. "You don't have to do the paperwork until tomorrow. Just let me back in."

Finally, they reluctantly relented.

While the guards wanted to be in my movies, my fellow prisoners, almost to the man, wanted to join my gang. I never had any problems with anyone in any of the prisons. Made men are kings among criminals, and the strict underworld social structure holds true in prison more so than on the outside. If there was violence, brutality, or homosexual rape going on, I never saw any of it anywhere.

I could have taken advantage of the standard business opportunities in prison, from bringing in illegal contraband to directing criminal activities on the outside. I declined virtually all of them. All I wanted was extra visits and phone privileges, my television, and sometimes a better meal. Other than that, I played it straight. I wanted to rack up all the gain time I could get. Each day I was a good prisoner, I would get two days knocked off my sentence. If I stayed out of trouble, I could be free in three and a half years.

CHAPTER 22

Shortly before Thanksgiving, 1987, I was roused out of my bunk at Terminal Island by an unfamiliar guard. "Wake up," the corrections officer demanded. "Pack your things. You're leaving."

I instinctively glanced at my watch. It was just before three A.M. That wasn't a good sign. "Why?"

"You're on the list, Franzese," the man said, showing me a sheet of official-looking paperwork.

I knew that statement was probably the full extent of the guard's knowledge. Everyone had his job in the rigidly organized prison. The answers that morning would have to emerge in bits and pieces as I went through the system.

It took a surprisingly long time to pack. I marveled at how much I had accumulated in my one-room home. The guard kept rushing me, but I gathered my possessions at my own pace. A shaving kit. Soap. Notebooks. Legal paperwork. Photographs. Letters and cards from Cammy. A few items of clothing. And my books—*Fatal Vision, Iacocca, Born Again* by Watergate burglar Charles Colson, and some escapist novels by Sidney Sheldon and Jackie Collins.

I was escorted through the dark prison and taken to the receiving and departing room. "What's going on?" I asked the officer there.

"You're being transferred."

"Where?"

The man looked at me, paused, and flashed a sympathetic expression. "Marion, Illinois."

I recoiled. Marion means nothing to most people; few could even find it on a map. But every two-bit burglar knows the significance of Marion, Illinois. That's the location of the only Level Six federal prison in the United States. Maximum security and beyond. Absolute lockdown, twenty-four hours. Home for 350 of the most undisciplined inmates in the federal prison system.

Marion, Illinois, is also the last whip the federal corrections system uses against prisoners. Even Death Row inmates and lifers have to fear something in order to be controlled. Marion is the sword of punishment that hangs over the heads of every federal prisoner.

"What the hell for?" I asked.

The guard shrugged. He too didn't know. It was just on the list.

My thoughts spun. My first were of Cammy. She was scheduled to visit me later that day. If she arrived and found me gone, she'd freak. When she learned where I was going, she'd *really* freak. I didn't risk considering that a young Christian girl like Cammy wouldn't know Marion, Illinois, from Omaha, Nebraska. Normally, she wouldn't have. But my wife wasn't the innocent she had been when we met. Two years of standing in jailhouse visitors' lines, chatting with the wives, lovers, parents, and children of other inmates, had educated her on the prison system. She no doubt knew what the levels meant, and what the differences were between Level One and Level Five. She no doubt had heard of Level Six, one level below hell. The guards at Marion were rumored to be as twisted and sadistic as the prisoners. They sometimes wore full riot gear complete with flak jackets, helmets, Darth Vader face masks, gloves, and heavy boots. They often carried pistols, rifles, and shotguns, along with three-foot-long clubs with ends weighted by steel beads.

I had to call Cammy. It was imperative. I had to ease her fears, even if my own were still vivid. I'd ask her to contact my attorney so he could find out what was happening and take measures to stop it. The task would not only take her mind off the perceived horrors of Marion, it would make her feel that the process could be thwarted. As soon as I could get to a phone, I'd call.

As I waited, I tried to guess what had sparked this latest development. An obvious answer came quickly to mind—*Life* magazine. A lengthy article about me had hit the stands three days before. I had consented to a rare interview, and the story was given a big play. *Life* proclaimed me "the mob's young genius" and once again hinted at favored treatment. It detailed my wheeling and dealing with the government and my unusual plea arrangement. It also mentioned that Cammy had given me an ultimatum to quit the Mob and had threatened to leave me if I refused. That part of the story made me furious. Cammy made no such demand. It was *my* choice. I quit because of my love for her.

I steered my thinking back on course. It had to be the same thing that had happened after NBC News showed me serving my sentence by cruising down Wilshire Boulevard in a convertible. Somebody in authority must have read the *Life* article, became angry over the depiction of my less-than-horrid life in prison, and decided to give "the mob's young genius" a big dose of Marion, Illinois.

"How can you do this in the middle of the night?" I demanded.

"What can I do?" the receiving and departing clerk said. "It came over the teletype. It's a writ."

A supervisor appeared. I confronted him. "How can you writ me to Marion?"

The supervisor seemed surprised. "Marion? Who said anything about Marion? You're going to Chicago."

It was probably an honest mistake. Chicago, Illinois—Marion, Illinois. The other guy just assumed. Chicago was still too close to Marion for comfort, but the supervisor insisted there was no connection.

Chicago, welcomed as it was, created a whole new set of confusing scenarios. "Why Chicago?"

"I don't know," the supervisor said. "You have to appear before a grand jury on Tuesday. We have to get you there."

It must be a mistake, I thought. I had made no agreement to testify in Chicago. I couldn't testify. In La Cosa Nostra, to testify is to die, or worse, to be imprisoned in the witness protection program.

"I've never been to Chicago," I said.

The supervisor knew what I meant. Chicago had its own hierarchy dating back to the days of Al Capone. That was Anthony "Joe Batters" Accardo's and the late Sam Giancana's turf, and their crime families. I had nothing to do with them.

It was mid-morning before the prison bus arrived at the small San Pedro airport. I still hadn't been given any answers, nor was I allowed to get anywhere near a telephone. I asked another prisoner to call Cammy and have her phone my attorney. I was confident that by the time I got to a phone, my lawyer would already be on the job.

Handcuffed and manacled, I was herded onto a beat-up 707 sitting on the San Pedro runway. The marshals' jets were generally broken-down machines inherited from some other department or confiscated from drug dealers. The insides had been altered just enough to shift from carrying illegal freight to transporting human cargo. The jet was slowly filling with criminals of one sort or another being transferred around the federal prison system for whatever reasons. By takeoff, the lumbering jet was packed with nearly one hundred convicts. Most quietly accepted their fate. A few, those who didn't quite know their fate, knew their fate and didn't like it, or were afraid of flying, had to be dragged onto the aircraft. They screamed in anger or terror.

As the battered 707 lifted off, the anguished wails of the prisoners who feared flying acted to drown out the disquieting creaks of the old jet's fuselage and engines. In a strange way, that eased the minds of the other prisoners. Screaming we could understand; rattling motors we could also understand. Better the first.

Lunch was served shortly after the jet leveled off. I struggled to maneuver the handcuffs enough to be able to eat the baloney sandwich, apple, and cookie I had been given. Some of the food ended up on my shirt or bouncing down my chest to the seat or floor. Most of my fellow prisoners were more skilled at eating with cuffs, and fared far better.

Shuffling slavelike off to the restroom, I took in a full panorama of society's underbelly. Instead of picture-perfect families, foreign tourists, college students, and the suited businessmen who populate commercial flights, each seat on "Convict Airlines" was occupied by some craven-faced criminal with hard eyes. Most were forgotten men who'd started life with nothing and had sunk even lower. I saw the same pathos in every face. It made me wonder whether I too now looked that way. I decided the first thing I would do in the tiny restroom would be to get as close as possible to the mirror and search for any sign of prison eroding my features.

There was no mirror—a mirror could be broken and turned into a weapon. No one on that plane needed to see himself anyway. After relieving myself, I leaned over to flush the steel toilet. Instead of swirling down the dark hole, the foul water shot back up and splashed across my face, hair, and shirt. I shuddered in revulsion and quickly washed off as much of the fluid as I could. No matter what I did, I couldn't kill the creepy feeling, or the smell.

"The Mob's young genius," I thought as I returned to my seat. The billionaire Cosa Nostra prince, ushering in a new age of smooth, white-collar crime. People were reading those sentiments in *Life* magazine at that very moment. And there I was, getting splashed with rancid sewage on a Convict Airlines flight to nowhere.

A couple of hours after takeoff, the jet's whining engines changed their pitch. I could feel it descending—apparently by design. It was too early to be arriving in Chicago, but that hadn't been a consideration. Most prison flights landed in El Reno, which acts as a way station for convicts in transit.

I was bused to the El Reno holding pen. No one there had any answers for me. No one there ever does. El Reno's just a post office for the human equivalent of junk mail.

I was finally allowed to get in line for a telephone at 11:45 P.M. It was Friday night, so the authorities knew a prisoner's chances of reaching a troublesome attorney had diminished. With me, they hedged their bets even further. Phone privileges at El Reno shut down at midnight. Although there were a dozen or so phones up against the far wall, the last-minute crunch had resulted in lines of six or more agitated convicts snaking out from each phone.

For a prisoner, every call is an emergency; one con's predicament is no more urgent than another's. Pleading for a chance to cut to the front of the line is usually fruitless, and can sometimes be hazardous. Still, made men have an advantage, even in unfamiliar prisons. I pulled rank and promptly made it to the front of the line.

Cammy tried to sound calm, but the quaver in her voice betrayed her. Her day had been as emotionally charged as mine. The Terminal Island inmate came through and called her, and she had immediately contacted my attorney, Bruce Kelton. As I predicted, she had focused her thoughts on coming to my aid. Kelton assured her he would take control.

Cammy was concerned with having to uproot the family and move to Illinois to be near my new prison. Although she was ready to do so without hesitation, she wasn't happy about the prospect. I told her I didn't think a move was going to be necessary. I couldn't elaborate, and she didn't force me to. The conversation lasted only a few minutes. I wanted to save my remaining minutes for Kelton.

Bruce Kelton was formerly the assistant chief of the Los Angeles Organized Crime Strike Force (OCSF). In the world of attorneys, experience in a specialized government field gives prosecutors valuable training that enables them to do an about-face in the private sector. State prosecutors, skilled at convicting thieves, rapists, and murderers, become defense attorneys and work to free wealthy thieves, rapists, and murderers. Federal prosecutors learn how to free federal criminals. Drug-task-force prosecutors learn how to best defend drug kingpins. IRS attorneys learn how to defend against IRS investigations.

In the old days, this legal seesaw didn't hold with the Mob. The first-generation mobsters were too full of rage, revenge, and paranoia to trust a former OCSF attorney. They preferred to rely upon traditional Mob lawyers or family members with law degrees. That changed as the second-generation mobsters became educated and sophisticated, and as the overcrowded court system became even more of a legal casino. Instead of public trials, prosecutors and defense attorneys increasingly face off in cubicles and plea-bargain. In such an atmosphere, those in need of a good defense attorney have learned that connections are more important than sharp legal minds or courtroom skills.

Bruce Kelton had given notice of his pending career change in March 1986. He was well liked by his bosses, well respected by law-enforcement agencies, and his credibility and ethics were unquestioned. I had been alerted to Kelton's professional movements by New York OCSF man Jerry Bernstein, the same Jerry Bernstein who had hunted me so feverishly. Bernstein recommended Kelton.

Kelton retired from the Los Angeles OCSF on May 1, 1987. I contacted him on May 2 and hired him a short time later.

I reached him just before midnight at his Los Angeles home. Cammy had called him late Friday afternoon. With the week quickly winding down, Kelton was unable to learn more than the Terminal Island supervisor. There was a writ and some hoped-for grand jury testimony, but the subject remained a mystery. He told me to hang tight and he'd stay on it.

The corrections officers began barking orders to end all the telephone conversations. The prisoners in line grumbled. I ignored them, talked for thirty seconds more, then hung up.

The worst was yet to come.

At the federal detention center in Oakdale, Louisiana, known as "La Isla Bonita" for its unusually colorful decor, and at the notorious Atlanta federal penitentiary, the fallout from the ill-fated 1980 Freedom Flotilla between Mariel, Cuba, and Miami, Florida, was about to explode.

On the Friday I was flown to El Reno, the United States and Cuba reached a tentative agreement to deport about three thousand Cuban prisoners whom Fidel Castro had shipped to America among the one hundred thousand refugees who arrived during the flotilla. In a reverse of Milton's statement about preferring to rule in hell rather than serve in heaven, the Cubans preferred to be incarcerated in an American prison rather than roam free in Castro's Cuba. With baffling speed, they took control of both prisons, taking 122 hostages and torching sections of the historical Atlanta facility, the jail that once housed Al Capone.

The rioting Marielitos had a ripple effect across the entire federal prison system. Everything froze while officials dealt with the Cubans. For me, being in transit during a prison riot, even a distant riot, was like being in the elevator of a tall building when the electricity goes off. I was locked in place in the massive receiving and departing corral at El Reno. Cots were brought in so the mobs of stalled prisoners could sleep. It was a mess, even for prison.

On Monday, Kelton was able to trace the writ to Howard Pearl, a federal prosecutor in Chicago. Kelton knew Pearl from his strike-force days and called him. Pearl, knowing he was speaking with a former strike-force prosecutor, didn't bother with coyness. He told Kelton they wanted me to testify in the Norby Walters case.

Pearl didn't have to explain what the case was about. Norby Walters was a onetime bar owner, entertainment manager, and booking agent; at that time, he was a successful sports agent. He was a longtime friend and music-business partner of my father, and partied with other top mobsters at his various bars and nightclubs. Walters was and remains flamboyant, gregarious, and quick to entertain friends and strangers with an endless supply of war stories culled from a lifetime of colorful activities. A favorite story was how he got his name. Born Norby Meyer, he and his brother Walter opened a jazz club in Brooklyn in 1953 called Norby & Walter's Bel-Air. The ampersand on the club's neon sign burned out, and the brothers didn't bother to replace it. Everyone began referring to the club as "Norby Walter's." Quick to jump on a good thing, he changed his name to Norby Walters. His brother likewise changed his name to Walter Walters.

Walters's biggest claim to fame was managing or booking superstar black recording acts through his successful agency, Norby Walters Associates. His main associate was his silent partner, my father. They set up the agency in 1968 and were fifty-fifty partners. Norby acquired a

notable list of clients, including Janet Jackson, Rick James, Dionne Warwick, Lionel Richie, the Commodores, the Spinners, the Four Tops,
Cameo, Miles Davis, Luther Vandross, Patti LaBelle, Kool and the
Gang, the New Edition, and Ben Vereen. Walters, a Jew, had a special
talent for communicating with blacks. He could slap hands, talk jive,
walk jive, and blend in. He was quick to provide them with seed money
to help launch their careers.

Walters's latest venture had been to buy his way into the sports-
agentry business. It was a perfect target—lucrative and totally unpoliced.
Anyone with a smooth tongue or some ready cash could convince a disadvantaged athlete to let him be his agent. Once the talent was signed,
the agent could cut himself in for a 5 percent share of a professional
sports contract that might total as much as $20 million. Better yet, there
was little skill or knowledge needed beyond recruiting the athletes. The
top players' agents set the market each year depending on how high a
player is drafted by the professional teams. All that the other agents have
to do is wait until the veteran agents set the year's price range, then sit
back and catch the rain of dollars.

Walters teamed with Lloyd Bloom, a crusty young man with a thick
New York accent and a smattering of sports connections. Bloom had
been a bouncer at New York's Studio 54 nightclub, once a hot celebrity
party palace. Even though the pair had personalities that clashed like
snake oil and ammonia, Walters and Bloom threw in together and
formed World Sports and Entertainment, Inc. In 1985, they set out to
become big-time sports agents.

Not long after the company's creation, Walters convinced me to
invest $50,000 in the operation. Aware of the huge contracts being
awarded to professional athletes, I felt it was a solid investment.
Cammy's brother Dino acted as the bag man and delivered a grocery
sack stuffed with cash to Walters's office in the Brill Building on Broadway in Manhattan—the former office of music-biz power broker Morris
Levy, the mob associate my father had chased away from Buddah
Records two decades before.

For a time, it was money well spent. Business boomed. Within three
years, Walters and Bloom had signed forty-three top athletes. Among
their catch were such big-name professional football players as Tim
McGee of the Cincinnati Bengals, Reggie Rogers of the Detroit Lions,
Brent Fullwood of the Green Bay Packers, Rod Woodson of the Pitts-

burgh Steelers, Tony Woods of the Seattle Seahawks, Terrence Flagler of the San Francisco 49ers, Ronnie Harmon of the Buffalo Bills, and Paul Palmer of the Dallas Cowboys. During the recruiting process, Walters talked such fluent jive that many of the black athletes who spoke with him over the phone thought the New York Jew was black—no small feat. One athlete told *Sports Illustrated* that Walters affected a walk complete with a juke in his step, like a hip black man.

It wasn't all walk and talk. Walters bragged about introducing the athletes to all the famous music superstars he knew, and backed it up. He sent several on trips to New York and Los Angeles where they mingled, wide-eyed, with the stars. He even took Palmer, a Heisman Trophy candidate, to the Grammy award ceremonies.

The trouble was, according to prosecutors, the National Collegiate Athletic Association, *Sports Illustrated,* and the targeted athletes, Walters and Bloom went after sports stars the same way Walters had gone after entertainers. They showered the prospects with cash—a total of $800,00 worth, according to Bloom—to get their attention. After that, it was easy to get their signatures on the dotted lines of postdated contracts. That last measure was taken to skirt the law and preserve the athletes' amateur status until they completed their college eligibility. Bankrolling a prospect is perfectly legal when dealing with a hot new singer down at the local club. It's unlawful when dealing with college athletes.

To complicate matters, whenever Walters and Bloom hit a snag, they brought in some muscle. In the early music days, my father had provided the muscle. His appearance at a meeting was usually all it took for Walters to iron out contractual difficulties, keep an unhappy act from jumping ship, or keep the entertainers' noses out of the books. After my father was imprisoned and I was made, I replaced my father as Walters's muscle.

When Dionne Warwick wanted to cut her ties to Walters in 1982, he called me. I hopped on a jet to Los Angeles, met him, and the two of us went directly to the Sunset Boulevard office of Joe Grant, Warwick's manager. After a few minutes of listening to Walters talk his jive, and Grant explaining that Warwick sought a more "prestigious" agency, I took over. I asked Walters to leave so Joe and I could chat.

"I don't like what I'm hearing," I explained. "I want you to do me this favor. Stay with Norby another six months. If you still have complaints, we'll talk about it again."

Warwick stayed with Walters.

A similar visit between me and the Jacksons' manager, Ron Weisner, nearly resulted in Walters bagging the group's 1981 tour, headed by the then-rocketing Michael Jackson. An unrelated snag killed the deal, allowing another booking firm to take over. I was also called in to lay down the law to the manager of the New Edition when that supergroup wanted to dump Walters.

Since such activities are commonplace in the Mob-saturated entertainment industry, our activities drew little attention. The same couldn't be said for the undeniably corrupt, but less visibly so, world of big-time college sports. The feds got wind of Walters's new sports agency venture, tapped Bloom's phone, and turned up a bonanza. They taped Bloom threatening to have his Mob pals—presumably me—break the valuable arms and legs of a few college football stars who figured they could take the money and then pull a double-cross by signing with another agent. Other athletes told the National Football League Players Association they had received similar threats from Walters. The Packers' Fullwood took it one step further. He testified before a Chicago grand jury that Bloom had threatened to kill his agent, George Kickliter.

In the midst of all these threats, which Walters and Bloom steadfastly deny, Kathe Clements, an associate of Chicago sports agent Steve Zucker, was roughed up in her Chicago office by two hoods wearing ski masks and gloves. Clements, wife of former Notre Dame quarterback Tom Clements, had squabbled with Bloom over Zucker taking three of World Sports and Entertainment's clients. The feds suspected that Walters, Bloom, and their muscleman, me, were responsible for Clements's beating and intensified their investigation.

Then the incredible happened. In March 1987, Walters had the gall to file suit against some of his former clients for breach of contract—contracts that were illegally postdated and gained through illegal cash payments, which Walters wanted repaid. Then he followed this strange action by telling the *Atlanta Constitution* that the players had wronged him by taking his money. The bizarre act is similar to someone calling the police to report that an acquaintance robbed him of his cocaine stash.

When the authorities came down on Walters and Bloom, a nasty scandal erupted that quickly became national news. Sports reporters dubbed it "Jockgate" and covered every angle. Walters and Bloom were made to symbolize everything that is corrupt and evil in big-time college and professional athletics.

The more press it received, the bigger the case became for the hotly pursuing prosecutors. When the lawmen connected Walters to me and my father, they could hardly conceal their elation. The high-octane element of organized crime invading college athletics fanned the media fires even brighter. The press, fed by the FBI and Chicago prosecutors, had a field day. The hallowed halls of academia, places like Notre Dame, Pitt, Miami, Nebraska, and Oklahoma, were supposedly being invaded by bent-nosed mobsters.

The last thing I needed was a messy national scandal, especially one that starred me as the chief leg-breaker. I was keenly aware that a case publicized to such an extent could turn me overnight into a "godfather" figure of Al Capone proportions. Walters and Bloom were already becoming household names. If I was suddenly pegged as the pin-striped mastermind behind the operation, it would open me up to an onslaught of media attention that would all but paint a giant bull's-eye on my back. Ambitious prosecutors from New York to L.A. would come gunning for me. Any convict looking to make a deal would be quick to sell me out.

That kind of heat I didn't need.

What I failed to realize, viewing the matter from my own perspective, was that the Walters and Bloom case had grown bigger than me. They were getting all the press. Therefore, in the prosecutors' minds, Walters and Bloom were the big targets. For the first time in my life, I would be on the other end. Instead of being the prized red bowling pin everyone wanted to topple, I was now one of the white pins needed to knock over the red one.

Once I knew what was happening, my next move was to get a better grip on the expected grand jury testimony. The problems that such an appearance presented were enormous. Testifying anywhere about anything is against Cosa Nostra rules. But that giant dilemma could wait. There was a more immediate hell to deal with. The Jockgate trial wasn't scheduled for two years. That meant the prosecutors might try to stash me in some dreary, overcrowded, inner-city, metro correctional center in Chicago with no exercise field and what amounted to a twenty-four-hour lockdown.

I wanted no part of that. It certainly wasn't part of my plea agreement.

"No way," Bruce Kelton told Howard Pearl, former prosecutor to prosecutor. Kelton explained that I was already steaming about getting stuck in El Reno during the Cuban riots. I would simply play my ace and take the Fifth. Pearl hinted that such a posture could lead to my indictment in the case and could also result in a contempt-of-court charge. If cited for contempt, I would be held in a Chicago prison for up to three years with no credit toward finishing my federal term. Kelton explained that we weren't shutting the door, we just wanted to establish ground rules before we officially opened communications. I wanted to go back to Terminal Island. That was nonnegotiable. Pearl would then be invited to pay me a visit and explain exactly what he wanted. We'd discuss it and take it from there.

Pearl agreed.

Everything had been worked out—in Chicago and Los Angeles. In Atlanta, things were still festering. The Cubans were hanging tough, refusing for weeks to relinquish control of the eighty-six-year-old facility. When they finally caved in, it took another week for the federal corrections system to clean up the mess and get back to its normal snail's pace. I sat fuming in El Reno for three weeks before I was sent "home" to Terminal Island. The worst part of the ordeal was spending a miserable Thanksgiving Day in El Reno. A slab of some kind of compressed turkey was all I received. At Terminal Island the previous year, we had a complete dinner with fresh turkey, stuffing, and cranberry sauce.

Pearl and FBI agent George Randolph flew to California during the normally slack work week between Christmas and New Year's. That action spoke volumes about the importance of the Norby Walters case. The prosecutor and the agent laid out their evidence. They even read the transcript of a tape where Bloom threatened to break a Texas wide receiver's hands if the athlete signed with another agent. Randolph, an honest straight-shooter who doesn't play games, knew the extent of my involvement, how much I had invested with Walters, how Cammy's brother delivered the cash, and precise details of the Dionne Warwick, Michael Jackson, and New Edition shakedowns. It didn't take me long to realize the prosecutors had Walters and Bloom nailed.

Although he wasn't saying it, Pearl also knew that I had little to do with the sports agency or the threats against the athletes. In addition, Pearl had nothing to connect me—or Walters and Bloom, for that matter—to the brutal beating of Kathe Clements.

There was little doubt, however, that Walters had been readily dropping my name to push his way around the sports world. And even though I was in prison, I remained Walters's prime muscle. That was enough, the prosecutor explained, to indict me and toss me into the sensational case. And not only me but my father as well. At the very least, they wanted my father to testify about his longtime dealings with Walters.

That threat got my attention. My first reaction was to protect my father.

"My dad's been in jail seventeen years. He's sixty-eight years old. Leave him out of this," I said.

Pearl made no promises. It all depended upon how cooperative I was. "We don't want your father. Just between us, we don't even want you," I was told. "I don't know if we can make a case against you, or if it will stick. But we have enough to get an indictment."

I briefly tried my "I'm out of it, let me do my time in peace" routine, but I could see that wasn't going to get anywhere. The Norby Walters case was too big. The Chicago prosecutors, Pearl and Anton Valukas, were in a national goldfish bowl on this one.

I also knew what the game was. It didn't matter what I could testify about. My story made no difference at all. My presence was what mattered. All the prosecutors had to do was connect Walters and Bloom with the Mob, and the jury would raise their eyebrows, shudder, and convict the pair of anything the government wanted. I merely had to appear, give my name and Mob rank, and admit to investing $50,000 in World Sports and Entertainment, Inc. To help the jury members with their imaginations, and to juice the national headlines, the prosecutors would get me to chat about visiting Weisner and Dionne Warwick's guy Joe Grant on Walters's behalf.

That was it. I wouldn't have to admit to any criminal activity. I wouldn't have to say anything to directly implicate Walters or Bloom. I didn't have to finger them in any criminal act whatsoever. I could testify and still stay semiclean. The prosecutors would take the ball from there. They would be able to take my testimony, stand before the jury, hum the *Godfather* theme, and paint a portrait of Walters's operation that would make Mario Puzo and Francis Ford Coppola proud.

Pearl and Randolph gathered their evidence and headed back to Chicago. I did some investigating of my own. Despite being in prison, my lines of communication were operational. What I learned was distressing. Word on the street was that Bloom was dealing and was going to roll on Walters. (The information was good. A year later, *Sports Illustrated* reported that Bloom had made a deal with state prosecutors in Tuscaloosa, Alabama, to testify against Walters in a separate but related case involving a University of Alabama basketball player. If Walters was convicted, Bloom would be sentenced to wash police cars for a week.)

That was the final straw. The Chicago prosecutors had Walters and Bloom by the balls. Everything they told me was true. They had the documents, the wiretaps, and the dirty athletes to prove it. The case was getting too much media attention for them to allow Walters and Bloom to slip away. If the case continued to its end, it would not only grow but would start sucking others down into the muck. I knew what I had to do.

A one-line order, complete with the official Colombo stamp, was promptly dispatched to Walters: "Take a plea. End it for all of us."

At the time, Walters could have walked away with eighteen months, Bloom less, and he wouldn't have had to turn. Both could have been paroled in three to six months.

Walters refused.

"Tell Michael they got nothin'—nothin'!" Walters responded. "I ain't takin' no plea. Tell Michael not to worry. I can beat it. Just tell him not to testify."

A second, more urgent message was sent through the Mob courier system.

"Michael strongly suggests you take a plea. End this!"

Walters refused again.

I was infuriated. Walters had benefited from his Mob associations his entire life. He used the Mob when it helped him and denied it when it hurt. Now he was disobeying a direct order and putting family members at risk.

The Norby Walters mess was screwing up my plans. I was determined to do the minimum, forty months, and get the hell out of prison. Now Walters was putting me into the position of possibly having to do the whole ten years. And that was just my current sentence. If I was dropped into the fetid Jockgate stew, I could have another decade or so tacked on—all to save Norby Walters from doing six months soft time in a case he was going to be convicted in anyway. "I'm not doing one extra day for Norby Walters," I vowed.

But the vow meant doing the inconceivable—testifying.

Trouble was, that inconceivable clashed with the unthinkable—being locked in a prison cell away from Cammy for up to seventeen more years.

"I'll answer truthfully. No lies," I told Kelton. "Just the honest truth. I had Dino give Norby $50,000. I don't know what Norby did. I never met a single athlete. I never met Lloyd Bloom. I never heard of Kathe Clements. I was in jail when all this happened. End of story."

CHAPTER 23

had more than a year to sit in my cell and contemplate my pending testimony. Messages filtered in about my decision. I was reminded about my oath never to reveal or acknowledge La Cosa Nostra. Yet, at the famous Cosa Nostra commission trials in New York, the heads of the five families had acknowledged its existence. That section of the oath appeared to no longer apply.

I briefly considered seeking advice from my father. I abandoned the idea when I realized how tough the communication would be between two prisoners three thousand miles apart. Short messages could be delivered, but the process didn't allow for give and take. I felt he needed a face-to-face, two-way communication to explain my decision.

Being unable to arrange such a meeting wasn't critical. I knew my father well enough to know what he would say. He would listen, nod his head, and agree to all my arguments. He would agree that the price was too severe to protect Norby Walters. He would agree that Norby wasn't worth making any sacrifice for, much less one so grave.

Then, after I presented my overwhelming case, my father would furrow his considerable brow and advise me not to testify. The reason was cut to the bone. It just wasn't right. It wouldn't look good. It was embarrassing to the family. And most of all, it went against the all-powerful oath. Even though my father himself sometimes questioned the allegiance to the oath, he remained loyal.

I knew my father so well I could almost hear him rendering his judgment. "We took this oath, Michael, and we are just going to have to live by it," he would say, ignoring the dire consequences. "We made our bed and now we got to sleep in it."

It was all so screwed up, I thought. How could my father still feel that way after all he had suffered, after a life squandered in prison, after putting his family through twenty years of pain and financial hardship, and after being forgotten, betrayed, and demoted by his own organization? How could my father hold true to a rigid pledge that no longer held any meaning?

I thought about the oath, the blood oath I sealed twelve years before. It seemed exciting back then—a secret brotherhood based upon honor and integrity. I repeated the ominous words and became a made man like my father. As I lay on my prison bed, Thomas DiBella's words echoed in disjointed segments.

"If your mother is dying and you are at her bedside, and the boss calls, you leave your mother….

"If you are ordered to kill, you kill. Even your best friend. Even your father. You do it. No question. If you fail, you will be killed…." Harsh words, but such power was supposed to be tempered with a strong sense of evenhandedness and uncompromising honor.

"Those who obey will be protected. Those who disobey will be killed."

But it hadn't been like that. Those who obeyed were sometimes killed. Those who disobeyed often escaped unharmed. There was little honor to be found in anything. Instead, it was a business of worshiping money, a business full of jealousy, envy, lust for power, savage treachery, torture, and death.

I hadn't failed the oath, I reasoned, however conveniently—the oath had failed me! It had destroyed my father and mother and brothers and sisters, and now was trying to destroy me and my family.

An even if one obeyed, if one followed the oath without yielding, what good was it? My father blindly followed. My father never bent. My father was the ultimate Mob soldier. What good did it do him? He was framed for a crime he knew nothing about. Twenty years rotting in jail, facing thirty more. Some say the Mob set my father up to begin with. Maybe the enemy wasn't the prosecutors and FBI but the Mob itself. And maybe they kept setting my father up each time he was released.

And still, my father kept quiet. Ten, twenty years in prison. The iron man. A man of rare honor and integrity. Everybody deserted him, but still no testifying. No plea bargains. No deals. No nothing.

No lasting parole.

Just fifty years in prison.

And who cared? Who cared about Sonny Franzese rotting in some Virginia prison? What honor was there in that? Rotting in prison for your "brothers" who want you to stay there.

And now *I* was supposed to follow in my father's footsteps? Even my mother waffled on her stance. She had initially supported my decision, expressing a disdain for Walters and inciting me with tales of how Walters had been disrespectful to her and my father. She repeated how Sonny's long imprisonment had torn at her and her family. But my mother could shift directions in a blink of an eye. She confided to others that she was revulsed at the thought of her son testifying. She even went as far as putting me in the same class as the men who falsely testified against my father. She proclaimed Norby Walters a dear family friend and decreed that I should stay quiet and be a good soldier like my father.

My mother's feelings not only stung, they enraged me. Her bashing of Walters had figured strongly in my decision. She had never given me any indication that what I was doing was wrong. Then, after all that, I couldn't believe that she could play "Don Tina" and tell people she wanted me to zip my lips and follow in the shackled footsteps of my perpetually imprisoned father. Hadn't that stance hurt our family enough? And all for the likes of Norby Walters?

No way, I thought. Regardless of what my father would say, and what my mother would say at any given moment, there was no honor in silence. Norby wasn't a "brother," just a fringe player who boasted about his organized-crime clout when it benefited him.

And Norby had disobeyed. Norby broke the code by refusing a direct order to take a plea. Norby wasn't thinking of the good of the family. Norby didn't give a damn if anybody had to do an extra seven—or seventy —years. He was trying to save his own ass from a six-month sentence.

And besides, as much as I loved her, my mother's opinions didn't carry much weight anymore. They had been supplanted by my feelings for another Franzese woman—my wife, Cammy. And Cammy wanted me out.

In March 1989, two marshals came to Terminal Island, handcuffed me, clamped on leg irons, then chauffeured me to Los Angeles International Airport for the trip to Chicago. Stopping at the terminal, they ordered me out of the car.

"I'm not going out like this—you must be out of your mind!" I said, nodding toward the leg irons.

"We can't do that," the lead marshal said.

"I'm not shuffling two miles through a crowded airport chained like a slave. You can turn around and take me right back to Terminal Island."

The marshals huddled for a few minutes.

"Okay, we'll take them off—but if you try to make a run for it, remember, we've got guns."

"Give me a break," I said. "Just get these stupid things off me."

The trial of Norby Walters and Lloyd Bloom was a star-studded affair played before a courtroom mobbed with reporters. The media conglomeration at the U.S. District Court in Chicago was a strange mix. The hard-news reporters were there, covering it as a news story. The sports press was there, covering it as a major sports scandal and reveling in the parade of big-time sports stars who took the stand and testified about wads of dirty money and threats of broken legs, arms, and hands. And the long-haired rock press also fought for seats, dispatching reports to *Billboard, Cash Box, Variety, Rolling Stone,* and other music magazines about the music-biz angle. They perked up when the Jacksons' and Dionne Warwick's people, Weisner and Grant, testified about my visits.

In the midst of all this sensational testimony, I took the stand and hushed the courtroom audience with my mere introduction.

"Michael Franzese. Capo in the Colombo crime family."

Few of the spectators, even among the hard-bitten journalists, had even seen a real live Cosa Nostra captain up close. I could feel the jury hanging on every word as I went through my lines. I talked for ninety minutes on direct, and another sixty on cross-examination, about my investments with World Sports and Entertainment, my father's involvement with Walters, and my visits with Grant and Weisner. I was the sexy connection that would juice the headlines in the newspapers and magazines. I was the link from the Mob to both sports and rock and roll.

As the prosecutors predicted, what I said didn't matter. Not even with the media. They could write between the lines.

The show closed after five weeks. The jury huddled, then threw the book at Walters and Bloom. They were convicted of conspiracy, racketeering conspiracy, conspiracy to commit mail fraud, mail fraud, wire fraud, and extortion. The judge sentenced Walters to five years and Bloom to three.

I returned to Terminal Island. A few weeks later, I was released.

It was over.

And it had just begun.

EPILOGUE

FROM DARY MATERA

What lies ahead for Michael Franzese?

A successful career producing movies and dealing in real estate?

Personal appearances witnessing and giving his testimony as a born-again Christian?

A seduction back into the Mob?

A bullet?

Depending upon whom one speaks to, all are possibilities. But possibilities are all anyone can offer. There's no precedent. No one of his stature has turned his back on both the Mob and the witness protection program.

Whatever happens, he won't be strapped for money. Government and Mafia sources estimate that he has between $200 million and $400 million in cash buried in Long Island, Florida, and California in sealed steel boxes. He has another $400 million stashed in banks in West Germany, Austria, Panama, South America, and the Caribbean, including the Bahamas and the Cayman Islands. Because he testified during his plea bargain that he had no money or assets other than the real estate and motion pictures he turned over, he must leave his treasure untouched until 1993, when the seven-year statute of limitations runs out on a possible perjury charge. If he weakens and grabs a shovel or makes an overseas dash, the FBI and the IRS could locate and confiscate the cash and/or accounts, revoke his parole, and try him for perjury.

The odds are the government won't find the the money in time.

The odds on whether he will live to spend it are harder to determine.

Rumors abound. The most sensational says that Sonny Franzese has ordered his son's death from his cell in Virginia. It's doubtful, but not incomprehensible. The Mafia oath presents that option.

Tina Franzese's heated reaction to her son's testimony may have stirred such rumors. "He's my son, but he testified," she says. "I can't make an exception. I can't. How can I? I know how informers can hurt people. That's wrong. I know what happens to people who testify. I pray every night for Michael."

Michael views the prospect of the ultimate parental punishment with amusement. "If that happens, then it will make a great ending for the book. I'll call my dad and see if we can accommodate you."

Norby Walters and Lloyd Bloom have neither the connections nor the expertise to have Michael hit, nor is there any reason to believe they would if they could. If the disgraced sports agents are intent on knocking off everyone who testified against them, they'd have to kill dozens of people, including a solid contingent of the National Football League. Plus, it appears that the pair have gotten off scot-free anyway. In September 1990, the 7th U.S. Circuit Court of Appeals reversed their convictions on the kind of legal technicality that makes the public furious. The appeals court ruled that the trial judge improperly refused to call certain testimony to the jurors' attention during his routine instructions to the panel. Norby Walters continues to deny that he was ever a partner of the Franzese family.

More serious are the reports that Michael's death contract was officially signed on April 12, 1990, shortly after a New York newspaper published a story saying he was going to testify against Colombo acting boss Victor Orena. The newspaper report was erroneous, but it was enough to prompt an assassination squad to make a trip to California. FBI agents visited Michael and advised him to get out of town. "The word is that you'll be dead by Mother's Day," the somber agents told him.

Michael stayed put. Mother's Day passed without incident. It's not known why the effort failed—possibly because it was merely a scouting expedition to arrange a future hit.

The strike force prosecutors who helped put him away remain mixed in their feelings about both the deal he received and his prospects for a long life. Edward McDonald, former chief of the New York Organized Crime Strike Force, Eastern District, said he was satisfied with Michael's punishment. It wasn't so much the jail sentence that sated McDonald but what he viewed as its chilling aftermath. "I think the deal he received was fair and reasonable. He's going to be in hiding and he's going to be looking over his shoulder the rest of his life."

When informed that Michael was neither in hiding, surrounded by bodyguards, nor looking over his shoulder—that, to the contrary, he was living a cautious but carefree California existence—McDonald seemed taken aback. After a long pause, the ex–strike force commander offered a carefully worded warning. "In my experience, considering the substance of his public testimony, what he admitted in Chicago [that he is a Mafia capo], I think he's nuts if he's not in hiding. If he's roaming around the streets of Los Angeles unprotected, I'd suggest that he mend his ways."

Suffolk County DA Ray Jermyn, who studied and hunted the Franzese family for more than a decade, holds a different view. "The Chicago prosecutors traded a Mafia don in his thirties, a guy who stole a billion dollars, for a sixty-year-old Jewish booking agent. That was shrewd. Nobody cares about Norby Walters. Franzese will probably live to be a hundred."

Whatever the truth, for the first year after his release, Michael stubbornly continued to "roam" unprotected. He dined out frequently and traveled around California in a Porsche convertible rather than in a more enclosed auto. Following the Mother's Day visit from the FBI agents, he's taken a more cautious approach. Never one to underestimate his former associates, he's recruited a gang of tough, street-smart Mexicans to watch his home and subtly shadow his movements.

In a rare moment of candor late one night at his new, $3 million mansion, he paced the room, peered out the window into the dark California night, and was moved to admit the inevitable.

"I know that they're going to take a shot at me. It could be today, tomorrow, or ten years from now, but it'll come. Instead of being happy that at least one of us made it out, they can't live with it. They'll never leave me alone. I'm not the kind of guy that they'll easily forget.

"I'm not going to make it easy for them. They're never going to be able to call me into a room, or take me for a ride, and put a bullet in the back of my head. If they're lucky enough to catch me on a street corner or in a restaurant, so be it."

Michael has since disavowed these comments, saying he was speaking metaphorically about the Mafia in general and was not referring to himself.

Consequently, even as he beefs up his security, he continues to downplay his personal danger. He argues that he sold out no one in La

Cosa Nostra. If he's been secretly tried and convicted and sentenced to death by his former Mafia brethren, his crime was turning away from the Mafia oath—and quitting the Mob.

Unfortunately, that's enough.

The fate of one of Michael's former partners is enough to give anyone pause. On May 2, 1989, in the early morning hours, Michael Markowitz left a poker game at a friend's Mill Basin home, got into his silver-and-maroon Rolls, and headed into the night. At Sixty-sixth Street, he noticed a familiar car, stopped, rolled down his window, and was greeted by three bullets. Two hit him in the chest; the third penetrated his shoulder. He survived long enough to steer the Rolls down the street until he crashed into a gray Buick parked by the curb. Blood dripping from the three holes in his body, he struggled to the door of a nearby home and began crying out for help. The residents, fearful of a crazed drunk or a madman, refused to open up. A neighborhood security guard passed by on his rounds, dashed over, and found the dying Rumanian sprawled in front of the house. As the life drained from his body, Markowitz kept trying to name his assassin. Nobody could understand him, though it was related afterward that he mumbled some foreign name. Markowitz died before anyone could decipher it.

The case has never been solved.

On the morning of Thursday, October 18, 1990, Metro Dade police homicide detective Jim McDermott was dispatched to room 431 of the Suez Motel in Sunny Isles, a cheerful section of North Miami Beach, Florida. There he discovered the body of Gia Franzese face-up on the floor; she was wearing green shorts and a white tank top. Gia had checked into the $59-a-night, two-story oceanfront motel four days before while waiting to move back into a luxury condominium her boyfriend rented at Aventura, an exclusive country-club development seventeen blocks away. The Suez, a Collins Avenue motel popular with foreigners, was overflowing with German and Canadian tourists.

Dade County medical examiner Dr. Jay Barnhart found superficial scratches over Gia's left breast, apparently self-inflicted, and wet towels scattered around the motel room. Dr. Barnhart knew from experience that the towels were a sign that Gia was trying to "combat hyperthermia," or simply, was attempting to cool her soaring body temperature.

The scratches pointed toward "formication"—the sensation of bugs crawling on her body. Both the scratches and the towels were indications of a bad cocaine high. During her last hours, she also suffered from "extreme paranoid delusions" of people trying break into her room, some by coming in through the sink. Detective McDermott found a lamp cord with one end tied to the base of the room's metal suitcase stand and the other looped around the closet door—presumably to keep intruders from entering through the closet.

Outside was a yellow Cadillac Coupe de Ville registered to Camille Franzese that Michael had given to his sister. Cammy and Gia had been close friends.

McDermott found a four-page fax on the dresser sent from Israel the previous day. The letter was from Gia's boyfriend, an Israeli businessman. The man professed his love and his desire to marry her. The letter also reiterated his request that Gia convert from Catholicism to Orthodox Judaism. The conversion issue had been a sore spot between the couple. They had a heated argument about it during a transatlantic phone call the night before.

After a thorough police and pathological investigation, it was determined that Michael's youngest sister had died from a severe physiological reaction to cocaine, a powerful stimulant that, despite its widespread use, can kill without warning. Her death was classified as accidental.

Gia, who never got over the murder of her boyfriend Larry Carrozza, was two months pregnant when she died.

Lawrence Iorizzo is said to be having a miserable time bouncing in and out of the witness protection program. Federal investigators located and confiscated an $11 million slush fund he had hidden in a safety deposit box in Austria. Many of those he testified against have already been paroled. Others, including the volatile and vengeance-minded Frankie Gangster, will be paroled in the next year or so.

"How do you hide a five-hundred-pound man in a Hawaiian shirt?" noted one wary prosecutor.

As if twice wasn't enough, Michael and Cammy were married a third time, on June 3, 1990, at a Westwood Hills Christian Church renewal ceremony. The previous year, Cammy presented Michael with a son, Michael Jr. The child was born July 15, 1989, two months after Michael's release from prison. Cammy had become pregnant while Michael was out on the eight-hour pass from Boron.

The financial cushion Michael set up for Maria and their children collapsed when he entered prison. The million-dollar investment that was to provide them with a steady $7,500 a month was embezzled by William and Howard Finger, the attorneys who handled the account. William Finger was dying from heart disease and lost both his ethics and his fear. With Michael in jail and the stolen tax money hidden and unavailable, Maria had to work to support the family.

"I let my kids down and feel bad about it," Michael admits. "I'm unhappy with myself. I wanted to stay close. I wanted them to live comfortable, but between prison and the thieving attorneys, it didn't work out. I didn't want to make excuses why I wasn't seeing them regularly, so I just let the time pass. I can't let that happen anymore. They're great kids, and Maria's been a great mother. I love them and I'll prove myself to them again."

Michael left the Brookville mansion snarled in so much red tape it has taken the banks and the government eight years to try to evict his former wife and children. They were able to live in the home, currently valued at three to four million, without paying the mortgage or property taxes. That helped.

Michael appears to be able to transfer his business ability into the legitimate world. The government's given him no deadline on repaying the $10 million. One good motion picture will wipe that away. Meanwhile, he's happy in his new life. Cammy's happy. They are together, and in love as never before.

Yet the rumors remain. Admittedly, when I wrote the first chapter of this book, I wondered if he would be alive by the last.

The odds seemed to plunge in late 1989. I sent a pair of photographers to his church to snap a shot of Michael, Cammy, and Michael Jr. playing the Holy Family in a manger scene during a Christmas pageant. Speaking with him afterward, he said he never noticed the two professional photographers focusing on him with their thousand-dollar cameras among the crowd of parents wielding cheaper Instamatics.

Cammy, however, did make the pair.

His behavior certainly doesn't speak of a man living in hiding and looking over his shoulder. It does portray a calm, collected man who harbors no fear or paranoia, a man determined to live his life on his terms.

A courageous stance, but as TV's Tony Baretta was fond of saying, "All the tough guys I know are either in the cemetery or the jailhouse."

But we're here, at the end. And Michael is neither in jail nor in a coffin.

Or at least he wasn't when I wrote this, in the fall of 1991.

With each day, Michael Franzese's fascinating story continues.

FROM MICHAEL

I used to have a grand illusion about La Cosa Nostra. I idolized my father, and it was his organization, his life, so it had to be something special. I thought it was the Mob that gave my father the tremendous aura that surrounded him and the power and respect he commanded. But it was my father who gave those qualities to the Mob.

I learned this when I became a member. I looked around and found very few men like my father. Mostly, there were men of weaker character who labored under the belief that the Mob gave them their clout. To some extent, they were right. A certain amount of self-esteem can be gained through the tactics of fear and intimidation. But it's an illusion.

The men on top, men like Paul Castellano, Carmine Galante, Joe Colombo, Carmine Persico, Jr., Fat Tony Salerno—and Sonny Franzese—are either dead or in prison. For all their influence, they didn't have the power to keep themselves alive or to free themselves from a life that is hardly worth living.

What kind of power do the bosses have when they frequently end up being killed by their own "loyal" soldiers?

What kind of authority do they wield when a twenty-five-year-old kid fresh out of law school can become a federal prosecutor and put them away for a hundred years? Put them in a prison where a semiliterate nineteen-year-old high-school dropout in a guard's uniform orders them around? That's what hurts when I visit my father in prison. Instead of being smartly dressed in one of his expensive suits, surrounded by tough men who jump at his every command, he shuffles out in his worn brown khakis and says "Yes, sir," "Yes, Mr. Jones" to some prison guard who can barely write his own name.

No one has been able to rescue my father from two decades of misery. With all the Mob's might, they couldn't do a thing to free him, or Persico, or Fat Tony, or Antonio Corallo, or Jerry Langella, or anyone else from a life behind bars—even if they wanted to. With all the Mob's strength, they couldn't prevent a proud street warrior like Paul Vario, one of the men Henry Hill of *GoodFellas* fingered, and dozens more like him from dying behind bars.

Spitting in the face of my father's legendary reputation as the king of the tough guys is the sad fact that the four men who destroyed his life got away free. The four punks who put my father in prison are still walking the streets today, nearly twenty-five years later.

That says it all.

I've learned to see a different kind of strength and toughness, one that comes from the integrity and honesty of the inner person. I see a man like Dr. Myron Taylor at Westwood Hills Christian Church, a pastor who has dedicated his life to his church, doing the best he can to spread the word of God and help those in need. A man who believes in what he does, because what he is doing is right. That's the kind of man who should be admired. That's the kind of man they should write stories and make movies about. That's *real* power.

For most of the 1,231 days I spent in prison, I thought about the oath I took on Halloween night, 1975. I didn't take the oath lightly then, and I don't now. It was a pact between men who promised to honor a secret organization, respect each other and each other's families, and protect one another. I accepted it, and accepted the warning that violating such an oath would mean death. But the oath wasn't what it seemed. Death wasn't limited to the capital offenses spelled out in the solemn ceremony. All too often, men were killed out of jealousy, greed, ego, or a lust for power. There wasn't even a pretense of honor in that. The oath itself had become a sham.

As I evaluated my life, I realized that my family, especially my six children, are the most important things in the world. They're more important than money or oaths or jobs or secret brotherhoods. I don't want my wife and children to go through the agonizing stress and mental torture that my mother, brothers, and sisters and I endured. My father's trials and imprisonment twisted our thinking and left us all with deep emotional scars. I don't want my kids growing up hating and fearing law-enforcement officers and worrying that every cop they see might be coming to take away—or kill—their father. I want them to have a normal, healthy childhood.

Because of the decisions I've made, I now live with the possibility of retaliation. I don't underestimate the danger, but neither do I live in fear. In a sense, my life now is no different than it was before. In the Mob, you always have to walk a tightrope. You exist every day with the knowledge that death could be waiting around the next corner. All my life, there were people getting killed, people I knew and cared for. At every funeral, I wondered who would be next, and when it would be my turn.

My darling Cammy was the catalyst that changed my life. She's been the strongest influence on me, even greater than my father. However, loving her has not come without a price. I face an uncertain future because my love for her convinced me to turn my back on the Mob. Still, it's been worth it. If I had to do it again, I would without hesitation. I love Cammy more now than ever before.

People ask me if I feel guilty about what I've done. I feel a great deal of remorse. I find it repulsive that with all the millions I had, and all the millions I paid the men around me, I did almost nothing to help those in need. I tossed money away like water while children were starving all over the world. I threw lavish parties while sick kids desperately needed medical care. I bought hundred-thousand-dollar cars and ate at expensive restaurants while teenagers from disadvantaged backgrounds struggled to pay their way through college and scratch their way out of the slums. This haunts me, and has grown into a burning desire to find a way to right these wrongs.

Before I joined La Cosa Nostra, I wanted to be a pediatrician. Now I'd like to resurrect that part of me and concentrate my future efforts and resources on helping children and my church.

Cammy and I share a dream of building a dance studio where poor children can come and learn to dance. Another dream we have is to build a motion-picture company that produces family-oriented films with inspirational Christian themes. I know everyone in Hollywood thinks that philosophy is a sure way to financial ruin, but I disagree. I think the audience is out there, and if the films are made the right way, the audience will come. This is actually more than just a dream. This is something I'm going to do, and do soon.

I'd also like to tell my story and give my personal testimony about how I changed myself, or more accurately, how God and Cammy transformed me from a Cosa Nostra captain into a born-again Christian. I'm not sure if I want to do this in front of audiences and church congregations, or more directly through the counseling of troubled children and adults. Whichever, the urge in this area is strong.

I'm sure there are a lot of people who will think this is all just another Michael Franzese con. With my background, such criticism is justified. My answer is simply to say "Watch me." I invite scrutiny. I've changed and I'll prove it.

I believe everything that has happened to me happened for a reason. There's a master plan behind my life. God gave me the ability to make money for a reason. Regardless of how I got it, it was in his plan. God set the course of the first half of my life because he wants me to do something important with the second half. I'm not sure what it is, but I'm motivated and ready and things are going to happen. Maybe in ten years, there will be another book, this one without all the horror, bloodshed, and heartache of the preceding pages.

One thing I do know. My purpose is not to go around the country testifying against others. Just because I can no longer honor an oath I no longer believe in, that doesn't mean I should go out and try to destroy the Mob or the people in it. The government wants me to be a big Mob witness. I refuse to be placed in that position or to be used as a tool. I'm not going to travel around the country building the careers of young prosecutors.

Similarly, I have no desire to seek revenge against those who want me dead by testifying against them. I'm not happy that I've had to testify at all. Still, I never lied. I didn't volunteer or offer the government any deals. I didn't go out of my way to hurt anyone. I didn't try to buy my way out of prison with my testimony. I didn't try to keep my money in return for my testimony. I don't see anything noble about being an informant, especially the prevalent breed who will say anything the prosecutors want, frame anyone, to barter their way out of prison.

I've made my point with the government. They know I'm out. They know that life is over for me, and that I'm now following a different path.

I'd rather make my amends by channeling my resources and efforts into helping children, making cheerful, substantive movies, supporting my church, and participating in other charitable activities.

I'm determined both to survive and to make it as a legitimate businessman. I've always been able to somehow, someway, pull a rabbit out of my hat under the most adverse circumstances. I'll do it again. I'll straighten out the mess I made of my life and continue to stay on the right track. I'll get closer to God and my family and the things that are important.

With the help of God, I'll repay society ten times over for the damage I've done.

FROM CAMMY

I was very much against cooperating with this book when Michael first mentioned it. I felt it would draw attention to him and hold our family up to scrutiny. However, as it progressed, I could see how important it was to him. There were things he was able to get off his chest, and he wanted people to understand the truth about what he was and how he became that way. I think the most important message in the book is that no matter what someone has done in the past, with God's help, they can leave it behind and change. God will forgive them if only they ask. If we can get that message across to just one person, it will have been worth it.

My husband's been through hell. He's been under so much pressure since he was a child. Very few people could survive what he had to survive. During his trials, I'd awaken to find him kicking and punching the bed. Even when he was asleep, he was still fighting his enemies. He wasn't able to let down for a second. He had so much to worry about. His family. My family. His ex-wife and their children. Our children. His legal problems. His New York problems. Fortunately, he has an incredibly strong mind and will, and not only survived but has come out of it with only a few scars. He's been a model at being able to forget the past and work toward the future.

I can't say I don't worry about Michael anymore, because I do. I realize that I might lose him one day. God might allow them to take him away from me. But at least now I know he's a Christian and I'll see him in heaven. And besides, life has been so great since he's come home there's been little time to dwell on the negative. When we're together, we can't help feeling wonderful.

Sure, once in a while, if he's a half hour late coming home and doesn't call me, I become nervous. Last month, he was two hours late returning from a meeting and by then I was hysterical. I don't know why it affected me so much in that instance, but those moments are rare and are becoming rarer as time goes on. The joy of our new life together has worked to almost totally obliterate the last lingering waves of fear and anxiety.

I love and adore my husband more than anyone could ever know or understand. I don't know what he's done in the past, and I don't want to know. That's between Michael and God, and God is the only judge who counts. All I know is that he treats me better than I've ever seen any other husband treat a wife. I just can't imagine him doing anything to hurt anyone.

I know I changed his life, but it wasn't me in the flesh. It was God who put us together. God said that through this woman I'll save Michael Franzese. God wanted to save him. God could see into Michael's heart. He knew Michael was worth saving.

God's been unbelievably good to us. He's been the main factor in our lives. We've been married seven years and I love Michael more now than I did when I met him in Florida and he swept me away in a romantic fantasy. We're still like newlyweds.

When he was in prison, it was as if I was in prison with him. I used to cry myself to sleep every night thinking about him. I would take my children to the park and see happy couples together and it would make me so sad. When I was living at the Mirabella, the people saw only me and the children. I don't think they believed I even had a husband. I was so happy and proud when Michael finally came home. I wanted to go to everybody and say, "See, here he is. I have a husband. And he's gorgeous!"

Michael's changed so much since I first met him. He's so much more relaxed. He doesn't take life for granted. He appreciates things. Good food. A nice restaurant. Sunshine on his face. He's learned to choose his friends differently and he doesn't let people take advantage of him. I know how much it hurt him when his friends turned against him. I think that's what shocked him the most—not the testimony but the personal betrayals. He's said to me so many times, "Everybody I had around me turned on me. How could they do that? How could my friends do that?" It still hurts him so.

Leaving New York has been the best thing that has happened to him. He was able to leave that whole scene behind and start fresh.

As for me, my ambition to be a dancer is still there, but not like it was before. I'd like to keep dancing for myself, for the self-satisfaction of mastering the art. I'd enjoy dancing in a music video or choreographing some of Michael's movies, but if I don't, I won't regret it. I'm more interested in raising my wonderful children, who have proven to be never-ending joys. I'm also dedicated to strengthening my relationship with God and, most of all, to taking care of my dear husband.

Michael and I have a long, bright future ahead of us, and we plan to make the most of every second.

AFTERWORD

The call came late at night, after the manuscript of this book was completed. The revelation was the most staggering of all.

It followed a long, emotional argument with Tina Franzese over some of the information recounted here. Tina had vacillated in her telling of routine details about her early life with Sonny, a phenomenon that always speaks of an intriguing reality hidden beneath the veils. Sonny and Tina's marriage license shows that they married in 1959, not in 1951 as Tina insisted. Sonny and Ann Schiller's last child, Loraine, was born in 1952, a year after the alleged marriage to Tina. When confronted with the holes in her story, Tina reacted angrily, changed the subject, and temporarily refused to cooperate.

Tina had also become enraged over the prospect of Louis Grillo being mentioned in this book. She mirrored the strange reaction Michael said he observed all his life from Sonny when the subject of his biological father was broached. The explanation that Michael's biological father had to play some part, however small, in the foundation of his life, only angered her more. She hotly argued that Grillo and the "biological baloney" be blotted out from these pages. She was livid when she learned that to the contrary, Michael's memory of the eerie fast-food-restaurant meeting with Grillo was going to be recounted as an important part of his young life. She refused to explain why this infuriated her so.

Then came the late-night call.

"You want to know the truth?" she asked. "Michael is Sonny's son. He's not Louis Grillo's son. He's Sonny Franzese's biological son! He's Sonny's son!"

The confession was monumental. Michael's entire life had been shaped by his psychological reaction to being a stepchild of his beloved father. As a child, he had tried so hard to please because he was terrified of holding the short straw in a family shake-up. As a young man, he spent his life trying to compensate for the fact that he was the only one in a family of seven who was not blood-related to the family's powerful leader.

Could all of it have been a lie? Was the psyche of Michael Franzese, "the Long Island don," created by a bizarre genetic cover-up out of a William Faulkner novel?

And if so, why?

The first answer was that Tina may have invented her "Sonny's the real father!" confession in order to banish Grillo from these pages. Presented with this scenario, Tina laughed the laugh of a poker player holding all the aces—and a few extra up her sleeve.

"You're so smart. Tell me. There was no child support. There were no in-laws. No Grillo grandparents. No Grillo cousins, aunts, uncles, nieces. Ask Michael if he ever met or laid eyes on any of them. Where were they all? Why is that, do you think?"

As Tina repaints her story, this most preposterous story of all, it quickly becomes apparent that this is the only one without holes.

She was sixteen when she met Sonny. He was thirty-one. She wouldn't say where or how they met, only that it wasn't at the Stork Club as Michael always believed. She repeated her vague recounting that they met at a place for children, with lots of lights all around, and one particular group of children noisily playing nearby.

The telling goes dark again, zipped tightly for whatever reason in Tina's selective memory. Then the story emerges like a train blasting out of a black tunnel. She's sixteen and pregnant. The child's father, the most feared man in New York, still loves her. But he hasn't been truthful. He's married.

Tina reacted as young girls in that situation have reacted for centuries. She fell back upon another suitor, a young soldier who loved her. She seduced him and told him the child was his. As expected, he eagerly proposed. They quickly married.

It took Sonny Franzese eight months to sort out his feelings for the beautiful teenager and follow through on them. Try as he might, he couldn't strip her image from his head. He tracked her down, only to discover what she had done. He was devastated. But Tina's rash action had forced his hand. Instead of turning away in anger, it made him want her more. He would forgive her transgression if she would forgive him his. He wanted her. He wanted his son.

Tina wanted him. She confessed to Grillo. Whatever fight existed in the soldier was erased by the stunning one-two combination of learning that the child wasn't his and that his wife loved another man. Grillo let her go.

Sonny kept his promise and freed himself to marry Tina. It was Tina who now had the problem. Grillo, in a moment of weakness caused by a crushed spirit, had given her up. As the numbness wore off, his resolve stiffened. For eight years, he exacted his revenge by refusing to grant his young wife a divorce.

Neither Sonny nor Tina pressed him. "We didn't want to hurt him any more than he already was," Tina explained. "He was duped. What do you want from the guy? Sonny and I were together. That was all that mattered."

When it became apparent that Grillo had dug in for the long haul, Sonny and Tina skirted the entanglement by traveling to Juárez, Mexico, in the summer of 1959. Benefiting from the liberal Mexican laws, they obtained Tina's divorce and married in quick succession.

All of which explains Michael's spotty memory on where he lived the first nine years of his life, when his "stepfather" and mother actually were living together as man and wife, why Sonny was the only father he ever knew from the time he was a baby, and why the official marriage in 1959 was much later than anyone remembered.

It also explains why Sonny always reacted strangely to any mention of Michael's "real" father, why Sonny changed Michael's last name to Franzese without first asking for the teenager's approval, why Sonny raged every time the newspapers referred to Michael as his stepson; and solves the mystery of why Michael never had to prove his Italian heritage before he was inducted into the Mafia.

But it doesn't explain why Michael was raised as a stepchild.

Tina's answer, however unsatisfying, nevertheless rings true when studying the characters involved.

"I insinuated it many, many times. Michael just didn't listen. I told him 'Sonny's your only father. Forget the other. He doesn't exist.' I told him that the man feeding and clothing him and going to his football and baseball games was his real father, and that was all he should concern himself with." Presented that way, it's easy to see how Michael confused such imprecise statements with the beliefs adoptive parents hold about the mother and father who raise children being the "real" parents, and the biological parents being no more significant than a random couple united chemically in a test-tube experiment.

Even if one accepts Tina's explanation, it was obvious to both her and Sonny that Michael lived his life under the belief that Sonny was his stepfather. Not only that, but he was confronted with the specter of his missing biological father every day. His name was Michael Grillo on his birth certificate. He was registered in school under that name. He grew up with "stepson" ingrained in his psyche every time a teacher called roll.

"I never sat him down and seriously told him," Tina admits. "When I wanted to tell him, he was always too busy."

Sonny loved his son, showered him with affection, shrugged, and rode with the misconception. If Michael's mistaken impression made him work harder to gain his "stepfather's" respect, maybe it wasn't such a bad thing.

"Sonny wanted to tell him, but he left it up to me," Tina said. "Sonny knew it was his son, so that was all that mattered."

Tina absolutely refuses to accept her son's story of being terrified that he would one day be banished from the family because of his status as a stepson. "He had nothing to fear, ever. Sonny treated him like a prince. He treated him like his son. They had a great, great relationship. Everything was perfect. Michael was the happiest child in the world. He was secure. His brothers and sisters loved him.

"What difference did it make?"

"My whole life would have been different," a visibly stunned Michael said when he learned of his mother's confession. "I wouldn't have been so afraid of losing my father if I knew he was really my father. I wouldn't have had to try so hard to please him. Why did they put me under that kind of pressure?

"I wouldn't have had to join the Mob to please my father. I wouldn't be under a death sentence right now. And my mother asks, 'What difference did it make?' "

INDEX